Praise for *New England Beyon*

"Elisa New is a refreshing voice among critics and historians of literature. She has a keen sense of the nature of New England and its deep spiritual resources, reaching back to the Puritans, moving through the great nineteenth-century expressions of interior landscapes and visions. Her readings strike me as passionate, original, and very much at odds with a good deal that is now being said in academic circles. To say she is eccentric means, quite literally, that she stands outside of the center. In this, she seems in keeping with her Puritan fathers and mothers, those dark visionaries who gave birth to Hawthorne, Emerson, Thoreau, Dickinson, and others. This is a book I welcome and celebrate."

Jay Parini, Middlebury College

"Elisa New's book is a remarkable achievement. It is very rare that a critic manages to ask what seem exactly the right questions, then to answer them in a lively, brilliant, evocative, and supremely intelligent prose. New recognizes the force of criticism's critiques of traditional claims for the importance of New England writing in the shaping of America's images of itself. But she also recognizes how criticism tends to be limited by its academic protocols, so it cannot fully address the urgency of this writing to appeal to the full human being, hungry for meaning and idealization and passion challenged continually by that social reality on which the critics concentrate. New develops a critical stance fully responsive to what she calls the texts' 'powers' as they seek to come to terms with demands for conversion, challenges to imagine how people produce values, and the constant worry that these very ambitions may lead imaginations to cross borders where terror seems the dominant affective register."

Charles F. Altieri, University of California

Wiley Blackwell Manifestos

In this series major critics make timely interventions to address important concepts and subjects, including topics as diverse as, for example: Culture, Race, Religion, History, Society, Geography, Literature, Literary Theory, Shakespeare, Cinema, and Modernism. Written accessibly and with verve and spirit, these books follow no uniform prescription but set out to engage and challenge the broadest range of readers, from undergraduates to postgraduates, university teachers and general readers – all those, in short, interested in ongoing debates and controversies in the humanities and social sciences.

Already Published

New England Beyond Criticism

In Defense of America's First Literature

Elisa New

WILEY Blackwell

This edition first published 2014
© 2014 Elisa New

Registered Office
John Wiley & Sons Ltd, The Atrium, Southern Gate, Chichester, West Sussex, PO19 8SQ, UK

Editorial Offices
350 Main Street, Malden, MA 02148-5020, USA
9600 Garsington Road, Oxford, OX4 2DQ, UK
The Atrium, Southern Gate, Chichester, West Sussex, PO19 8SQ, UK

For details of our global editorial offices, for customer services, and for information about how to apply for permission to reuse the copyright material in this book please see our website at www .wiley.com/wiley-blackwell.

The right of Elisa New to be identified as the author of this work has been asserted in accordance with the UK Copyright, Designs and Patents Act 1988.

Wiley also publishes its books in a variety of electronic formats. Some content that appears in print may not be available in electronic books.

Designations used by companies to distinguish their products are often claimed as trademarks. All brand names and product names used in this book are trade names, service marks, trademarks or registered trademarks of their respective owners. The publisher is not associated with any product or vendor mentioned in this book.

Limit of Liability/Disclaimer of Warranty: While the publisher and author have used their best efforts in preparing this book, they make no representations or warranties with respect to the accuracy or completeness of the contents of this book and specifically disclaim any implied warranties of merchantability or fitness for a particular purpose. It is sold on the understanding that the publisher is not engaged in rendering professional services and neither the publisher nor the author shall be liable for damages arising herefrom. If professional advice or other expert assistance is required, the services of a competent professional should be sought.

Library of Congress Cataloging-in-Publication Data

New, Elisa.
    New England beyond criticism : in defense of America's first literature / Elisa New.
        pages cm
    The final chapter, A Fable for Critics: Autobiographical Epilogue, is about the author.
    Includes bibliographical references and index.
        ISBN 978-1-118-85453-2 (hardback) – ISBN 978-1-118-85454-9 (paper) 1. American literature–New England–History and criticism.   2. Literature and society–United States–History. 3. New England–In literature.   4. New England–Intellectual life.   5. United States–Intellectual life.   6. New, Elisa.   7. College teachers–Biography.   I. Title.   II. Title: In defense of America's first literature.
    PS243.N49 2014
    810.9'974–dc23

A catalogue record for this book is available from the British Library.

Cover image: Marsden Hartley, *The Last Stone Walls, Dogtown*, c.1936-7. Photo: Yale University Art Gallery. Gift of Walter Bareiss, B.S. 1940S, 1951.1.2.

Set in 11.5/13.5 pt BemboStd by Toppan Best-set Premedia Limited
Printed in Malaysia by Ho Printing (M) Sdn Bhd

1   2014

Contents

Contents

Acknowledgments

Like all books of this kind, this one is far better for the support, feedback, interventions, and complaints of colleagues, editors, assistants, anonymous readers, students, friends, and family.

The Harvard English Faculty Colloquium and the Harvard Graduate Americanist Colloquium heard various parts of this book and provided sharp and sympathetic feedback on its strengths and weaknesses, as did thoughtful audiences at the Modern Language Association, the American Literature Association, the University of Utah, SUNY Buffalo, Suffolk University, and the American Academy of Arts and Sciences. Chapters One, Four, Five, Seven, Nine, Eleven and Twelve all appear in print here for the first time. Chapter Three – excepting a few brief sections that appeared first in *Early American Literature* and the *New England Quarterly* – is original to this book as well. Earlier versions of Chapters Two appeared in *Religion and Literature* and then in *Infinite Conversations*. A version of Chapter Six appeared in *The New Republic*. A version of Chapter Eight appeared in *Reading The Middle Generation Anew*. Chapter Ten appeared in *American Literature's Aesthetic Dimensions*: the current chapter also includes excerpts from an essay originally published in *The New Republic*. Those chapters previously published are far better for the excellent readings and suggestions offered by editors and readers. I am grateful to Barbara Packer and Roger Lundin for their searching responses to "Variety as Religious Experience" (Chapter Two); to Leon Wieseltier for his smart and lucid editing of what became "Growing up a Goodman"; and I thank Eric Haralson for many excellent suggestions on the book chapter that is here, "Disinheriting New England." I am grateful to Chris Looby and Cindy Weinstein for helping me with "Upon a Peak in Beinecke". In a world where disinterested feedback is sometimes hard to come by, these editors provided suggestions both generous and practical. Among colleagues I want especially to thank Ramie Targoff and Stephen Greenblatt, Peter Sacks, Stephanie Sandler, and especially my friend Larry Buell, the most generous of mentors, and friends. Jay Parini was wonderfully supportive; so was Paul Dry. I am grateful to Emma Bennett at Wiley Blackwell for soliciting this manuscript and to Deirdre Ilkson for her skillful piloting of the manuscript through the review process. Combining imagination and efficiency, the Wiley Blackwell editorial team has been exemplary. I am grateful to Annette Abel, Zeb Korycinska, Kevin Fung, Jeffrey Goh, and Sara Henning-Stout for their professionalism and unfailing intelligence.

Most of the insights in this book originated in the classroom. One's best teachers, and critics, are always the students one teaches – or teaches with. Animated discussion – or stony stares – these must be critics' best guide to validity in interpretation. The list of those whose insights, sometimes years and years old, continue to detonate or evolve in my mind is very long. But it must include Gina Bloom, Jeremy Sigler, Jim Dawes, Jennifer Jordan Baker, Mike Magee, Bernie Rhie, Hester Blum, Dan Chiasson, Katie Petersen, Odile Harter, DeSales Harr, Jim von der Heydt, Emily Ogden, Erica Levy, Adam Zalisk, Andrew Goldstone, Adam Scheffler, John Radway, Ingrid Nelson, Martin Greenup, Sharon Howell, Andrew DuBois, Lauren Brozovich, Dave Weimer, Kaye Wierzbicki, Maggie Doherty, Cara Glatt, Leah Reis-Dennis and Orli Levine.

I owe an immense debt to the talented assistants, research and editorial, who worked with the manuscript, in various versions, through a period of years. Sol Kim- Bentley has seen this book through many drafts. She painstakingly deciphered and transcribed penciled, penned, or sticky-noted insertions into some chapters three and four times:

Acknowledgments

Sol sometimes smiles to see the same chapters return again and again to her desk, but she never complains. Still going strong at age 90, my dear friend Charlotte Maurer read and helped me rethink and clarify several parts of this book, some of whose passages I know she found too academic by half. Her wisdom as editor, and reader, will be with me always, although she is now gone. Superb undergraduate research assistants who worked on this book include Madeleine Bennett, Antonia Fraker, Sarah Hopkinson, and Elizabeth Tingue, and, in a break from her own career, my daughter Yael Levine. Through Yael, I am lucky to have found Caroline Bankoff, whose unfailing intelligence, dispatch, and professionalism help me get pages out the door: I count on her. And I owe deep thanks to Yang (Linda) Liu, who began work while writing her senior thesis as my undergraduate research assistant and then, two years into her own graduate training, helped me finish the manuscript. Linda's literary insights and her editorial pen, both delicate and sharp, gave this book a clarity and polish it would not otherwise have had.

I also wish to express my gratitude to the readers, many anonymous, who have liked —and have disliked —this book, in earlier and in later versions. Those enthusiastic about the book's approach helped me to persist in completing it. Those who objected to it have been, in some ways, even more helpful, for from them I learned the real stakes of my argument. But for their objections, I might not have known that what I wrote was a manifesto.

Finally, a different sort of thanks must go to my husband, Larry Summers, for first inviting me to visit, and then inviting me to share with him, James Russell Lowell's – the Harvard President's – house, Elmwood. As I describe in my Epilogue, living at Elmwood and with Larry changed my whole literary disposition; changed the way I see the meaning of what we do as teacher and scholar. No matter where our adventures take us, Larry and I will always share our very own Harvard, along with everything else.

1

Introduction

New England Beyond Criticism

Once, in the mid-twentieth century, children all over North America learned that a nation was born in Plymouth, Massachusetts. On bulletin boards outside classrooms across the continent, Pilgrims, cut out of black and white construction paper, were displayed to represent the purposeful beginnings of the nation. Orange and brown Indians stood by to assist the United States find its destiny. In the classrooms of secondary schools and institutions of higher learning, and in the public culture, the legacy of the doughty Pilgrims furnished the academic, and also the civic, curriculum for the nation. From New England, this curriculum taught, came America's founding rituals and folkways, its most enduring democratic practices, and its greatest, classic works of literary art.[1]

There are surely classrooms where this story is still being told. But the prestige of New England, in professional literary circles at least, has never been lower. Among the highest priorities of critics working in American literature in the second half of the twentieth century was the unseating of Protestant New England as the capital

New England Beyond Criticism: In Defense of America's First Literature, First Edition. Elisa New.
© 2014 Elisa New. Published 2014 by John Wiley & Sons, Ltd.

of American literary culture. As late as the 1960s, it was still axiomatic that the origins of American culture were to be found in this one region, its area extending north and east of Boston to the Canadian border, west and south of Boston to the Connecticut Valley, a region whose civilizational outline was already distinct by the end of the seventeenth century. Never mind this region's size relative to the vastness of the eventual United States. With its twin epicenters at Harvard and Yale, its links to high culture and high office, its roster of Adamses and Websters striding the national stage, this region of subcultures, frequently quite distinctive and frequently quite parochial – Separatist, Federalist, Abolitionist; Cantabridgean, Brahmin, WASP – somehow came to represent the quintessentially American.

But by the time a New England (San Francisco born) icon, Robert Frost, got up on a January day in 1961 to offer poetic tribute to the New England born (Catholic) President, this era was nearly over. Starting in the 1970s, and gathering force through the 1980s and 1990s, a rigorous and exciting revisionist scholarship began to expose the cultural processes and ideological interests by which Pilgrim grit was identified with the national Spirit, the Protestant mind with the national idea, and the New England classic with literary excellence. Distinguished critics joined forces to show how, through sermons, pedagogy, and print networks, through academic dynasties and intellectual oligarchies and self-reinforcing ideological formations, New England's primacy and representativeness were invented, established, and packaged for wide distribution.

Such scholars pointed out the obvious – that New England, an English outpost on a continent the French and Spanish had already explored, was not in any sense "first," and so could not have struck the template for all American culture. The Americanness of New England literature was revealed as a fiction, a back formation, or, in the catchall phrase, an ideological construction. Indigenous peoples had long populated the "wilderness" which Spanish, French, and English settlers laid claim to, and those settlers were themselves proud subjects of European kingdoms. For its first one hundred and fifty years, New England was in every sense colonial: geographically removed, culturally in thrall. Early modern explorers might have found it expedient to call densely populated Indian lands "howling wilderness," as, in subsequent decades, and then centuries, their descendants would find it similarly convenient to wrest national integrities, to claim national destinies, out of circumstances even more ambiguous. One simply had to overlook sea trade, slave trade, book trade, and sundry other transatlantic, trans-hemispheric, and transnational complications to claims of discrete and integral nationhood.

New England was always cagey about its associates (bankers in London; middlemen in Africa; sugar planters in the West Indies), self-conscious about its provincialities, insecure about its innovations, and, in the case of literature, deliberate when not outright desperate to show off its local product. Just as early "American" literature's founding texts had been written by the King's loyal subjects, written not only in the language but within the cultural orbit of Europe, so as late as seventy-five years after the Revolution many of the authors best known for establishing New England's primacy – Emerson, Hawthorne, Melville, Longfellow, Stowe – remained completely dependent on publishers and readers in London, Philadelphia, and New York. As New England mills relied on Southern cotton produced by African slaves, so the idea of New England's literary primacy depended upon networks of European distribution and approbation, on transatlantic and also intra-American pirating and reprinting. The premium the Virginia-raised Edgar Allan Poe sought in claiming his first book of poems authored by "A Bostonian" was (as Poe shrewdly surmised) more hype than reality, but it certainly lent cachet.

The academic revisionists who expressed skepticism about New England as founding region were naturally also interested in how New England's special prestige had been constructed; by whom, and to what ends. To be sure, to read the early literary histories of America, especially the criticism produced from the 1880s through World War I, is to encounter learnedness mingled quite noticeably with partisanship. A national literature commensurate with so great a nation had long been wanting, long sought and sometimes despaired of in the period between the 1790s and the 1890s. And so it was perhaps not that surprising that by the turn of the twentieth century the first Ivy League canon-makers would have been delighted to find the requisite materials so close at hand: the canon right outside their windows. But could it *really* have been the case, as Professor Barrett Wendell of Harvard intimated at the turn of the century, that virtually all of the nineteenth-century poets meriting attention should have had addresses along Brattle Street; that virtually all of the "major" writers of prose could have belonged to that cozy set that drank each other's claret in Cambridge, dug each other's gardens in Concord, and, when summer came, carried each other's picnic baskets up Berkshire summits? Could it have really been, as the critics of the 1930s to the 1950s who founded American Studies as a branch of New England studies implied, that the most salient literary challenges to Massachusetts hegemony should have come from no further than Connecticut, from a set of Hartford and New Haven based "New Lights" (headquarters: Yale) whose major difference from Boston's coastal, more liberal, Christians amounted to their yet fiercer determination to guard orthodoxy's flame? Or that the rigorous clerical literature of frontier Deerfield and Stockbridge was actually more productive of the American spirit than the vigorous and virile writings of Virginia's Tidewater? Could it really have been the case, later revisionists were justified in asking, that an entire national culture should have depended on the lucubrations of a few generations of Congregationalist ministers, Edwards to Emerson, Mather to Niebuhr, their ranks filled out by ministerial womenfolk – Rowlandson, Phelps, Stowe? Not to forget, either, the way these women had, despite immense readerships, received short, and invariably patronizing, shrift. The romanticization and canonization of the homiletic writings of certain Massachusetts Bay, Narragansett, Stockbridge, and New Haven ministers, and then the critical partiality to writers of "lyric" and "romance," all white men, effectively left out Rowlandson, Stowe and Warner, Child and Sedgwick, left out Wheatley, left out Du Bois, left out Occum; left out race

4

and gender, class and caste; left out slavery and the women's "sphere" and the ubiquitous sway of capital.

Fair enough, then, for critics of the 1980s and 1990s to pursue the question of whether those professors who discovered the roots of American culture in New England had not been themselves somewhat blind to how parochial they were, how chauvinistic even, creating America's canon in their own, in their region's – and, of course, in their gender's – image. White, male, Protestant, and over-whelmingly holding posts in the Ivy League, these had enjoyed a bit too much, and written a bit too much about, the world in which they were ever so comfortably ensconced. The critics who heralded the development of the New England literary tradition as a "flower-ing," a "renaissance," who not only described – but embraced – the idea of New England's "errand" – evinced excessive confidence in their own labors – the professing of literature – and excessive will-ingness to use the curriculum to shape the very souls of their students. With agendas extending beyond the literary into the civic, they presumed to impose two-semester courses in New England writers, and they had intimated that those who took those courses would be better people, and Americans, for having heard the lec-tures. Regarding teaching as more than a profession, they had endeavored more than the fostering of aesthetic pleasure – but also less than the inculcation of critical thinking. They had presumed to try to change people, and to change them for good.

Even if one granted their benign motives, were not the methods deployed by these earlier champions of New England themselves part of the problem? Partial to organic unities and pat typologies (delighting in designs and patterns, ready to cut through historical difference in order to suture Pilgrim Fathers to Minute Men to the Greatest Generation) and, what's more, moving with disquieting facility between lectern, pulpit, and Washington DC, had not these canon-makers missed how even the most liberal and dissentient discourses are co-opted by power? Had they not failed to discern that the New England literature they extolled for its rare capacity to preserve ambiguity, complexity, and nuance was, in fact, readily co-opted, and that the premium they placed on spiritual, aesthetic, intellectual, formal, and moral excellence was itself exclusionary, pushing to the "margins" (as came to be said) discourses just as, or more, central and revelatory, if sometimes less refined? The very practice of close reading (its meticulous and time-consuming rhythms indispensable in the classroom) and the discipline of the History of Ideas (its largeness of scope and rhetorical sweep easily pasted verbatim into State of the Union addresses) were Ivory-Tower/Halls-of-Power practices – practices giving undue primacy to highly privileged forms of culture and eventuating in a national canon remarkably unrepresentative. This canon that had pushed other literatures to the margins, this tradition imposed on college students and school children, this region whose values so drowned out other values – if these had circumvented general criticism, literary criticism would put them in their place.

The title of this book, a provocation, is meant to raise the question of whether academic literary criticism can, or should, be left to play that role. Its subtitle – another provocation – is meant to authorize rereadings in the texts of New England fully alert to their claims of cultural priority, yet still open to their primary power. Claims to priority were, from the beginning, constitutive of this tradition fully invested in the text, the Word, as a sort of prime mover: in literature's generative capacities. New England writing is committed to the charisma, the magnetism, and the force of print on a page, and it vests meaning in reading as a revelatory and inspiring experience. This is writing, moreover, that reserves a key cultural role for that literate interpreter (whether minister, essayist, novelist, poet, or professor) who opens the text to others, rehearsing and applying, animating and revitalizing its meaning. Whether they practice homiletics or metrics, write essays or historical narrative, or, even, criticism, these interpreters to do not dissolve into or disappear behind the literature of New England: they often emerge as full-bodied artists of, and characters within, this canon they strove to establish. Thus it is that this book, *New England Beyond Criticism*, hails many a forgotten, superseded, or rejected critic along its way. Although these pages will adjure readers to risk a re-encounter with the New England canon "beyond criticism," it will also, by its last pages, have embraced a larger than usual number of critics not much read anymore, the out-of-print and out-of-favor interpreters of remoter periods of literary history. Living and dead, symbols of the passé mingling with stalwarts of the Modern Language Association (MLA) – the critics of New England will receive in these pages attention both critical and uncritical.

Now it is obvious that each scholarly generation brings its own, and its particular historical epoch's, biases to what it reads. It is probably also true that the relatively accelerated history of America's ascent among the cultures of the world lent urgency to the project of canon making, providing fertile conditions for ideological distortions. That the distortions of one period are rarely legible until the next is an argument for the value of vigorous review, for a scrupulous and empirical attitude to prior claims, for a criticism ready to vet and correct. Or so the disposition of our own epoch tells us – an epoch in which the experience of American literature is mediated by the protocols of university research and the exactions of literary scholars, rather than, say, by the tastes or enthusiasms of a large and engaged readership.

Our own biases are best exhibited in, and announced by, the rarely questioned prestige of the very term "critical" – an assurance of probity and care, though not one aspiring to impact, outreach or even accessibility. A fitting term for an ethos rigorous, restrained, and insular, the function of the "critical" is to ground reading, to preserve it from enthusiasms too flighty (aesthetic or pedagogical, institutional or political) and from apprehensions amateurish or personal. This grounding, just as it sounds, safeguards soundness. The prestige of the critical certainly does not require us to cauterize all the surplus feeling that literary texts might evoke (indeed, the classroom functions, for a great majority of literary scholars, as a space of joyful unrestraint, and sometimes a refuge from the strictures of their critical lives). But the latitudes permitted by pedagogy are deemed problematic in criticism – where the task is to delimit and incise, not amplify, the power of the literary text; to contextualize and contain rhetorical strategies, so protecting understanding from mystifications. Implicated in all of these, a primary office of the critical is corrective. Criticism moves forward by detecting, and correcting, misapprehensions that past interpreters have perpetrated.

The very strong tilt toward the contemporary, characteristic of a critical age, is abundantly in evidence in scholarship on New England. Though historicist and materialist in orientation, our criticism maintains a bias toward literary advance, toward new findings, that discourages lending too much credence to the work of prior generations. It is naturally disposed to distrust characteristics that other eras prized: breadth and brio, conviction and accessibility, lyricism and vision, and a readiness to meet readers beyond disciplinary boundaries. Advanced readers of literature, and especially professional scholars of literature, take for granted that they are to maintain a distance from the texts they read, and distance too from the readings of these texts advanced by prior generations. Especially in the case of New England, a case where prior critics – those overzealous canonizers – proved too soft, it is for us to hold the line.

The task is made less simple, of course, by the fact that the New England canon bestowed on us by prior generations continues to have a quite vibrant life in the culture. Like it or not, our predecessors' canon stuck. The disposition of the critical establishment notwithstanding, it is still the case that readers of all kinds, both inside and outside the classroom, reserve special attention, regard, and devotion for the texts of New England and, what's more, for the civilization that these texts invented and continue to represent. Readers look to these texts for aesthetic pleasure, for spiritual succor, and for insight into the common good. They consult them while traveling to historical sites with their children, listening to inaugural addresses, watching *John Adams* or *The Abolitionists* on PBS (Public Broadcasting Service), passing through village greens in Vermont or deep woods in Maine. Twenty-first-century novelists and poets continue to mine this archive; the president of the United States and playwright Tony Kushner dine on its wisdom; New Urbanists and Hollywood directors, twentieth-century composers like Ives and Rorem, environmentalists and techies and political consultants all return to New England, confident they will find in its archive the classic, the iconic, American forms. Every public figure confessing to adultery inevitably has to don his "scarlet letter" for several news cycles, the stigma affixed not by literary critics but by the anchors of cable news, and every midlife career changer sees two roads diverging in a yellow wood. Images from Jonathan Edwards's "Sinners in the Hands of an Angry God" enter the cultural mainstream every few years when we count down to the End of the World: again. And one cannot stop at a historic village, Sturbridge or Plymouth Plantation, or walk through Harvard Yard or Mt Auburn Cemetery, or visit a historic writer's house ever so inconspicuously tucked off the highway, without finding tourists there. My physician reports that he took only one book with him on a late adolescent hike through the wilds of the Monongahela Valley – *Moby Dick* – because he knew that this book, a guide to finding himself, would announce his vocation. College sophomores, New Hampshire ministers and Vermont backpackers, adults in night courses and alumnae returning on tour buses, and visiting scholars from China and Japan and India continue to cherish the literature of New England. When Marilynne Robinson, whose work I treat in Chapter 11, titles a book *When I Was a Child, I Read Books*, the books she means are New England's.

As for me, the longer I've taught and thought about the literature of New England, the less comfortably I've lived in scholarly harness, the greater elbow room, the wider scope, I've come to feel is due the largeness, the strangeness, the beauty and power, of my subject.

Although the literature of New England was already at the center of my scholarly life before I began to teach at Harvard University in 1999, until that time my attachment to New England – or at least what part I confessed – was perfectly professional; or, even, as we say, academic. When friends and family inquired what I worked on, I'd reply that I worked on early, or classic, American literature, and when pressed further, I'd report that my scholarly specialty, my subfield, was the literature of New England. But, in fact, even before I moved to New England, when I asked *myself* the question of why

I worked on this tradition, my reasons were more along the lines Emily Dickinson had given Thomas Wentworth Higginson for how she recognized a poem: this stuff simply took the top of my head off.

The thinking, the teaching, the writing about literature of the region happened to fill certain criteria for scholarship, happened to contribute to a body of knowledge to be laid up in libraries. But the truth was – as again, I increasingly quoted Dickinson to myself – there was a "palsy" this writing "just relieved," a species of excitation to be indulged in private sessions of reading, in the woods or leaning over Cape Cod Bay; or, in the classroom. There one found secret sharers. Though my students may have come in believing that the Puritans were "puritanical," those who left themselves reasonably open were liable to find themselves, as Perry Miller himself had said they would, "staggering and reeling." The most "puritanical" of writers supplied experiences of sheer aesthetic rapture; and, at the same time, tutored varieties of mental discipline, complex states of consciousness, of alienation and uses of obscurity and difficulty rivaling anything attempted by the Modernists. The psychological intensity and candor of Puritan introspections; the etched sharpness of Transcendental observations of the natural world; the clarity and definition of New England civic precepts; the ferocity, and reach, of New England social strictures; the care in craft, the intrepidness about form, the esteem for creative activity, the honor paid to all literate forms of expression. Add to this the way, as Frost himself promised, certain New England sayings – proverbs, epigrams, bits of vernacular and portable folk wisdom – begin to give a rhythm and organization to the way one thinks (you *can't get there from here*; *if you don't like the weather, wait five minutes*; and even the contemporary, local use of *wicked* – as in *wicked* cold or *wicked* smart). And the way certain poems – Dickinson's "There's a Certain Slant of Light" and this one by Frost: "The way a crow / Shook down on me / The dust of snow / From a hemlock tree // Has given my heart a change of mood / And saved some part / Of a day I had rued" – more than once proved their therapeutic utility.

10

It is popularly thought that the "Protestant ethic" is an ethic of diligence and of duty. And superficially it is. Except, of course, that this ethic's central precept is remembering the barrenness of duty. With its wariness about "works," New England Protestantism abhors regularity, distrusts norms and protocols, and reserves special suspicion for the self-regard of the specialist. Writing, whether that of a seventeenth-century minister or a nineteenth-century prose writer or a twenty-first-century poet, is not self-justifying and requires a highly paradoxical attitude to the daily round: assiduous, yet – detached; mindful, yet – distrusting mere application; feet on the ground – heart tugging on kite strings. Though the object of knowledge may never be fully known, still the knower's obligation is greater, not lesser, for it. And whether the particular calling be selling nails or sowing beans, whether it be working in a Customs House or on a whale ship, whether standing before the community as a minister or as a lyceum speaker or as a professor of New England authors, the person long exposed to the New England Way will become liable to certain (as Thoreau called them) "extra-vagances."

I am certain this is why some of the apparently mildest of New England authors turn out to be daredevils when it comes to literary form. Such writers eschew rhetorical elegancies and regularities in favor of "plain" – which is to say frank, stark, immoderate, copious, surprising, improvised, ragged and jagged – modes of expression. Theirs is an art that cuts across the apparent grain of things into deeper tissue – back toward secrets, toward origins and reckonings. These are writers who conceive the relationship of visible to invisible phenomena somewhat as Cubists imagined the relationship of noses to napes, backgrounds to foregrounds. Puritans at their purest, New England writers at their most classic, are less orthodox than avant-garde.

New England Beyond Criticism is a book informed by my own experience as a critic and teacher of the literature of New England, as a transplanted resident and citizen of Massachusetts, and as a member of the faculty of New England's, and America's, oldest institution, Harvard. I hold the chair occupied before me by some of the most renowned, and controversial, New England scholars of the twentieth century, and, in ways I never expected, my personal life has led me deeply into Harvard history. I came to Harvard in 1999, where, by my very good fortune, I met and fell in love with, in 2001, Harvard's new president, Larry Summers. I married him in the Harvard President's house just a few weeks before, in 2006, his turbulent presidency ended: the five years of that term gave me access to, and perspective on, aspects of my University's, and New England's, history and culture I would never have come to see otherwise. Though not without their sting, my institutional adventures with Larry Summers were emancipating, helping me to see my field, my profession, and the meaning of my work in ways that were not hitherto obvious to me. These adventures, I am sure, played their part in inspiring me to step beyond certain disciplinary norms, beyond the mores of the day. They emboldened me to risk, sometimes, what Thoreau called extra-vagance.

I offer in the coming chapters a work of advocacy, an attempt to express, and to foster, a passion for the literature of New England not fully authorized by the protocols of literary criticism. This book is personal, sometimes explicitly so, taking the function of a "manifesto" to be different than that of a monograph or reference work. A manifesto is – it must be, in some significant part – a work of conviction and of emancipated passion. A manifesto must be ready to hazard drama, to suspend critical disbelief, to demonstrate, testify, and sometimes to marvel. Thus, in the coming chapters, I offer rereadings of New England texts open to their experiential potency – and open, too, to their canonical power, the role a given text may play in relation to the larger archive of texts of which it is a part. For canonicity is itself a literary effect, a crucial one, encouraging – and even sometimes commanding – responses not comprehended by a purely critical attitude. While it is certainly appropriate that a canon receive, from time to time, close and even suspicious scrutiny, those valuing its preservation do well, too, to cultivate modes of reading responsive to its influences. In the case of the New England canon, a canon so explicitly invested in the transformative, indeed converting power of the Word, one may as well not read at all as read too guardedly. With such a canon, too fortified an attitude of insusceptibility is, finally, impertinent. The chapters ahead would thus preserve, rather than interrupt, susceptibility to the text's power to excite and stir, its power to summon and convene, its power to touch the present with the very finger of the past. These chapters venture readings open to the spiritual excitations, the civic aspirations, and the institutional influences shaping many of the works produced in New England.

The first section, called *Excitations*, explores religious experience and its aftereffects in the poetic tradition. This section asks what I take to be the fundamental, though not frequently enough asked, question: Why would anyone have ever *wanted* to be a Puritan? Are not at least some of the questions we ought to be asking the early literature of New England experiential and aesthetic ones – questions going to the affective power and even appeal of Protestant writing: to how it makes us feel? Thus: what intellectual and spiritual longings did the sermonic and poetic literature of a Protestant establishment actually satisfy? How did beauty figure in texts of Protestant faith, and what were the pleasures of terror? What did it mean to seek to live "in this world but not of it" and how might such a creed have licensed, incubated, and fertilized poetry? What satisfactions were there in imagining the End of Days? Or, in directing attention to Hell, a pit of fire a long way down? Or, to Heaven, which is, and is yet not, in the sky? One answer I propose to all of these questions: for the thrill of it. These three chapters reintroduce Protestant excitations – the ups and downs, the drastic and exhilarating features of a belief system asking, permitting, licensing human beings to stretch their imaginations far beyond what their senses perceived.

In the second section, called *Congregations*, I pursue matters of community and individuality. Are Americans, as they sometimes like to think, "individuals," tested by wilderness, tempered by struggle, their individuality forged by their forebears? If so, what has proven so powerful about the New England Town Hall, the Commons,

13

about that idea of the People to whom, and for whom, statesmen still address their rhetoric? How best to describe the role of the podium, stump, and pulpit within New England, and American, civilization? Where do the dead figure in the tally of the People; and in what ways can rhetoric – and art – summon congregations impossible within any one historical moment? And what are individualism's costs; and alternatives? These chapters take us back to some key sites and moments in communal life: to the New England Way as it seeks to forge civic congregations; to artists who find in language itself a space of social converse; and to critiques of the New England flintiness and the Protestant ethic from within. The texts of New England may give sanctuary, and even an honored place, to the individual. Meanwhile, however, human need, human softness and vulnerability will also stake out territory within the very region of Pilgrim fortitude.

In the book's third section, *Matriculations*, I return to the incubator of the New England canon, and to what are perhaps New England's most hallowed institutions to this day, its universities. In these chapters, I probe the strong role learned culture has played and still plays within New England's literary tradition. These elite institutions – with their great libraries and mythic reputations; with their prestige within, and antagonisms with, the cities they dominate; with their imposing architectures, their eccentric calendars, their rituals and rosters – these enter, bear on, New England literature in quite literal ways. Professors are teachers, icons, gatekeepers, ancestors, heirs; students, members of classes, pass through classrooms over four years, over epochs, over centuries; curricula are evolved and canonized, contested and dislodged; there are reformations and counterreformations of literary fashion and taste; there are in-groups and out-groups, clerics and heretics, and again and again, there is the defense of The University, and its higher calling. The phrase itself, raised by its definite article, looks down from churchly heights. New England's first universities were, not incidentally, Divinity schools; its professors not merely instructors, but moral arbiters and guides. And even now, hundreds of years after their establishment – just how the professor stands behind his lectern, just where the canon stands in the curriculum, just how the oldest rituals stand up to the present's innovations – these questions exercise, stimulate, and imbue the newest writings.

In this third section of the book, and in the Epilogue that finally closes the book, my focus tightens. I keep in view the figure of the scholar, and of the literary critic, and I give increasing attention to those twentieth-century scholars and critics who have left real marks, whose vitality remains, once we open their pages, still bright. Intellectual impact: What is that? How long does it last and how does a field (say, the field of New England studies) accommodate the influences, and personalities, of the past? To be sure, in earlier chapters I will have already endeavored various trans-temporal, trans-disciplinary experiments, working to bring the work of prior critical generations into quite direct communication with those of today. Chapters 2 and 4, for instance, deploy different approaches to representing Emily Dickinson's manuscripts: Chapter 2 employs the typographic conventions contemporary critics prefer – those of R.W. Franklin – while Chapter 4 hews to conventions Thomas Johnson had established in the middle of the twentieth century. Chapter 5, to use another example, makes the legendary critic and teacher Perry Miller, and his student, Ann Douglas – my own graduate mentor – recipients and transmitters of a pedagogical narrative begun by none other than William Bradford. Moreover, this chapter works across period and genre boundaries, putting to the side some of those contemporary methodological protocols that keep discussions of seventeenth-century New World exploration entirely separate from discussions of twentieth-century poetic texts. In this chapter the findings of historicist critics of early America are allowed to penetrate poetry studies, while the surmising of poets – and the music of poetry – are ushered into the precincts of research. And in Chapter 7, on the other hand, I endeavor to treat historical crisis in a particular epoch (post-Civil depopulation) as the thread connecting the work of writers practicing in quite different registers and genres (statecraft, fiction, non-fiction, poetry).

Contemporary critical strictures, and especially critical categories, make quite it rare to encounter such writers as Edward Arlington Robinson, W.E.B. Du Bois, and Sarah Orne Jewett together (Du Bois so often placed within African American Writing; Jewett within Regionalism; Robinson among those, alas, of decaying reputation), and yet the writings of these three New England contemporaries describe nothing less than the postbellum rediscovery of poetry's convening power.

Finally, in the book's last (frankly autobiographical) Epilogue, I look back at the intellectual and literary history of New England, and at my Harvard predecessors, a colorful cast of characters! Belletrists and partisans, poetasters and editors, popularizers and obscurantists, New England promoters and New England debunkers, the many figures who appear in this chapter represent the different critical values and priorities. Our idea of the "critical" would have seemed to many of them an anything but essential category – as some of their ideas of New England now seem, from our vantage point, too decorative and dilettantish, or too jingoistic and exceptionalist, now (in the case of late twentieth- and early twenty-first-century work) even perhaps too cool, too surgical, too certain. Not a critical history so much as a critical walking tour or intellectual album, I endeavor in this last chapter to share my own esteem – and my affection – for critical forebears whose wisdom I am sure I have not outgrown.

There is an old Puritan saw – one of the most famous – I've kept in mind as I've completed the chapters of this book. Describing their position in the world, Puritans framed the ideal of living "in this world but not of it." A mode of double consciousness, this ideal acknowledged one's footing on *terra firma* and in human history while still evincing faith in meanings less localized, larger and less empirically comprehensible. "In this world but not of it" is the ideal of a profoundly imaginative, and profoundly literary, civilization, one that germinated in orthodox faith, but, when orthodoxy's hold loosened, retained that salutary openness to uncertainty and what William James called the will to believe. This openness is characteristic still, and for those who find the literature of

New England worth rereading, it guarantees posterity a New England still beyond criticism.

Note

1   Of the hundreds of books published in the last 30–40 years, those in the chronologically arranged list below are among the most influential and/or characteristic. Generally historicist in orientation, these books nevertheless exhibit a great range of methods, from the archival to the polemical, and they cover a very wide range of subfields, from Native American studies to avant-garde poetry. My larger question as to the drawbacks of our "critical" epoch notwithstanding, these are books reflecting the great fruitfulness of the turn to history for our understanding of the literature of New England. The reader seeking an education in contemporary New England – and Americanist – writing could not do better than to read through this list:

1973: Richard Slotkin, *Regeneration Through Violence: The Mythology of the American Frontier, 1600–1860*
1975: Sacvan Bercovitch, *Puritan Origins of the American Self*
1977: Ann Douglas, *The Feminization of American Culture*
1979: Michael Paul Rogin, *Subversive Genealogy: The Politics and Art of Herman Melville*
1981: Carolyn Porter, *Seeing and Being: The Plight of the Participant Observer in Emerson, James, Adams, and Faulkner*
1982: Jay Fliegelman, *Prodigals and Pilgrims*
1984: Philip Gura, *A Glimpse of Sion's Glory: Puritan Radicalism in New England, 1620–1660*
1985: Michael T. Gilmore, *American Romanticism and the Marketplace*
1986: Cathy Davidson, *Revolution and the Word: The Rise of the Novel in America*
1986: Myra Jehlen, *American Incarnation*
1986: Jane Tompkins, *Sensational Designs*
1987: Donald Pease, *Visionary Compacts: American Renaissance Writings in a Cultural Context*
1988: David S. Reynolds, *Beneath the American Renaissance: The Subversive Imagination in the Age of Emerson and Melville*

1989: Nina Baym, "Early Histories of American Literature: A Chapter in the Institution of New England," *American Literary History* 1:3

1989: Andrew Delbanco, *The Puritan Ordeal*

1989: Wai Chee Dimock, *Empire for Liberty: Melville and the Poetics of Individualism*

1990–2006: Paul Lauter and Juan Bruce Novoa (eds.), *The Heath Anthology of American Literature* (2 vols.)

1990: Michael Warner, *The Letters of the Republic: Publication and the Public Sphere in Eighteenth-Century America*

1990: Donald Weber, "Historicizing the Errand," *American Literary History* 2:1

1991: Lauren Berlant, *The Anatomy of National Fantasy: Hawthorne, Utopia, and Everyday Life*

1991: Ross Posnock, *The Trial of Curiosity: Henry James, William James, and the Challenge of Modernity*

1993: Karen Sánchez-Eppler, *Touching Liberty: Abolition, Feminism, and the Politics of the Body*

1993: Eric J. Sundquist, *To Wake the Nations: Race in the Making of American Literature*

1994–2006: Sacvan Bercovitch (ed.), *The Cambridge History of American Literature* (8 vols.)

1994: William Spengemann, *New World of Words*

1995: Lawrence Buell, *The Environmental Imagination: Thoreau, Nature Writing, and the Formation of American Culture*

1995: Walter Benn Michaels, *Our America: Nativism, Modernism, and Pluralism*

1995: Laura Dassow Walls, *Seeing New Worlds: Henry David Thoreau and Nineteenth-Century Natural Science*

1996: Christopher Castiglia, *Bound and Determined: Captivity, Culture-Crossing, and White Womanhood from Mary Rowlandson to Patty Hearst*

1996: Christopher Looby, *Voicing America: Language, Literary Form, and the Origins of the United States*

1997: Myra Jehlen and Michael Warner (eds.), *The English Literatures of America, 1500–1800*

1998: Susan L. Mizruchi, *The Science of Sacrifice: American Literature and Modern Social Theory*

1998: Nancy Ruttenburg, *Democratic Personality: Popular Voice and the Trial of American Authorship*

1999: Christopher Irmscher, *The Poetics of Natural History: From John Bartram to William James*

1999: Samuel Otter, *Melville's Anatomies*

2000: Renée L. Bergland, *The National Uncanny: Indian Ghosts and American Subjects*

2000: Sandra Gustafson, *Eloquence Is Power: Oratory and Performance in Early America*

2000: Christine Stansell, *American Moderns: Bohemian New York and the Creation of a New Century*

2001: Gillian Brown, *The Consent of the Governed: The Lockean Legacy in Early American Culture*

2001: Susan Castillo and Ivy Schweitzer, *The Literatures of Colonial America: An Anthology*

2001: Russ Castronovo, *Necro Citizenship: Death, Eroticism, and the Public Sphere in the Nineteenth-Century United States*

2001: Joseph Conforti, *Imagining New England: Explorations of Regional Identity from the Pilgrims to the Mid-Twentieth Century*

2001: Louis Menand, *The Metaphysical Club: A Story of Ideas in America*

2002: Kirsten Silva Gruesz, *Ambassadors of Culture: The Transamerican Origins of Latino Writing*

2003–2012: Stephen Gould Axelrod, Camille Roman, and Thomas Travisano (eds.), *The New Anthology of American Poetry* (3 vols.)

2003: Lisa M. Gordis, *Opening Scripture: Bible Reading and Interpretive Authority in Puritan New England*

2004: Mary Loeffelholz, *From School to Salon: Reading Nineteenth-Century American Women's Poetry*

2004: Eliza Richards, *Gender and the Poetics of Reception in Poe's Circle*

2005: Jennifer J. Baker, *Securing the Commonwealth: Debt, Speculation, and Writing in the Making of Early America*

2005: Anna Brickhouse, *Transamerican Literary Relations and the Nineteenth-Century Public Sphere*

2005: Virginia Jackson, *Dickinson's Misery: A Theory of Lyric Reading*

2005: Paul Lauter and Sandra Zagarell, "Literature," *The Encyclopedia of New England: The Culture and History of an American Region*

2007: Michelle Burnham, *Folded Selves: Colonial New England Writing in the World System*

2007: Max Cavitch, *American Elegy: The Poetry of Mourning from the Puritans to Whitman*

2008: Lisa Brooks, *The Common Pot: The Recovery of Native Space in the Northeast*

2008: Meredith L. McGill, *The Traffic In Poems: Nineteenth-Century Poetry and Transatlantic Exchange*

2013: Caroline Levander, *Where is American Literature?*

Part I

Excitations:
Protestant Ups and Downs

2

Variety as Religious Experience

Four Case Studies: Dickinson, Edwards, Taylor, and Cotton

Open Emily Dickinson's poetic daybooks of 1862–1863 on virtually any page and find the same scene – the light altered, a new array of objects standing at the ready – in process. A reversal of hemispheres is under way. The poet, a student of reversal's laws, is breasting the streams and updrafts of a richly currented environment which the poem fits her to navigate. The transformations find the speaker now liquid, now solid, now diffused in the elements, now given density by their admission. Committed to changes, she uses the poem to make passage from one state to another.

Thus, in #255 (Franklin) she is "The Drop, that wrestles in the sea –" and so "Forgets her own locality." Knowing herself "an incense small –" she yet "sighs, if all, is all, / How larger - be." A distinct drop, atomized in "an incense," occupies a space simultaneously limited and indefinite. The drop's spatial ambiguity evokes a corollary enigma of the emotional life: namely, the power of a sense of insignificance to plumb, then fill, the basin of what's large. The awe that small things feel, that wishful diffidence that releases itself

New England Beyond Criticism: In Defense of America's First Literature, First Edition. Elisa New.
© 2014 Elisa New. Published 2014 by John Wiley & Sons, Ltd.

in an exhalation, is uncannily expansive; smallness's sigh gives "an incense" breadth, or raises a plangent tide, each individual drop agitating the swell with its turmoil. Or take another poem, #413, "Heaven is so far of the Mind" where the speaker imagines that "were the Mind dissolved- / the Site - of it - by Architect/ Could not again be proved." The lines intimate the solidity of a Heaven undiscoverable on ordinary blueprints, but more, they also hint at this Heaven's eclectic situation in a zone far "of the mind." This "of," grammatical cousin to the "an" of "an incense," puts Heaven – where? Somewhere between deep in mind and far off from mind: just not, it is clear, among plain ideas. Heaven is not simply a dream we sustain until empirical tests prove it moot. Nor is it a form, a Platonic template, or realm of "intellectual beauty." Rather, Dickinson passionately surmises a reality, which, while not internally confined, is yet guaranteed by internal life. Her poems' repeated conviction is that poetic experience sustains states, opens worlds, whose properties remain inexplicable to all but the delicate instruments and sensitized adepts of this same experience.

The most delicate of these instruments is metaphor, which functions for Dickinson to catch meaning's pulse, and so, by extension, to register the inmost character of things. Following Dickinson's lead, here I use "metaphor" in this most general sense to describe a linguistic realm where phenomena discover and catch their truest likenesses by entertaining unlikenesses. The poetic vehicle's contravention of identity is key to that identity's truer realization as something other than, more alive than, its mere self. Dickinson's development and advancement of metaphor has, as Emerson would say, a very long American foreground. Her resistance to institutional Christianity very much to the point, Dickinson's understanding of metaphor as *just* enigmatic enough to indicate that the soul resembles no one's more than John Cotton's. Minister to the Massachusetts Bay migrants of the early seventeenth century, Cotton offered a challenging, imaginative, and poetic account of Divine grace. One might expect of an early "Puritan" a dogma depicting the soul in far more monolithic terms. But for Cotton, the outward signs of grace were always "mixed" or "coupled." Cotton's own

24

favorite metaphors for the state of grace prefigure Dickinson's own, but, even more fundamentally, his theological reliance on metaphor, his certainty as to grace's essentially poetic structure, predicts hers. As it happens, Cotton (himself attracted again and again to conceits of the "drop" in suspension – waterfalls, clouds, and, of course "Christ, the Fountain") found many ways to call the soul "an incense": to aerate grace's fluency, to consolidate faith's buoyancy; but more: to source the figural turns of his own homilies in grace's most ordinary motions.

Presumably, Puritans favored "plain" rhetoric, and what I am describing here may seem, by contrast, rather fancy. A good idea, then, to revisit just what "plain" may have included, what it may really have meant. By the end of this first chapter of this part of the book, therefore, we'll have found our way back to John Cotton himself, whose sometimes extravagant understanding of what plainness permitted gave scope and quite serviceable latitude to later American believers in beauty's revelatory power. "Puritan plainness in style," Kenneth Murdock succinctly warned, "did not imply tameness." And if Perry Miller's argument – that plain-stylists relied on the logical method of Peter Ramus to deliver doctrinal truth without embellishment – has not worn well, yet Miller's essential observation – that Puritans suspected "harmony . . . as the lighter part of rhetoric," resisting "likeness of sounds, measures and repetitions" in favor of "similes, metaphors, illustrations and examples" – has.[1] Indeed, in Harry Stout's words, Puritan preachers found in "metaphor or 'similitude' all the latent extravagances of the minister's imagination" (43).[2] Beauty's faculty for ringing changes on sameness, for summoning variety out of monotony, remains an article of both aesthetic and Christian faith for practitioners of a distinctive American poetics.

I'll proceed backward through New England literary history here, from Dickinson (writing in the 1860s) back toward the early seventeenth-century work of John Cotton, by way of two other virtuosos – Jonathan Edwards, America's premier impresario of gravity, buoyancy, and complex beauty, and Edward Taylor, American champion of the mixed metaphor. In all of these we see

25

confirmation of Andrew Delbanco's rich assertion that for Cotton, "to be a Christian is to grasp the essence of metaphor,"[3] a claim with implications as important for the study of New England poetry as for New England preaching. A poetic tradition oriented away from apparent (and therefore accessible) and toward more enigmatic (and necessarily less accessible) forms of poetic pleasure incubates in a faith oriented toward the unseen, the unglimpsed, the non-apparent; and moreover, toward the various, the mixed, and the complex. This is not to say that American poetry, like American faith, does not sometimes fall prey to ostentation, to the very decorative effects Protestant reformers reviled. There are inglorious moments in metaphor's New England career, moments when the fullness of grace, an exquisite condition, attenuates itself in more conspicuous convulsions of style. Allowing for these, the goal of the coming pages is to show where the metaphoric not only describes, but sustains, spiritual liveliness.

In the end, for those committed to it (whether poets or theologians) metaphor functions to keep open that valve between – as the Puritan saw goes – life in, and of, this world. Cleared by the grateful helix of metaphor – tenor and vehicle transfusing revelatory experience back and forth through an aperture of rare situation – the self is stirred out of stagnancy and made a place of access and movement. Protestant innerness is delivered from self-absorption, and the regimens of the spirit from mere occultism or priestcraft. From Luther we recall that Grace, while inward, should never be reclusive. The sign of its presence is, indeed, an expressive versatility not context dependent but, rather, never alone where the Word goes with it: Protestant grace is, we might say, consent dependent. Thus, Cotton insists, grace is not outgoing; not even its signs go alone: "but how is it coupled, for God couples every grace with another grace that they may poise one another, as Christ sent out his disciples two and two together; for all the Graces of the spirit join one another" (Cotton 125).

"How it is coupled?" is, of course, the enigma motivating Dickinson's own method. In poem after poem, Dickinson tracks meaning to its origin in what she calls "Internal difference," a seam of encounter which neither purely external observation nor solely inner intuition detects[4]. There, summer can have a "further" (as in poem #895 beginning "Further in Summer than the Birds -") as light can have a "Heft" (as in the poem – analyzed at length in Chapter 4 – beginning "There's a certain Slant of light"). The torque of the poem, rearranging vectors in the course of its action, reveals all the iridescences which either the removed or the privileged view will occlude. By the 1860s, and by such poems as "I dwell in Possibility," Dickinson simply takes for granted that any spiritual endeavor with half a chance must find its dwelling place not in "prose" but in this mixed zone of "possibility."

> I dwell in Possibility -
> A fairer House than Prose -
> More numerous of Windows -
> Superior - for Doors -

Prose, dispatched by the poet to describe, all at once, linguistic univocality, dull perceptual wit and religious literalism, will prove inadequate to discern the many mansions within the Father's house. Poetry, on the other hand, discovers planes, divines proportions that while manifold are not – and this is crucial – simply many. The poem manages a dense internal complication of the many in the one, but without exiling that complication in merely mimetic, or repetitive, excrescency. To be sure, if, as Kierkegaard showed, the common symptom of poetic superfluity and spiritual deadness is a willed and meaningless repetition (which confirms, rather than relieves, atrophy of structure), Dickinson develops a complexity free of repetition where, for instance, degree is an internal dynamic of structure itself, rather than an anxious mimetic chafing of structure's fixed extremities. Under this degree's auspices, even the most extravagant predicates of possibility may escape hyperbole, and language itself maintains that fidelity to function which Puritans had called plain. For instance, "numerous" and "superior" in "I dwell in Possibility" do not impound or engross merit but rather recognize, admit, and give play to its many shades. Like marvelous hinges, "numerous" and "superior" open the poem to fresher and fresher drafts: to full, partial, and still invisible planes of implication. This is why in this poem we see, or think we see, all at the same time: Pentateuchal tabernacle, Solomonic Temple, and City of God.

> Of Chambers as the Cedars -
> Impregnable of eye -
> And for an everlasting Roof
> The Gambrels of the Sky -

The mansions of possibility are not ranked as to genre. The Kingdom of Revelation by other lights, after all, is just a castle in the air. By still others, half-up, its open portals admit even homelier scents: cedar chest, sawdust, beams; the smell of changing weather. Frontier, the poem reminds, is one of our words for possibility.

Such connotative impasto might be heavy, to be sure, but for the sheerness of each element, so that an evanescence of image prevents the poem's surface from that over-elaborated obscurity Marianne Moore later had in mind when she reviled sophistication for its way of muddying "prismatic color." Prevents it too from that certain decadence Hart Crane had in mind when he made Poe, whose work the next chapter treats, poetry's fallen prince – and not so much for his Gothic themes as for an actually grislier trespass for a poet: love of the dead letter; love of effects. In Dickinson's poem, though, the images here lie translucent on each other, or simultaneous with one another; or, they prefigure and recall one another, each the penumbral hint or echo of the other, contrapuntal ciphers of a less visible, still unrealized, but eagerly expected order of Being. The temporal dimension is as crucial as the spatial since the images we see seem to depend on an eccentric temporality of possibility that retains the affective tones and halftones of life in time – eagerness, anticipation, anticlimax; giddiness, tedium, regularity – but dispenses with its workaday divisions – past, present, future (it happened then, it's happening now, etc.). Further, as time is pressed in this poem for its elixir of feeling (not the increments of sequence but the pangs that seam or "rivet" such sequence together), tones too will disclose many faces, the least telling of which, the emptiest, will be the self-evident.[5] We know from other poems that monochromatics of tone belong to very dull personages, to those "somebodies" who evict the more vital nobody ("I'm nobody! Who are you!"). The croak of self-declaration, of identity, proves beyond doubt a usurpation, a frog installed in a nobody's place to service the tone-deaf.

Tones mixed in a suspension, on the other hand, indicate the happy disappearance of this doughty personage behind one whose glimmering coexistences indicate vitality and changefulness. Thus, the tonal complexity of "I dwell in Possibility," is compounded, alchemized, out of lesser moods, greedier selves, now relieved of assertion and mass. The final lines, in which the speaker "spread[s] wide my narrow Hands / to gather Paradise," hint at these less subtle somebodies – the social pugilist or queenly diva of circumference who "sneered softly" at lesser transports. Or, she of nebulous outline and existential emergency, she whose terror of empty space her various "columnar selves" ("On a Columnar Self - /How ample to rely/In Tumult – or Extremity/How good the Certainty") fore-stalled. These confute each other. The poem's final pose, relieving any vacancy of self, transfigures antinomian overassertion as well. This self neither incorporates nor incarnates.[6] It knows over-reali-zation, literalization, for the surest way to run afoul of meaning, to strand expectation, like the prince, in green warts in a "bog." Rather, by means of a certain subtle process that metaphor enables – a poise in space, of time, by mood – she who gathers wide her narrow hands is graced with openness and fullness both.

Or, perhaps this poem is not simply graced with fullness (a pleas-ant but honorific condition) but full of grace. What we are seeing here are the near and further ranges of a grace which Dickinson's most accomplished lyrics labor to achieve; as well as the poetic tools she deploys in achieving that grace. The grace itself, however, had already been brought to a rather advanced sense of development by Dickinson's precursors. Its gestalt necessarily imbued Calvinist rigor with distinctly aesthetic, specifically poetic, kinds of sense.

This rigor is of a character that contradicts still quite live assump-tions about the Protestant subject. But the significance of an internal dynamism not equivalent to solid self-presence (or identity) can't really be overstressed, since it is not yet generally recognized just how normative for early American Christians, was the idea of Christian as grace's ductile and even eclectic character. Attention to purities and identities detracts from the more recondite discourses springing up not around selves, or even subjects, but around souls.

Unlike the self, this soul has, in place of identity, a knack for what Jonathan Edwards calls consent – which is to say a gift for living doubly, contrapuntally, responsively: or, to invoke a favorite Protestant figure for this adjustment, musically. The graced soul is that gifted with talents for modulation and transposition: in place of an identity it has – and we want to use this word spatially and musically – *range*. While selves seek selves, disporting themselves in such binary choreographies that give identity center and ballast, souls, on the other hand, sing, but as they sing, they also fly: both the singing and the flying – and here's the hard part – more like the other activity than like life itself. Souls are characterized by their variety and not their self-presence. Indeed, music that confines itself to mere singing exiles itself in its most obvious talent – like Dickinson's frog in its bog. Music, however, that transposes chords in flight as, in turn, flight finds tempo in it, achieves diviner scale. Such music ranges in possibility.

This capacity for transposition is the salient virtue, for instance, that Jonathan Edwards finds to praise in his love letter and saint's portrait of Sarah Pierrepoint, whom he later married.

> They say there is a certain young lady in New Haven, who is beloved of that Almighty Being, who made and rules the world and that there are certain seasons in which this great Being, in some way or other invisible, comes to her and fills her mind with exceeding sweet delight, that she hardly cares for anything except to meditate on him – that she expects, after a while to be raised up out of the world and caught up into heaven; being assured that he loves her too well to let her remain at a distance from him. . . . She will sometimes go about from place to place, singing sweetly; and she seems to be always full of joy and pleasure; and no one knows for

what. She loves to be alone, and to wander in the fields and on the mountains, and seems to have always someone invisible conversing with her.

Sarah is a person whose habit of singing exemplifies a spiritual reciprocity of inner turns and outer forms not to be confused with mere grace of carriage, nor with the admirable, but finally one-dimensional, accomplishments of the Proverbial woman of valor. Self-possessed but in constant converse; living in sacred space while among local hills; eager for, but not impatient of God's visitations; expressive but impressed, open and mysterious, Sarah Pierrepoint's excellency recalls that of the Hebrew Scriptural Woman of Valor, of the Book of Proverbs. But while Proverbs catalogues virtues and enumerates competencies, Edwards stresses not discrete acts or observances, but the effortless choreography undergirding Sarah's usual round; Sarah Pierrepoint's external movements are what Protestants deem the effects, rather than the satisfying conditions, of her soul's justification. Her loveliness, her efforts at virtue, do not secure her redemption; they rather simply illustrate and exhibit her redemption. Her characteristically weightless bearing is but the visible face of her soul's multifacets. The model for what Edwards will identify as true virtue, Sarah walks in variety.

Later on in Edwards's career, it is, of course, precisely the lack of such variety that finds out the sinner. In "Sinners in the Hands of an Angry God" it is the sinner's inert and pedestrian identity with himself, and his therefore base and cautious clinging to the clay – to known and visible plane – that will suggest his ultimate fate. While Sarah Pierrepoint moves "from place to place," her true, her only home, reciprocity, the sinner plays no part in the world's motions but to be vulnerable to them. Dead already, the fallen self is encumbered by an inner density and obscurity – a dark architecture – that parodies Sarah Pierrepoint's fullness with weight and burlesques her spiritual vitality with jumpy reflexes. Selves, "engrossed by finity," in Dickinson's Edwardsean phrase, contain nothing but themselves; limited to self-love, they are greedy for, engorged on, themselves. But that lightness Sarah Pierrepoint enjoys, as Dickinson herself will

31

testify, needs hold or hoard nothing. As Dickinson writes: "I take - no less than skies/ For Earths grow thick as / Berries, in my native Town -/ My basket holds - just Firmaments -/ Those - dangle easy - on my arm, / But smaller bundles - Cram."

Edwards's identification of beauty with attraction, and of the spiritual life as buoyant movement between disparate realms, will later inform his work on both the conceptual and rhetorical levels. Edwards always assumes that relation is the stamp on excellence, that truth is a drawing together. Echoing Cotton on the coupling of graces, he writes, "One alone cannot be excellent . . . for in such a case there can be no matter of relation."[7] Such a conviction will make it singularly satisfying to the young Edwards that it takes red and violet, the two poles of the spectrum, to make white. One great attraction in Edwards, for those who discover it, is his relish for lighting on the deeper logic behind the Creator's often counterintuitive moves. Edwards' oeuvre abounds in tensely sprung expositions, in surprising bridgings and daring landings. With considerable derring-do, he balances gravity on thin air; he finds freedom's scope within foreknowledge; he discovers Christianity's simplest axiom in Newton's *Principia*. Edwards shows how the God who expresses Himself in complex mixtures would naturally mix His scientific and His sacred law, would naturally make the Fall feel like falling. Meanwhile, as such unlikely conceptual marriages are forged at every juncture of Edwards's work, rhetorically too, he likes to work in a variety of idioms, each governed by the law of consenting opposites. For example, in such speculative essays as "Of Being," awe must accommodate empiricist rigor, and vice versa: the contemplation of nothingness, an exercise requiring that "we expel body from our thoughts," leads to where "the sleeping rocks dream." It is as if Locke and Augustine stood before one adamantine object: a metaphor mind will not penetrate it because it is made of mind itself. Just so, in his works of intellectual disputation, the particularity and partiality of doctrinal conviction are in a constant *pas de deux* with the urbanity of the international and "common sense." In his homiletics, uncanny pairings of scripture and science, colloquial directness and learned allusion spin like plates on either intellectual hand. Using multiple faculties at once, Edwards demonstrates, even as he entreats, grace's ambidextrousness.

All of these reciprocities and more had been predicted in Edwards's portrait of Sarah Pierrepoint – whose gift is for living largely but without being large. Finally, Sarah Pierrepoint's lightsome singing is a sign of her identity's, her subjectivity's, release into, and commerce with, that more diffuse and diverse environment which, here as elsewhere, is deemed God's true climate. If one effect of the Fall, as Edwards understood it, was to bifurcate and encrypt Being in a temporal and spatial geology (iron-edged, subject to impact), he lofts his saint in a more permeable region without fault-lines or preci-pices. There, her sanctification, her outer carriage, was never not aligned with her inner justification. Sarah has what no sinner enjoys – an elation we might as well call: fun.

It should not surprise us at all that Jonathan Edwards goes in, and goes in big, for such fun. His own intellectual barnstorming suggests as much, but fun is also an unmistakable aspect, and indeed persuasive evidence, of a saint's justification, for poet-minister Edward Taylor. Taylor devotes the whole Preface of *God's Determina-tions* to postulating fun on a Divine scale, conjuring for us just what precision of timing, just what gladness of touch was enjoyed by that Creator who fashioned a world and called it "good." The ordered, even the guided harmony of God's perfect creation is itself sug-gested in the rhythmic inevitability of a chiming and reiterated "Who?" As the questions court their closure, so too does the Divine creativity realize and pleasure itself in the rondure of form.

> Who Lac'de and Filletted the earth so fine
> With Rivers like green Ribbons Smaragdine?
> Who made the Seas its Selvadge, and it locks
> Like a Quilt Ball within a Silver Box?
> Who spread its Canopy? Or curtains Spun
> Who in this Bowling Alley bowl'd the Sun?

The lines give a human accounting of the divine satisfaction that pronounced "It is good." As if to induce a kind of prelapsarian reverie, to virtualize, if only as fantasy, the lost dream of man's infancy, the miniaturized images to follow afford the child a glimpse of that world where man lived as a God. The prospect the poem surveys is generous, rolling on and on, and the eye feasts on the cunning way it all fits: river in bank like cloth within selvage; the colors varnished, the design true, the very constellations made the brilliant appointments of a dollhouse, or, of a play-space that we are allowed, for the moment anyway, to command. By the end of *God's Determinations,* in the final poem, "The Joy of Church Fellowship Rightly Attended," Taylor can report that similar fun now flows to the Elect: "For in God's Coach they Sweetly Sing / As they To Glory Ride Within." Note well: Taylor's visible saints do not just fly or strum, let forth carols or wing through clouds in a coach. Rather, as recorded by a poetic informant with, by the way, similarly excellent timing – "In heáven soáring úp / I drópped an eár" – they finesse both, reposing on melody; caroling buoyancy, their interior scansion exactly adjusted to the external situation. The lines that transport the saints are sprightly – and ever so slightly softened with a certain mirth – yet the saints celebrated in them are no more lightweights than Sarah Pierrepoint. If their ease and mastery of the divine refrain are now more play than regimen, once they had not known their own strength. As Adam's progeny they *had* to have been exercised by the work of knowing. The enjoyment of grace accruing to the elect is not, in Taylor's version, relaxation but a kind of fruition or expanded range: heavenly assurance feels like know-how, like being in form, like literacy, though a literacy transcending mere mastery of the letter.[8] Indeed, as the text sharing, or even perhaps informing, the rhetorical figures of "The Joy of Church Fellowship" reminds, the saint's soaring is like the moment, hard to isolate, when a child fully comprehends his primer text. He need not any longer make out the letters, or even the words; reading raises him up, carrying him and the whole alphabet away. So the Word carries mere words into the wild blue yonder; spirit levitating its observances. Why else would the *New England Primer* designate that the reward for spiritual literacy is riding in style through limpid blue: "He that learns his letters fair / Shall have a coach to take the air."

Of course, there is perhaps no Christian figure more clichéd, more ridiculous than the figure of the airborne soul with its zither. But there is reason to consider it nonetheless, since the persistence of the figure, as well as its devolution into cliché, has much to tell us: first, about the persistence and appeal of a certain kind of Christian pleasure, but second: about the history and development of a poetic ideal informed by it. This ideal honors not the metaphor itself (not, to invoke the Calvinist analogue, outward behavior, or the beauty of the figure itself) but its kinetics on loan to "the figure the poem makes" (Frost). This ideal honors not meter, but, as in the even more influential, though enigmatic, formulation, the "argument" meter makes (Emerson). Both of these poetic principles emphasize a making, a mixing (or, as Cotton terms, a "turning") that is in fact latent in and deeded by Edwards and Taylor. Flying and singing, images of a proficient poise, depend on an updraft for their lift that is not internal to, or satisfied by, the figure, but rather dwelling just inside, filling the sheets of, its ductility. As a form virtue takes, it is airborne; as virtue's sufficient form: heavy as lead.

In other words, what the flying singer provides, as Emerson might say, is the meter in which a necessarily protean virtue can make its argument. The singer is an expediency, a cipher even for virtue's triumphant ascent to a manner of Being not just in, but of, time and space. Such emphasis on making will necessarily enforce circumspection as to the value of the made-thing, deferring and devaluing "works" or the more meretricious realizations of style. At the same time, though, it will lift constraints on figural extravagance, elevating genre and bestowing the prestige of Bezalel on refinements of craft. Thus, Edwards fashions his piece on Sarah Pierrepoint as a virtuoso piece, an aria or motet unabashedly elaborated in baroque detail. More formalized than a love letter, more lyrical than any theological explication, Edwards' highly stylized saint's portrait assumes that the godliness in Sarah is well served by deliberate art; and, the God who made her glorified also through the arduous discipline of the creative act. Though working in a different, homelier genre, Taylor does the same. He allows the sing-song and the charm of his refrain to coax a certain indulgence, or imaginative suspension of disbelief, requisite to full appreciation of the saint's joy (for "in Christ's coach they sweetly sing," etc.). Taking that same latitude Frost claims in *A Boy's Will*, Taylor essentially bids: "you come too." In both cases, the deployment of a particular highly stylized figure as mnemonic for grace holds literal investment in the figure at bay. Edwards's gliding, saintly Sarah, Taylor's merry flying saints are effects, somewhat surprising effects, of virtue's dynamics: their graceful conduct is result of what's conducted through them; the picture of harmony they happen to exhibit does not satisfy or resolve but rather simply betokens the force, the grace of argument.

When the argument fails, to be sure, there is little to prevent the strumming seraph from lapsing into the worst kind of cliché . Such lapses are common, even among the most angelic poets. Dickinson's "little Tippler," she quaffing quantities of that "liquor never brewed" ("Till Seraphs swing their snowy Hats - /And Saints - to windows run - /To see the little Tippler/ Leaning against the - Sun") swings very close indeed to kitsch; and Dickinson has, we might as well admit, a weakness for the stanza tuned to migrainal intensity. Dickinson is not above pillaging an adjacent stanza for some rare figure and then leaving it half-developed, not felicitously "mixed" in Cotton's sense, but just abandoned to congeal in its own cleverness. Then, Dickinson's technique can descend to so much china painting, and her uncanny spatial effects seem grandiose or ad hoc. There is not enough at such moments to distinguish Dickinson's heaven, a musicale with lanterns, from Huck Finn's same, where Miss Watson and the Widow Douglas hover and bob on the mauve and gold. However, when this does happen, what's gone wrong is telling: the effects of metaphor have overcharged and finally cauterized metaphor's life principle of relation. What remains is a stylistic or representational residue – a self-perpetuating extent of mimetic half-life parodying the more vital life it affects to maintain. What remains is sanctification without justification; or, in poetic terms, language attenuated in effects.

Such effects were, we might surmise, what Hart Crane must have had in mind when, in "The Tunnel," he used the images of "hair beyond extinction" and of "verdigris" – the green mold on copper – to introduce Poe's language of luxurious but moribund fecundity. Mourning the modern amputation of language from its source in soul, and following poetry's literal descent to the merely vehicular, Crane lets Poe punch tickets on poetry's last run to "Gravesend": "Why do I often see your visage here? Your eyes like agate lanterns – on and on." But these "eyes" deflect a light they do not see. They simulate quickness while they are, in fact, stone. There is, indeed, nothing behind the pupil's agate but the artful and potentially damned hand that fashioned them, as not incidentally, Poe had himself fashioned his agate-eyed mascot, Psyche, by smelting hell, Helen, and Hellenism, three bewitching vehicles to one phantom, absent tenor – no there there; no meeting on a seam of encounter. Synthesizer of beauty out of classical junk, Poe functions in "The Tunnel" as one of his own effects, his human visage frozen in a rictus signifying over-signification. And what Crane sees, and tele-scopes so brilliantly in this horrified, but resolute internment of Poe with his poetics, is that in, say, "The Bells," nothing changes, nothing alters – even though in stanza one we hear the "silver bells" that "tinkle, tinkle, tinkle"; in two, the "mellow wedding bells" that "swell" and "dwell"; in three, the "loud alarum bells" that "clash," "roar," and make "uproar"; and in four, the iron bells that "toll" and "roll." Each set of sonorities remains within its own geometry or ellipse. Each strikes the fixed set of variations in its complement of tones, heard by a hearing not likely to be changed by bells because identical with them.

> And the people – ah the people –
> They that dwell up in the steeple,
> All alone
> And who tolling, tolling, tolling,
> In that muffled monotone
> Feel a glory in so rolling
> On the human heart a stone

37

It is no more than poetic justice that Crane should reduce Poe's head to a prosthesis of the strap it hangs on. Poe's people do not just live in: they are "of" the steeple, clappers to sound's fuller body.

Poe's style is so revealing, and was so controversial, because it jumps the track running from Cotton through Edwards, Dickinson through Frost and Crane; Poe reminds us of how much these poetries actually may borrow from, how consistent are they with, that dialectical, as opposed to rhetorical, ethos so concerned to be plain.

For what is implicit in the pages on Poe above, and will receive a great more attention in the next chapter, is an essentially rhetorical aesthetics, an aesthetics of linguistic effects. It is this Emerson, like Dickinson, Taylor, Edwards, and Cotton before him, refused. "Give me truths / for I am weary of the surfaces, and die of inanition" wrote Emerson in "Blight." And again, in "Merlin," "The trivial harp will never please/ Or fill my craving ear." And again in "Ode" where Emerson implicates his own "honied thought" implicated along with "the priests can/or statesman's rant." These are only a few instances, of course, of what those familiar with Emerson's verse will recognize: that nearly every well-known poem of Emerson's is – or contains – an animadversion against poetry. Poetry assertive of surface but with plugged-up ducts; poetry shut in unity at the price of variety; poetry reaching prehensile, but empty inside: all such poetry, lacking Spirit, is, as Teresa Toulouse puts it, "dead formal performance" (174).[9]

Such dead formal performance, which substitutes external action for inner motion, is what Emerson's criticizes in his Divinity School Address. But it is, somewhat ironically, precisely what John Cotton had in mind in *Christ, the Fountain of Life*," a series of twelve sermons all parsing John 1:5:12, "He that Hath the Son, hath life, and he that hath not the Son, hath not life." Cotton's unjustified souls maintain an uncanny adjacency with life – not relationship, but the more mechanical dependency and contiguity of reaction to action. Cotton's soul that "hath not life" may be, he writes, likened to a thing that may "move in its place, and yet move from some kind of outward respects; as a Watch or a Clock it moves, but it is from the weight that lyes and hangs upon it, and so it is rather a violent motion than a natural." This juxtaposition of Poe's poetics and Cotton's homiletics gives us purchase in all that is actually at stake in New England debates on style, plain and ornate, and all that may later have given such ethical urgency to the development of various American poetics.

Metaphor is not only the favored device of Cotton's; it is also, according to the necessary tautology of Cotton's affectionate creed, that style's chief object. For Cotton, the graced soul is a soul adept at mixings and meltings, the soul habitually acting against its own identity, or integrity. Grace works on soul as metaphoric vehicle works on tenor, orienting it toward its truer − which is not to say its most *integral*, but rather its most responsive, and in some ways dis-integral − bearing.[10] To cite just one of Cotton's many formulations of this process:

> love, which was as heat and fire to thaw and warm, cold and hard hearts, it is as it were, cold water, which allays that heat and bitterness and harshness, which else our hearts are subject to . . . it both thaws our cold and still hearts towards our brethren, and also puts a watery temper to cool our wrath toward our enemies; it is a mighty power of the Spirit of Grace to turn itself so many ways. (121)

The turning, grace's primary faculty for Cotton, is, of course, another name for metaphor. Trope means turn. Just so, in Cotton, grace's infusion rhetorizes the self and gives it torsion and flex, so that phenomena strictly inner or outer, spiritual or earthly, are pressed until their tough husks loosen and dissolve and identity gives itself up. If, for Poe, the technical grace of the poem functioned in essence to make things more and more themselves, Cotton's grace knows identity for its nemesis.

For a final instance, then, of that variety that gives meaning to New England religious experience, we cannot do better than read Cotton's own description of the graced soul, a description that sums up the case for variety as a key attribute of religious experience while also exhibiting the literary complexity (what Edwards calls the complex beauty) that accompanies such experience. "This is a combination of graces," Cotton wrote:

> that are not wont to be found in men mixed together, but it is found in the people of God, that live a sanctified and a holy life. I know not better what to instance it in than the liquid air, of all other things the most easiest to be pierced through; of itself it give way to every creature, not the least fly or least stone cast into it, but it gives way to it of its self; yet if God say it shall be as a Firmament, between the waters above, and the waters below, it then stands like a wall of brass, and yields not; it will not suffer the water in the clouds to fall down, but if it do fall to water the earth, it shall strain through the air as through a sieve, the clouds sometimes are so full that one would think they would burst through the air, and fall upon the earth, but God having set the air to be a firmament, or expulsion between the waters above, and the waters below, though of itself a very liquid thing, yet it stands like to a wall of brasse. And truly so it is a Christian.[11] (114)

Cotton's explicit aim is to explicate Moses' kind of holiness, a holiness capable of great strength, but a strength more elemental than apparent. Like the weather, which later supplies Taylor, Edwards, and Dickinson − not to mention Emerson and Frost, too − with some of their own most fertile figures, Cotton's Moses channels a force not mistakable for authority; he has currency rather than identity, a capacity for flow and turn, realizing Creation's, and Christianity's, own idiom. Indeed, Moses' virtue is appropriately expressed in a language itself mingling Genesis and John, two sources of his liveliness. Moses' conservancy with fluid, vapor, gravity, and ground tutors his ready acceptance of other forms: if Genesis flows through him as a force of creative dynamism lifted above chaos, it is John that specifies the shape this dynamism will take. And so Cotton's Moses is himself a range of possibility: a cloud bursting with latency, a live acoustic primed to vibrate with Christ, the Fountain's, gush of sound.

Finally, Cotton's Moses is made by and of metaphor; his outward carriage is the meter in which God makes argument. Cosmetic sanctification and baroque embellishment – doppelgangers in the theological and rhetorical realms – will ultimately expose and discredit one another. Grace and metaphor, committed to mutual recognizance, will, in John Cotton's words, "poise one another." In Cotton's homiletics, as in later American poetics, the test of grace is not unity but the variety that gives life to religious, as to aesthetic, experience.

Notes

1 Perry Miller's insistence on Ramus as the key to the plain style has not, by and large, been persuasive to other critics. Bozeman, Daly, Toulouse, and Knight all concur, contra Miller that, as Bozeman puts it, "the Scripture was approached . . . not as a logical structure, but as a dramatic event . . . the 'first work' of the preacher thus was to engage the imagination with 'lively representations'" (*To Live Ancient Live* 37). More specifically, later critics have, contra Miller, followed Murdock in seeing in Puritan preaching an "attachment to dialectics rather than rhetoric too deep rooted to be attributed to the influence of one man" (97). Defining the "dialectical" element has been quite productive. For analysis of Cotton's plain style as it fuses discrete moments in Christian history, see Bozeman's *To Live Ancient Lives*. For the dialectical relationship with Scripture, see especially Jesper Rosenmeier's *New England's Perfection* as well as Lowance on Canticles and, more recently, Gordis in *Opening Scripture*.

2 The student of plain style will want to study the indispensable work by Harry Stout, *The New England Soul: Preaching and Religious Culture in Colonial New England* (and such introductions to New England preaching as can be found in Larzer Ziff's *Puritanism in America: New Culture in A New World*, Andrew Delbanco's *The Puritan Ordeal*, Janice Knight's *Orthodoxies in Massachusetts*, Peter White and Harrison Meserole's *Puritan Poetry and Poetics*, Robert Daly's *God's Altar* and the excellent introduction and relevant headnotes in Heimert and Delbanco's *The Puritans in America: A Narrative*. Also tremendously valuable are studies focused on individual ministers, including Sargent Bush's study of Hooker, *The Writings of Thomas Hooker, Spiritual Adventure in Two Worlds*, Larzer Ziff's *The Career of John Cotton* and Everett

Emerson's *John Cotton*, and Teresa Toulouse's study of New England preaching through Emerson, *The Art of Prophesying*. All of these works serve to remind the reader that "plainness" was not a denial of the aesthetic but a criterion for the aesthetic's necessarily experiential and affective character. Plainness is a description of directness of impact, of the capacity of imagery to enter and move the believer. As Murdock quotes Thomas Shepard, "The word is like an exact picture, it looks every man in the face that looks on it, if God speaks in it."

3 See Delbanco's *Puritan Ordeal*, chapters two and three, "Errand out of the Wilderness" and "City on a Hill," for gripping accounts of the rigor and idealism of the early Puritan experiment. Delbanco's description of "sermon-drunk" Puritans, hanging their hopes of a new, better social order on homiletics, offers an extraordinary portrait of a culture given over to literary experience.

4 This "internal difference" is precisely what homiletic plain-stylists like Cotton sought to achieve in the breast of the believer: the "heavenly hurt" of a purely internal movement toward faith. On the subject of the plain style's affective dimensions, its dialectical power to "move" the believer, I have learned much from Knight and especially from Toulouse, on whose description of the non-rational, experiential, and affective tradition from Cotton through Emerson this essay builds. See also Ivy Schweitzer's fascinating chapter on John Fiske's elegy on John Cotton, a chapter that explores Cotton's penchant such for such "dense internal complication." In Fiske's elegy, Cotton's plainness is what allows the believer to experience, or even to connect, and thus to understand.

> The knott sometimes seems a deformity
> It's a mistake, tho such be light set by
> The knott it is the Joynt, the strength of parts
> The bodies-beauty, so this knott out-starts
> What others in that place, they ought to bee
> Even such a knott exemplar'ly was hee . . .
> When knotty theames and paynes some meet with then
> As knotty and uncouth their tongue and pen
> So 'twas not heere, he caus'd us understand
> And tast the sweetnes of the knott in hand.
> When knotty querks and quiddities broacht were
> By witt of man he sweetely Breathed there

Schweitzer explicates this text interestingly, showing how the knot stands both for spiritual difficulty and the ministerial rhetoric that plainly presents that difficulty's sweetness. The "knot is a point of connection that permits articulation; movement, cohesion and the body's beauty" (59–63).

5   Bozeman is especially effective in describing how temporal layerings of this kind are paradoxically characteristic of Puritan "primitivism." This concern to preserve the coincidence of temporalities in one, the deepest time within the most contemporary, is fundamental to Dickinson's and later poets of New England.

6   Jehlen's argument in *American Incarnation* is that self and continent, subject and nation, invariably reinforce each other. Jehlen's and other arguments for the imperial self in the American context get considerable attention in my *The Line's Eye*.

7   Stout's and Minkema's *Jonathan Edwards Reader* offers a rich selection of readings in Edwards' theology and an excellent concise introduction to Edwards' life and thought. For more suggested reading, see notes to chapters in my *The Line's Eye*.

8   Michael Colacurcio writes wittily and accessibly about Taylor's conjurings and mixtures, linking his theology back to the "inspired recklessness" of John Cotton and crediting both Taylor and Cotton for making Christian experience "fun." He has less fun with Edwards, which I find inexplicable.

9   See Toulouse's excellent description of the Emersonian poetics as it draws on earlier, more orthodox models. And see also Barbara Packer's excellent chapters on transcendental preaching in Bercovitch's *Cambridge History*.

10   Knight describes Cotton's peculiarly persuasive theology as, in effect, oozing, grace just where the edges of a figure soften and tenderize each other.

11   Cotton's fondness for climatic, fluent and evanescent metaphors is one way in which he protects his sermons from deadness. As Larzer Ziff explains, for Cotton, the sermon is an event in time, an essentially transitory "act" rather than a product, which succeeds insofar as it "affects" but fails when it relies on merely mechanical, that is, rhetorical stimulations. Such images and figures as the sermon deploys should, ideally, be as self-consuming as weather, lest liveliness go moribund in rhetorical effects. Teresa Toulouse goes further to suggest that Cotton's own method is essentially "lyric," and she draws on

Sharon Cameron's work on Dickinson to claim that "particular means of presenting religious truth" dramatize the "heart of an experience rather than its outward form."

References

Bozeman, Theodore Dwight. *The Precisionist Strain: Disciplinary Religion and Antinomian Backlash in Puritanism to 1638*. Chapel Hill: University of North Carolina Press, 2004.

Bozeman, Theodore Dwight. *To Live Ancient Lives: The Primitivist Dimension in Puritanism*. Chapel Hill: University of North Carolina Press, 1988.

Bush, Sargent. *The Writings of Thomas Hooker: Spiritual Adventure in Two Worlds*. Madison: University of Wisconsin Press, 1980.

Cameron, Sharon. *Choosing Not Choosing: Dickinson's Fascicles*. Chicago: University of Chicago Press, 1992.

Cameron, Sharon. *Lyric Time: Dickinson and the Limits of Genre*. Baltimore: Johns Hopkins University Press, 1979.

Colacurcio, Michael. *Doctrine and Difference: Essays in the Literature of New England*. New York: Routledge, 1997.

Cotton, John. *Christ, the Fountaine of Life, or Sundry Choyce Sermons on part of the Fifth Chapter of the Fifth Epistle of John*. New York: Arno Press (New York Times Company), 1972.

Daly, Robert. *God's Altar: The Word and the Flesh in Puritan Poetry*. Berkeley: University of California Press, 1978.

Delbanco, Andrew. *The Puritan Ordeal*. Cambridge, MA: Harvard University Press, 1989.

Edwards, Jonathan. *A Jonathan Edwards Reader*. Ed. John E. Smith, Harry S. Stout, and Kenneth P. Minkema. New Haven, CT: Yale University Press, 1995.

Emerson, Everett. *John Cotton*. Twayne Authors Series. New York: Twayne, 1965.

Gordis, Lisa. *Opening Scripture: Bible Reading and Interpretive Authority in Puritan New England*. Chicago: University of Chicago Press, 2003.

Heimert, Alan, and Andrew Delbanco. *The Puritans: A Narrative Anthology*. Cambridge, MA: Harvard University Press, 1985.

Jehlen, Myra. *American Incarnation*. Cambridge, MA: Harvard University Press, 1986.

Knight, Janice. *Orthodoxies in Massachusetts: Rereading American Puritanism*. Cambridge, MA: Harvard University Press, 1994.

Lowance, Mason. *The Language of Canaan.* Cambridge, MA: Harvard University Press, 1980.

Miller, Perry. *Errand into the Wilderness.* Cambridge, MA: Belknap Press of Harvard University Press, 1956.

Miller, Perry. *Jonathan Edwards.* New York: Sloane, 1949.

Miller, Perry. *The New England Mind: The Seventeenth Century.* Cambridge, MA: Harvard University Press, 1954.

Murdock, Kenneth. "The Puritan LiSterary Attitude." In George Waller, *Puritanism in Early America.* Lexington: Heath and Co., 1973.

New, Elisa. *The Line's Eye: Poetic Experience, American Sight.* Cambridge, MA: Harvard University Press, 1998.

Packer, Barbara. "The Transcendentalists." In *The Cambridge History of American Literature: Vol. 2.* Ed. Sacvan Bercovitch. New York: Cambridge University Press, 1994–2005.

Rosenmeier, Jesper. "New England's Perfection: The Image of Adam and the Image of Christ in the Antinomian Crisis." *The William and Mary Quarterly, Third Series.* 27.3 (1970): 435–459.

Schweitzer, Ivy. *The Work of Self Representation: Lyric Poetry in Colonial New England.* Chapel Hill: University of North Carolina Press, 1991.

Stout, Harry. *The New England Soul: Preaching and Religious Culture in Colonial New England.* New York: Oxford University Press, 1986.

Toulouse, Theresa. *The Art of Prophesying: The New England Sermon and the Shaping of Belief.* Athens: University of Georgia Press, 1987.

White, Peter, and Harrison T. Mesersole. *Puritan Poets and Poetics: Seventeenth-Century American Poetry in Theory and Practice.* University Park: Pennsylvania State Press, 1985.

Ziff, Larzer. *The Career of John Cotton: Puritanism and the American Experience.* Princeton: Princeton University Press, 1973.

Ziff, Larzer. *Puritanism in America: New Culture in a New World.* New York: Viking Press, 1973.

Further Reading

"A Bishop's Benediction." *Christian Register,* April 27, 1850.

Ahlstrom, Sydney. *A Religious History of the American People.* New Haven, CT: Yale University Press, 1972.

Bushman, Richard. *The Great Awakening: Documents on the Revival of Religion, 1740–1745.* Chapel Hill: University of North Carolina Press, 1989.

Colacurcio, Michael. *The Province of Piety: Moral History in Hawthorne's Early Tales*. Cambridge, MA: Harvard University Press, 1984.

Dickinson, Emily. *Bolts of Melody*. Ed. Mabel Loomis Todd and Millicent Todd Bingham. New York: Harper & Brothers, 1945.

Dickinson, Emily. *The Complete Poems of Emily Dickinson*. Ed. Thomas H. Johnson. London: Faber and Faber, 1970.

Dickinson, Emily. *The Manuscript Books of Emily Dickinson*. Ed. R.W. Franklin. Cambridge, MA: Belknap Press, 1981.

Dickinson, Emily. *The Poems of Emily Dickinson: Reading Edition*. Ed. R.W. Franklin. Cambridge, MA: Belknap Press, 2005.

Dickinson, Emily. *Selected Letters*. Ed. Thomas H. Johnson. Cambridge, MA: Belknap Press, 1971.

Edwards, Jonathan. *Basic Writings*. Ed. and Introduction by Ola Elizabeth Winslow. New York: New American Library, 1966.

Edwards, Jonathan. *Sinners in the Hands of an Angry God: A Casebook*. Ed. Wilson H. Kimnach, Caleb J.D. Maskell, and Kenneth P. Minkema. New Haven, CT: Yale University Press, 2010.

Edwards, Jonathan. *The Works of Jonathan Edwards*. Ed. Perry Miller and John Edwin Smith. Vol. 11. New Haven, CT: Yale University Press, 1957.

Emerson, Ralph Waldo. *Essays*. Boston: Houghton, Mifflin, and Company, 1882.

Florence, Anna Carter. *Preaching as Testimony*. Louisville, KY: Westminster John Knox Press, 2007.

"John Foster's View of the Bible and the Future State." *Christian Register*, January 29, 1849.

Keller, Karl. *The Example of Edward Taylor*. Amherst: University of Massachusetts Press, 1975.

Moore, Marianne. *The Complete Poems of Marianne Moore*. New York: Penguin, 1981.

Neibuhr, H. Richard. *The Social Sources of Denominationalism*. New York: H. Holt and Company, 1929.

Schleiermacher, Friedrich. *A Critical Essay on the Gospel of St. Luke: With an Introduction by the Translator, Connop Thirwall*. London: John Taylor, 1825.

Taylor, Edward. *The Poetical Works of Edward Taylor*. Edited with an Introduction and Notes by Thomas H. Johnson. Princeton: Princeton University Press, 1971.

Tracy, Joseph. *The Great Awakening: A History of the Revival of Religion in the Time of Edwards and Whitfield*. Boston: Tappan and Dennet, 1842.

3

The Popularity of Doom

From Wigglesworth, Poe, and Stowe through The Da Vinci Code

Cotton Mather famously predicted that Americans would be reading Michael Wigglesworth's *Day of Doom* "Till the Day itself Arrive."[1] That day of reckoning has not arrived, and Wigglesworth's readers are certainly far fewer than Mather predicted. But at least one factor accounting for the disappearance of Wigglesworth's 1662 poem must be that it was literally read to pieces, passed from hand to hand until all extant copies fell apart. Although its vaults contain texts far older than Wigglesworth's poem of 1662, not even Harvard's Houghton Library has a complete copy of the first edition – only scraps.

Day of Doom was early New England's one runaway bestseller. Adults committed long sections of the poem to memory. Familiarity with it provided crucial evidences of faith: the poet-minister Edward Taylor confessed that an element of his intended wife's appeal was that her breath was much "perfumed" with "the Doomsday verses." Children apparently enjoyed hearing Wigglesworth's stanzas, especially at bedtime. Our solicitude for juvenile feelings did not concern

New England Beyond Criticism: In Defense of America's First Literature, First Edition. Elisa New.
© 2014 Elisa New. Published 2014 by John Wiley & Sons, Ltd.

most Puritan parents, but those who might have wanted to protect their young ones from nightmares had to contend with the children themselves, for whom *Day of Doom* was their Dr Seuss. As Perry Miller pointed out in an essay in *Errand into the Wilderness*, it was precisely because *Day of Doom* "drove Puritan children crazy . . . [that] they loved it" (Miller 218).

Day of Doom is, of course, preserved in academic treatments of the Puritan period, usually as an example of the "jeremiad," a form paradoxically advancing communal cohesion via the concept of a chastened, even scourged, nation. Whether in sermons, poems, pulpit exhortations, broadside imprecations, or rhetorical warnings, texts written in the mode of the Biblical prophet, Jeremiah, cautioned New Englanders to slip from God's Way at their peril. At the same time, these direst warnings to a backsliding people also helped consolidate that People and its destiny. As Sacvan Bercovitch so aptly showed, the jeremiad and the federal covenant of which it was part supplied fertile conditions for what was eventually called Manifest Destiny. For if it was collective "declension" the jeremiad thundered against, it was also collective regeneration it secured, transforming miscellaneous backsliders into a congregation, and then a nation of the collectively redeemed. Historical guilt, acknowledged and then paid for in suffering; unregenerate souls, identified and once and for all purged; glorious destiny, glimpsed and then embraced as necessary telos – out of these elements, solidarity and the nation were forged.

But *Day of Doom* merits attention beyond that which scholars accord the jeremiad, for the poem struck a template and bestowed a vibrant literary legacy still very much alive in American mass culture. If the fall from grace ("Thy foot shall slip in due time," in Jonathan Edwards's later words) encouraged the turn toward faith, a lingering, delicious emphasis on those "backslidings" (and their awful costs), along with certain highly engaging methods evolved to dramatize sin's wages, provided something more. The threat of the "slipping" foot and of the long drop into hellfire filled a reservoir of images not only frightening, but exciting and, what's more, readily adapted to mass purposes. Fertilized by periodic revivals of millennialist cliffhanging, and advanced by such technicians of effect as Poe and such students of these effects as Harriet Beecher Stowe, American popular art internalized and conventionalized all the special effects of the End of Days: gory spectacle and adrenaline rush; deferral and ineluctability; fire and blood, hairsbreadth escape, and there-but-for-the-grace-of-God-go-I. The consequences of human backsliding, thus revealed, are spine-tingling: suddenly, terrifyingly, and titillatingly, all faculties of human control fail, and the senses are narrowed and sharpened into one intense channel of delirious helplessness. In other words: the Fall as Tilt-a-Whirl, the postponement of the Judgment Day as matchless suspense.[2]

In its mass cultural versions, the Fall bestows a host of thrills. Not just of figuratively, metaphorically, descending – but of really plummeting, hurtling through screaming space into the endless void. And not just of hurtling – not just of suffering one's own excruciating punishment – but, better, experiencing vicariously the torture of others. The Fall brings the thrill of drastic moral reversal and cosmic vindication: of watching the complacent brought low, and the low raised up. In one unified line of aesthetic voltage, the subject overtaken experiences all the risks human beings are heir to.

To entertain one's fallen state is very terrible. And very entertaining.

Wigglesworth was, of course, not the first to turn the "opening" of scripture to aesthetic account, nor even the first to imbue religious persuasion with thrills. Earlier American adherents to Luther's creed, *sola scriptura*, understood that to render doctrine less dry, to make obscurity an enticement, required a certain activation of a congregation's imaginative faculties. Faith itself is a "leap," and so the suspension of disbelief is achieved through a practice – and by an audience habituated to leaping pulses. The most successful ministers were the ones who understood this. John Cotton combined scouring thoroughness with a tendency to riddling, tantalizing ambiguity. Thomas Shepard was so in love with the text, so possessed by its Barthesian *plaisir*, he liked to rhyme his own words (Shepard: "Comfort thyself; Christ is thine") with the Biblical texts'

(Bible: "I am Beloved's and My Beloved is Mine").[3] The more robust Hooker bore down on his auditors with exhortative Biblical quotations and the high risk exploits of various Biblical agonists – some saved, others doomed – to keep the believer in constant suspense and thus invested in his own soul's drama.[4] Differences in sermonic method between Cotton, Shepard, Hooker, and Williams – for those who church-hopped – gave rise to various famous intranecine disputes. Meanwhile, the task of keeping salvation's hopefuls hoping focused ministers on their art, with ministerial popularity closely tied to the craft and charisma of the sermon.

But by the 1660s – Wigglesworth's moment – waning of faith had stimulated various doctrinal adjustments necessary to keeping the pews occupied. Chief among these was the Halfway Covenant, which permitted the children of parents not yet "saved" to enjoy partial church membership. It was a compromise calculated to foster anticipation and to whet the desire for salvation. There were also new latitudes, new definitions of what could count as "plain" in the rhetorical realm. The poem that would become the runaway best-seller of the seventeenth century may have aimed for nothing but the "plainest" exposition of what manner of Doom awaited the unsaved. And yet Wigglesworth's *Day of Doom* was fated to introduce into American literature, and to teach American readers, a pleasure in the letter they had not yet known.

The poem's use of setting and spatiotemporal imagery is its first and most striking innovation. From its very first lines, Wigglesworth's poem puts his readers, like their proxies (souls under judgment), at the psychic and cognitive disadvantage of not knowing where they *really* live. Soon, sooner than they think, they will absorb full face (and from behind) a breakdown of the most fundamental givens.

> Still was the night, Serene and Bright,
>   when all Men sleeping lay;
> Calm was the season, and carnal reason
>   thought so 'twould last for ay.
> Soul, take thine ease, let sorrow cease,

much good thou hast in store:
This was their Song, their Cups among
the Evening before.
(Wigglesworth 9)

Sleeping off their dissipations, blithely unmindful of what is coming, Wigglesworth's sinners have no fears for the future. Today's apocalyptic horror films rehearse the same convention, opening on a scene of innocence: an everyday street in everyday United States; a suburban living room strewn with toys; a neighborhood tavern, its denizens laughing. The costs of snoozing through the date are colorfully illustrated in *War of the Worlds*, which opens with Tom Cruise waking up, hungover, to the Day the World Ends. In this film, as in *Day of Doom*, normality is broken by a sweeping light from above. Still half sleeping, Cruise runs through the ravaged geography (ground cracking beneath his own feet, seas rising, thunder thundering) of his own erstwhile complacency. If he awakens just in time to save himself, the destruction of his neighbors all around remind him of the doom that might have been his. As Wigglesworth had it: "all Kindreds wail; all hearts do fail: / horror the world doth fill" (12). The bodily terror of Gog fighting Magog is laid bare in the decimated landscape. Those not "saved" will be reduced to gobbets of crimsoned flesh, meat for the Beast's maw. Awake, awake! *War of the Worlds* warns, or *your* blood – not your neighbors' – shall soak the ground.

   In the age of the camera, images of subtly cracking earth and gradually rising seas, of clogged highways and of news anchors "on the scene" who suddenly disappear from the scene – such visual data first unsettles and then blasts open the complacency of the everyday. These contemporary conventions work by allowing a genuinely cosmic irony to engulf those living in a world more pedestrian and stable, those blithely savoring "the Evening before."[5] Wigglesworth, for his part, shatters the complacency of enjoying this evening before by letting the three syllables of "evening" fill out the metrical pattern like a sort of bull's-eye in the line. Time is not what we think it is. Day and Night are only apparent, not real, for the real "Day" comes at night – and then in its full brightness. The poet's aim in this first stanza is to prepare ground for the shocking collapse, the violation of norms that will show us where we *really* live: directly in God's sights. For it turns out that sleep's universality, night's cover, is no protection against the guilt or menace that "lurks beneath." "Calmness of season" does not quell, though it may conceal, that turbulence waiting to erupt. Rather, the concealing is requisite to the revealing: the calm before the midnight cry becomes the chamber the cry fills.

Perry Miller, in his book on Jonathan Edwards, inventoried Edwards's techniques for raising fear in his auditors. There was Edwards's evocation of Newtonian force as violent potentiality, his conjuring of the violent, rising tide of entropy only God's Hand can stay ("the bow of God's wrath is bent, and the arrow made ready on the string . . . and it is nothing but the mere pleasure of God . . . that keeps the arrow one minute from being drunk with your blood") and his deployment of Lockean sensation to shape Christian understanding. Wigglesworth's management of temporal irony techniques in fact predict those of Edwards: the longer restrained, the harder flies Judgment's arrow. All Time, no matter how uneventfully it *seems* to pass, is pregnant with what, from God's vantage point, has already occurred: the letting loose of the wrath of his judgment. This "was their Song," the poet cautions, "the Evening before." Wigglesworth's retrospection vacuums Time from the Day Before as though it had never been. In Wigglesworth's poem, when the "Day" arrives, all time is now elapsed, all clocks run out.

Having first awakened its reader to the evanescence of the past, having then disturbed that reader's circadian rhythms and reset that reader's pulses, Wigglesworth's poem now moves on to subtract that reader's complacent anticipation of a better future. Sin, it turns out, has not "improved," but squandered time; overspent on its credit, not only wallowing in present pleasures but compromising future improvement with bad practices. The rescinding of God's patience is worse for those who have mired their souls in habitual vice. Although drunkenness was, in fact, particularly worrisome to seven-teenth-century pastors, it works here as a metaphor for that open-eyed sleeping that is sin. Those "their cups among" represent all those doomed to meet their maker unawakened. We are only at the twelfth stanza of this two hundred and twenty-four stanza poem, yet for those sinners who have "rush[ed] from their beds with giddy heads and to their windows run," it is already too late (Wigglesworth 10). The sleep still about them is a sign of their escapist habits and of their chronic over-extensions. Now, brought to the edge of time's precipice – a cliff they never knew they approached – they stand in empty air. As time runs out, so space's firm organization gives way, and with it collapses the very earth's foundations:

> The Mountains smoak, the Hills are shook,
>   the Earth is rent and torn,
> As if she should be clean dissolv'd,
>   or from the Center born.
> The Sea doth roar, forsakes the shore,
>   and shrinks away for fear;
> The wild Beasts flee into the Sea,
>   so soon as he draws near.
>   (Wigglesworth 13)

Near and far, land and sea, tides and winds, liquids and solids – Creation's order and equipoise, all that cohered in Genesis – devolve into chaos, and with this devolution of physical boundaries comes, too, the dissolution of psychic ones. Now the compartmentalizing psyche, next the safe and stable hierarchies of the social world, next the protocols that regulate individual and social norms – all these will break down as the complacent throw off their defenses, running (if they only could!) for their lives. "Some rashly leap into the Deep, / to scape by being drown'd: / Some to the Rocks (O senseless blocks!) / and woody Mountains run, / That there they might this fearful sight, / and dreaded Presence shun" (Wigglesworth 12).

Violent social anarchy, the unraveling of normative behaviors and bonds, begins to turn Christian terror toward what we might recognize as modern "horror." In Wigglesworth's poem, a transvaluation of familiar, ethical values to values profoundly Other anesthetizes pity and even fosters relish for the suffering of others. Wigglesworth is not

53

at all squeamish in treating social adhesion, even kinship bonds, as a casualty of sin. Drastic reversals of fortune allow unrecognized saints to watch erstwhile estimable sinners burn: "Friends stand aloof, and make no proof / what Prayers or Tears can do" (Wigglesworth 58).

With "compassion . . . out of fashion," the line dividing saved from damned cracks open the family itself (58). No fellow feeling, not even family feeling, prevents the dispatch of the damned to their well-deserved Hell. With positive gusto, Wigglesworth shows how false attachments on earth are severed in a post-natural world:

> One natural Brother beholds another
> in this astonied fit,
> Yet sorrows not thereat a jot,
> nor pitties him a whit.
> (Wigglesworth 58)

> The pious Father had so much rather
> his graceless Son should ly
> In Hell with Devils, for all his evils
> burning eternally
> (Wigglesworth 59)

By subjecting high and low, without exception, to suffer common reduction – "Mean men lament, great men do rent / their Robes, and tear their hair: / They do not spare their flesh to tear / through horrible despair" (12) – the poet kicks away the substrate of norms, that bracing contextual realm whose baseline is the humdrum. Worse yet is to come, though, as the final, the most primary distinction – that between the living and dead – falls away:

> Both Sea and Land, at his Command,
> their Dead at once surrender:
> The Fire and Air constrained are
> also their dead to tender.
> The mighty word of this great Lord
> links Body and Soul together
> Both of the Just, and the unjust,
> to part no more forever.
> (Wigglesworth 13)

To wake to a world where those disencumbered of body, long dust, are re-encased in flesh (oneself among them!) is to experience, to recognize, the living body as the corpse it always was. To cling to it is not life but corporeal lock-up: "With Iron bands they bind their hands, / and cursed feet together, / And cast them all, both great and small, / into that Lake forever" (Wigglesworth 61).

Body consciousness – though an augury of living death – provides, however, certain compensating satisfactions. Students of Hitchcock know from *Psycho* the power of a scream. Wigglesworth knew it, too. Wigglesworth exposes trepidation to terror, lets fear, the contaminant, act on and erode the last traces of normality. The sight of panic, the release of a scream – these themselves disorder. The scream not only expresses fear; it creates it.

> Thus shall they ly, and wail, and cry,
>   tormented, and tormenting
> Their galled hearts with pois'ned darts
>   but now too late repenting.
> There let them dwell i' th' Flames of Hell;
>   there leave we them to burn,
> And back agen unto the men
>   whom Christ acquits, return.
>   (Wigglesworth 63)

Nor, however, is this scream – the emotional climax – suffered to interrupt the onward rush of Wigglesworth's galloping verse. Letting enjambments sustain forward motion, literally carrying the reader around corner after corner, Wigglesworth renders the sufferings of the damned into a scene – an exciting scene to be sure, but a scene nonetheless, not independent but part of a longer, unfolding drama. Or part, we might observe, of a plot. The scene of damnation lasts precisely the amount of time the wretches deserve: part of what damns them is their stasis relative to our forward motion. But it lasts, too, for an interval whose episodic quality is signaled by the invitation of the next, and the next, stanza. Pain's differential impact, selecting someone else for torture, feels – *should* feel, anyway – good, but so too does the sensation of "returning" to what fresh stimulations may be in store a little later along in this unexhausted, and still young, Day. While they wail and cry one has other fish to fry, for the story goes on and on – each apparent climax or denouement only part of the longer plot, one the reader does not want, ever, to end.

A key element in the pleasure, the entertainment even, provided by the poem, is the way forward motion provides spiritual escape, but within a form bestowing the benefits of escapism on those escaping Hell's tortures. When Cotton Mather predicted the long life, the enduring power, of Wigglesworth's poem, he had to have been influenced by the length of *Day of Doom*, a poem that seems measured to last as long, say, as it takes a soul to exhaust every last alternative. Too short and too exciting to read over several sessions, yet too long for a brief one, Wiggleworth's poem stipulates a period of excitation and fills that period. Its length is about that of an airport thriller, or a movie – which it is.

Wigglesworth was a better versifier than some of his critics allowed, but what kept his poem alive were not his galloping four-teeners. Rather, as Mather rightly surmised, Wigglesworth's poem achieved its effects by operationalizing exegesis as a mode of suspense. Understanding not only the importance, but also the relationship, of the two Protestant tenets – *sola scriptura* and *sola fides* – Wiggleworth's innovation was to let faith flower in the suspension of disbelief. In Wigglesworth's poem, an endorsement of reading's fullest capacity, the imagination learns its true office as self-reliant Revelatory mechanism. Not beholding the papal dumbshow from a cold pew, imagination by its own offices hoists Truth's very curtain. *Sola scriptura* ("by scripture alone") is harnessed to disclose and decode.[6]

Think of the international bestseller, *The Da Vinci Code*. Following its Boston "professor of Religious Symbology" and his muse (Sophie, whose name means knowledge) across an international landscape, the popular page-turner shows Romish obscurantism foiled and exegetical derring-do, American style, saving the day.[7] If his Boston symbologist is not just New World but New Age (his Christ, it turns out, had children; the Divine "transcendence" he

56

decodes includes sexual union with the sacred feminine and the great art of Europe), Dan Brown's Boston interpreter offers a syncretic reconciliation of the plain and its Poe-inspired travesty. Like his orthodox forebears, Langdon awakens each morning with an urge to "open" scripture, a conviction that worldly things have hermeneutic keys. An artist of (as well as in) Mystery, Langdon sees through the glass darkly for the fun of it. Truth, Brown's Langdon explains, is always "just below the surface." Full knowledge of it teases, just one airport, rental car, or elevator ride away. And yet this truth, like Sophie, keeps its chastity. The pleasure of the text is in – to the very last page – the next page.

Deferral has always been, since Wigglesworth, the essential structural feature of Doomsday art. Such art may or may not borrow Revelation's vivid imagery (its thunder, its bestial predators, its graves vomiting their dead). It gives new names to the betrayers and the loyal apostles, preserving the Gospels' own cast of valiants and hypocrites, doubters and pilgrims. But Doomsday art is not doomsday art without suspense. American cultural history confirms the attraction: "*It's coming . . . It's coming . . .*" warns both a Hollywood movie trailer and manifold popular web sites on the Second Coming. It is not to arrive but to not arrive; not to reach the end that keeps us going. It is rather to be teased, to encounter and re-encounter but never to consummate or submit to truth. In this, faith's deferrals mime and are sustained by the process of suspense, and especially when the act of reading and suspense can be coordinated in one process. The pleasure is active: the pleasure of peeling and peeling the onion of the Ultimate, of living in that sweet spot between the "re" and the "veil" of revelation: the pleasure of eternal *dénouement*, impendingness, the threat of time's sudden recoil, connects popular horror to the more pyrotechnic Christian web sites. "Time is running out. I can feel it," writes film theorist Wheeler Winston Dixon of the many cinematic visions of apocalypse.[8] Fear the date, warns "666 Watch." Fear the date 6/6/06, warns Hollywood, reprising not only the classic of 1976 but classics of 1666, 1776, and 1876 as well. In terms of entertainment value, the payoff to fearing the date is great: *The Omen 666* earned the highest box office receipts for a Tuesday ever recorded, its release at 12:06 on 6/6/06 making the film a true "midnight cry" in the tradition Wigglesworth invented.

After Wigglesworth, no one reanimates and exploits the mass potential of Christian apocalypse better than Edgar Allan Poe. In the rationalist turn against Calvinist awe, Poe finds unexploited literary real estate, and in the material of New England faith, a cabinet of repurposable props.

By the 1830s and '40s, the moral efficacy of Wigglesworth's scarifying effects was no longer obvious to all. Unitarian and liberalizing tendencies in nineteenth-century Christianity led Christians away from the more drastic, and vivid, aspects of Calvinist orthodoxy. The terrifying power of an Angry God, the depiction of the Church at Rome as devouring Beast, the razor-sharp line between sinners and saved, the spectacle of the tortured Christ, the leaping fires of hell – all these once persuasive images of Doom seemed to the liberal mind fantastical, ill-befitting a benign Creator. The liberal faith in growth entailed an unalarming repertoire of images, and it necessarily expunged material too raw.

Poe, for his part, saw in these materials time-tested riches, their rawness their value. Moralists might insist on more ambiguous and complex accounts of human beings, on the sacredness of spiritual agency. Poe, for his part, passed over these values of moral evolution as inimical to art. A meliorist gentility blunted excitations; a gradualist optimism, shrinking behind the thresholds of pain or pleasure, made no imprint on the senses, but an assault on the viscera inflamed the imagination. Thus Christianity might rid itself of gargoyles – saved and condemned, torturer and tortured, guilty and guiltless – but Poe was ready to use them. There is so much still to be made, it turns out, of the old Christian material. Poe keeps his evil-doers and angelic sufferers in distinct and antithetical realms, sharply divided by fire, water, or sword, helpless and dreading translation from one realm to the other. All the better to drop them in the Pit. To see them sucked into the Maelstrom. To watch them emerge from the grave.

Thus it is no accident that the sufferer of the "Pit in the Pen-
dulum" is a victim of the Inquisition, Protestant cousin to the
persecuted in Foxe's *Book of Martyrs.* Nor is it an accident that the
Narrative of A. Gordon Pym traces a journey downward from Cape
Cod's godly harbor to the "southern" underworld of an unredeemed
New World.[9] From the cryptic inscriptions found in this nether
region – "I have graven it within the hills, and my vengeance upon
the dust within the rock" – to its mists and shrouded figures, *Pym's*
place at the end of the world is purloined from the End of the
World of Revelation (Poe 736). The power of Poe's language and
imagery depends upon the pseudo-spiritual excitations always
secreted within Christianity.[10]

Poe's effects derive from an almost entirely synthetic and even
technical resonance he draws out of his materials. Plucking at
various themes in no particular order – Biblical prohibition, metem-
psychosis, the Visible, the Invisible, the restlessness of the damned
– he confects his stanzas to incite sensation rather than, say, to
prompt thought. Christianity dead or dying, reduced to a "shell" of
itself, is just what Poe's art thrives on.

Readers descending into the hellish zone of "City in the Sea,"
for example, experience a certain faux-Christian vivacity not to be
confused with life:

> Lo! Death has reared himself a throne
> In a strange city lying alone
> Far down within the dim West,
> Where the good and the bad and the worst and the best
> Have gone to their eternal rest.
> There shrines and palaces and towers
> (Time-eaten towers that tremble not!)
> Resemble nothing that is ours.
>
> (Poe 744)

As had been the case in Wigglesworth, in "City in the Sea" the
exhibition of the dead on "watery biers" ("There open fanes and
gaping graves / Yawn level with the luminous waves") is especially
fearsome for confusing, literally blurring, the line between living

59

and dead (Poe 744). Likewise for Poe's unlucky sleepers: beware an overly restful night, lest one join those resting unquiet forever! Indeed, in the world of "The Sleepers," sublimity and plain spookiness thrive and nurture one another:

> There the traveler meets, aghast,
> Sheeted Memories of the Past
> Shrouded forms that start and sigh
> As they pass the wanderer by –
> White-robed forms of friends long given,
> In agony, to the Earth – and Heaven.
>
> (Poe 751–752)

Note how the mere use of capitalization intensifies the last line, and how evocations of extreme affect – "aghast," "agony" – produce a shiver of frightened recognition utterly detached from any cause or origin or precipitating truth. The solemn pacing of the "traveler" and the possibilities, spiritual ones, his inquiry into the Past *might* produce – these are intersected by the weirdly perambulating "shrouded forms," now too reified to sustain any meaning. Indeed, rhetoric trumps logic; suggestiveness of tone overrules grounding. In the lines above, "Earth – and Heaven" – in any religious text discrepant, alternative destinations – become here stations on one itinerary, the substitution of "and –" for "or – [Heaven]" now raising new doubt and new suspense about this "Heaven." Hyperbole, overstatement, sonorities of tone, brazen illogic work in the lines above against any ingathering of meaning. The senses are roused, rendered alert and alive to the images, but the sensing is along the nerves and viscera, not the knowing faculties. Even when the language seems most allusively Biblical, the resemblances are surface ones:

> So wills its King, who hath forbid
> The uplifting of the fringéd lid;
> And thus the sad Soul that here passes
> Beholds it but through darkened glasses.
>
> (Poe 752)

St Paul's warning that mortal sight is "through a glass" does not inhibit but rather emboldens this poet. The beclouded vision of the sinner provides Poe with a sort of peek-a-boo keyhole, a perspective the artful poet opens and shuts with a flick of the double negative: "Never its mysteries are exposed. / To the weak human eye unclosed" (Poe 752). Spiritual sight is not serious here: the tease of the "fringéd lid" makes revelation a form of voyeurism or, worse, grave robbing. Indeed, if Poe's allusive use and reuse of Biblical material in such lines as the above has the feel of exhumation rather than explication, desecration rather than divination, that is because Poe's art works by abolishing and expunging the spirit (the soul, we might say, of a text), emancipating the Letter itself from the gravity of that spirit. The test of a poet's virtuosity is not, for Poe, in describing true phenomena – in getting at their essence or spirit – but rather in confecting simulacra, conferring liveness and a sensation of vivacity by linguistic prestidigitations.[11] Such lines as those above are manufactured out of still-warm Calvinist matter.

In his poetry, as we have seen, Poe gathered materials from the archives of Christian faith, from Revelations and the martyrologies of the Reformation, from the Apocrypha and from the Gospels, of flame-like, life-like, soul-seeming authenticity. But Poe, too, achieved his most important effects in manipulations of temporality. Master of detective fiction, of the horror tale, of the poison pen review, Poe worked across the full range of sensational literary modes, demonstrating, genre by genre, how provocation may substitute for cause, and deferral give utter vacancy great dimension, standing in for any more genuine stimulation. *Eureka*, his last major work (1848), is also a demonstration of how such effects, disposed across a linear text, establish the genre of suspense.

Eureka is, as critics have long since agreed, an apocalyptic – or, perhaps better, a faux apocalyptic – text, a treatise on aesthetic perfection as it achieves the Ultimate, but, just as saliently, a demonstration of how excitation is sustained by excitation itself.[12] Perry Miller puts Poe's text in the context of the Millerite excitements of the early 1840s; that is, he ties it to Baptist William Miller's perfervid, complexly documented predictions that the Second Coming, the true midnight cry, would occur in March 1843. *Eureka*, written during this very year, provides a rehearsal of the satisfactions of the coming, only minus the Coming, and so inaugurates a mode of literary pleasure that bears formal resemblance to, borrows thematic material from, and promises shattering closure in the way of apocalyptic literature. For what this class of literature understands is the very pleasure Poe's *Eureka* incites. Poetic, scientific, and theological all at the same time, *Eureka* is an inquiry into the nature of matter and the mystery of its continuance, one that defends somatic excitation rather than any more sober data or analytic procedure. Its famous first pages compare arriving at truth to spinning on one's heel: "Only by a rapid whirling on his heel could he hope to comprehend the panorama in the sublimity of its Oneness" (Poe 1261). Disorienting dizzying motion simulates and, Poe hints, perhaps even delivers a sense of oneness. For Poe, the achievement of sublime Oneness will depend upon a moving beyond "*extent*" and "*diversity of scene*," and beyond individuality, too: his text thus turns itself into a centrifuge, accelerating and distending discrete modes of knowing (science and poetry, theory and theology, allusion and citation, rhapsody and invective) till they blur into one surge hurtling toward fulfillment, one long dash or ellipsis bound for apocalypse.[13] As this strange text's strange expositor sums up, "My general proposition then is this: *In the Original Unity of the First Thing lies the Secondary Cause of All Things; with the Germ of their Inevitable Annihilation*" (Poe 1261).

With an argument that equates the sensory experience of receiving or experiencing revelation with the reality of that revelation (revelation is an *activity* realized in action and apprehension), *Eureka* frustrates the reader interested in the truth content of any of its discrete claims, while rewarding the reader simply along for the ride. To the extent that Poe gets away with it, it is because truth claims are beside the point, of far less moment than the urgency with which they are advanced: the style and rhetoric and character of the speaker bears them along, and bears along the reader. Poe creates in *Eureka's* narrator a desperate character, one torturing truth with factitious detail. He can neither hush nor die, but rather hangs on death's edge expostulating and theorizing, torturing the elusive All with the hectic motion of the ceaseless each. Expostulation and eloquence, pedantry and poeticalness overextend themselves, until the narrative and its narrator seem to cry out for the cleansing sweep, the lightning stroke, to cut through so much *"diversity"* and change of scene. One is not very long into *Eureka* before longing for its end, indeed for the same foregone conclusion of an End its hyperventilating, hypographic narrator craves. Are we not quiet yet? Have we not yet found our purpose? Has It not yet come?

Poe's work is, finally, an insult to New England theology, the more insulting because so intimate and interimplicated. There is gross impiety in the way Poe uses *Eureka* to exploit religious sensation for sensation's sake, to mine Christian texts – and especially the *Revelation* – as a source of artistic special effects. *Sola scriptura!* By Scripture alone, Luther had propounded, so sparking the great epoch of Christian literacy, so establishing the principle that the reading, the hearing, the tasting of the Word would itself save. And yet there is reading, and *reading*; hearing, and *hearing*.

In the throes of the so-called Great Awakening, Jonathan Edwards became so worried about the difference between genuine motion of the spirit and the overstimulated nerves of those craving such motion that he wrote *On the Religious Affections* to draw strong distinctions between religious affections and religious sensations. Before him, Thomas Shepard devoted whole sermons to adumbrating the dangers of "external efficacy," of speech with a semblance of godliness but without its inner meaning. Literalism worried him. "Do not trust to the external word," warns Shepard, wrapping up a sermon on "ineffectual hearing" (Warner 115): "'Tis but the blowing of the winde upon a rock, which blusters for a time, but when the winde is down they are still. Truly they hear the word spoken, but they do not hear God speaking" (98).

Poe's poetic principle is this very "blowing of wind upon a rock," and American escapist literature is born in it.

One writer who saw the danger of this – and who, indeed, used her most important book to warn against it – was Harriet Beecher Stowe. For among its many other projects, Stowe's *Uncle Tom's Cabin*

63

also includes a quite detailed analysis of the differences between a genuine Christian supernaturalism and the degraded imitation of that supernaturalism in superstition and, quite specifically, in sensational fiction.

Uncle Tom's Cabin is, of course, best known as a fictional treatise on the sin of slavery and as a work of sublime propaganda, constructed to persuade readers to revile the institution. The book is a genuine masterpiece, managing to provide sharp and scouring analysis of a nineteenth-century social world while also evoking and placing historical action within the ampler space of the Christian cosmos. Thus the book critiques the intellectual bankruptcy of American compromise on the subject of slavery and offers an in-depth look at the communal norms and mores resultant from that compromise. Thus it explores the separation of male and female spheres of influence as redemptive, at least potentially so, as Stowe imbues women (and men in their more feminine aspects) with the power to educate, to nurture, and to transform American society. The book scrutinizes a range of social practices – from the use of alcohol, to the norms of legal culture and interstate commerce, to the paternalist assumptions of the slave household, to the artificial class distinctions and regional dividing lines – and she offers a thoroughgoing program for the redemption of the American slave and his master through personal responsibility and social accountability.

And yet Stowe's social and secular analysis of slavery is bisected throughout, or rather superimposed upon, a Christian world of above and below, heaven and hell, where social redemption is a visible effect and sanctifying indicator of the deeper spiritual redemption. The book is plotted on an up and down axis whose apparent poles are Canada and Mississippi but whose more magnetic poles are Heaven and Hell. The slave who escapes North is rescued by the Grace of God and by the sacrifice of those whose sufferings secure their likeness to Christ himself. These rise into that greater Canada, Heaven, the home of all those who have found their redeemer, while those delaying their redemption in Christ descend the Red River down to Hell: a plantation in Mississippi where the Devil is his own worst tormenter.

Stowe also adapts that same temporality Wigglesworth adumbrated in such detail. One tends to hear the "Doom" in *Day of Doom* accented more strongly, but just as much emphasis falls on the "Day," an endpoint, punctilious, that cannot be deferred. A soul's purpose on earth is to improve his time, and woe to those who defer for tomorrow what ought to be done today. Wigglesworth's sinners are found supine, "in their cups," and sleeping away the last hours given them to repent. Dilatory about getting his house in order, Tom's first master is overtaken by an evil that a more attentive attitude to his affairs might have forestalled: he lets opportunities for good slip through his fingers and so is implicated in an institution he knows to be wrong. As Wigglesworth's poem literally stops the clock, catching his sinners unready and unprepared to meet their judge, Stowe shows how the well-intentioned but weak may miss their chances while the morally pure know how to use their time to spiritual advantage. Opportunities to hear the Word of God abound: every community includes one of its apostles in the person of a right-thinking Tom, or an angelic, aptly named, evangelistic Eva, or a Quaker family ready to give sanctuary. But only some recognize these apostles in time, and many more miss the chance to redeem themselves, thereby abetting the course of evil. Those on the side of good manage to outrun evil, spiriting themselves or others away from danger just in the nick of time. But the saintly Tom's delivery into the hands of the Devil himself, Simon Legree, occurs due to the lack of spiritual urgency on the part of Augustine St Clare, a chronic oversleeper and drinker. St Clare means well, but he dies before signing Tom's (his own redeemer's) emancipation papers. Thus are spiritual dereliction and temporal delay co-implicated, the slack pace of the morally weak bringing its own inertia. In Stowe, as in Wigglesworth, if one is not rising toward heaven, one is sinking toward hell, gathering weight as one falls.

Stowe's plotting of *Uncle Tom's Cabin* along an up–down/North–South/Heaven–Hell axis and her calibration of moral quality with temporal prescience show her exploiting all the spatiotemporal tools Wigglesworth bestowed on her. But perhaps her greater contribution to the literature of Doom lies in the subtle analysis she provides of the gestalt of faith versus the contrasting gestalt of faithlessness and of the respective spiritual, and even psychological, states bred in these two conditions. Since Stowe's cosmology does not allow for a world without some sort of supernatural realm, in her analysis the decline or loss of genuine belief can only lead to ungenuine belief. Thus she develops a picture of faith's opposite: of a morbid Christianity in which awe is attenuated in terror, belief in superstition, and the transforming motions of the Spirit are mimicked in hectic psychological states.

Faith responds and develops as a soul perceives its relation to Heaven to be its home, and so rests ever more securely in that orientation. Faith's motion is toward what (eternally) is: faith abides in time only in order to meet eternity, and moves from the letter to the spirit. Faith's external faculties are quieted as its inner compass finds Heaven. Those without faith, however, are moved by forces more external, their senses all nervously alive to, chafed and inflamed by, those same phenomena whose deeper operations soothe believers. If evil is, as St Augustine wrote, absence of the good, it is an exercised absence, repulsed by what it lacks, like the darkness made visible that Milton described.

Thus Simon Legree's restlessness. Legree, in Stowe's sharp analysis, is not in the least insensible to religious influences: they overstimulate him, inflaming his responses. Exposure to the faithful, and to the comforts of the faithful (hymns, Bibles, Tom), only madden him. It is as if unregeneracy were an exposed nerve that godliness is ever plucking. Memories of his own life's evangelists (his mother) do not aid the repentance, the inner change, of such a sinner so much as they drive his more violent repulse of the Good. While godly lives become part of a larger, simpler Christian narrative, moving with its flow and grain, the ungodly are aversive, restless, beset by cravings and in need of distractions, in constant agitated flight from their own souls. They cover ground, they fill days with incident, but they are not, ever, moved.

Stowe detects something crucial here: evacuated spirit craves plot. It is no accident that Simon Legree is a greedy dreamer, nor that he is easily manipulated by tawdry plots, and props, and tricks and, ultimately, brought down by precisely the kind of mass art that Poe had fashioned out of Calvinist leavings. Thus it is that Cassy, Legree's tormented mistress, is able to escape her tormenter by improvising for his psychic torment a cheap, customized set of special effects that disquiet but cannot ever change Legree. Stowe's analysis of such artistic claptrap as Cassy devises is, literally, damning. As against the sublime narrative that moves Tom, transporting him to the heavenly home, the narrative Cassy devises fosters restiveness: not peace but overactive inertia. Cassy's instrumental plot, contrived of delay and surprise, delay and surprise, sends the psyche on a gallop that does not, however, stir the spirit. It is, as Thomas Shepard had said, the "wind blowing on a rock." Thus when Cassy bends the sound of the wind in the attic eaves – rigging up a bottle in a knothole so that wind wails down the attic staircase like a host of wailing souls – Legree twitches on her line, tosses in his sleep. Hanging in dread, living in a frenzy of agitation, motion, disquiet, Legree is the victim of his own godless Doom. The sign of his complete unregeneracy is the cheapness of the narrative he lets consume him.

Between the 1660s, when Wiggleworth published *Day of Doom*, the 1840s and '50s when Edgar Allan Poe and Harriet Beecher Stowe turned Christian affect to impious, and pious, uses, and our twenty-first-century moment, other influences interposed themselves.

The imprint of the European Gothic, which proved so protean and adaptable in the New World; the conventions of utopian, and dystopian, science fiction (genres claiming Gothic as well as Christian antecedents); the cinema's, and especially Japanese cinema's, deployment of the Creature Feature as laboratory for special effects – all these have flowed into, enriched, and complicated the Christian apocalypticism whose drama Wigglesworth so aptly exploited. And yet the decades of the second half of the twentieth and beginning of the twenty-first century see the number of apocalyptic films released per year increasing every decade (the auspiciously numbered decade that opened the new millennium saw 55 films released), and even films tracing the advent of apocalypse to environmental or geopolitical causes – as many do – deliberately preserve the

Christian subtext, with such titles as "Damnation Alley" (1977), "Land of Doom" (1986), "Millennium" (1989), "Dogma" (1999), " End of Days" (1999), "Lost Souls" (2000), "Left Behind" (2005), or "The Omen" 1, 2, and 3, and, of course, "666." Whatever the precipitating cause of the world's end — thermonuclear war, virus, totalitarian takeover, environmental negligence — such titles suggest that, whatever the instrument, the End that is Coming is that same end augured in Revelation. Between the mass literature of the seventeenth century and our own, Revelation in this broad sense held its own — revelation not only as theme but as action, as kinesis and as pleasure sustained and self-sustaining, opening the seals, seal after seal, crypt after crypt. And then, too, it brings the thrill of detection, of breaking the seals and seeing once-inaccessible truths exposed to light. Neither chary of artifice nor sparing in stimulations to ear, eye, or viscera, *Day of Doom* is formally and technically, as well as psychologically, revelatory, exercising the auditor and training proficiency in revelation.

By the time Poe arrived on the scene, Wigglesworth had already taught Americans that God's fury had a beat a hermeneutics and a rhythm anyone could learn, and that the profoundest truths might be deployed across a relatively shallow surface area. As Poe's Dupin famously pronounced, "Truth is not always in a well. In fact, as regards the more important knowledge, I do believe that she is invariably superficial" (13). To seek the eternal in the virtual, to make imagination a black box where doom, guilt, bodily horror, mortal terror are played and reprised in combinations available and accessible to eye, to mind, to viscera — this Wigglesworth pioneered, Poe refined, Stowe exploited, and purveyors of Doom still release in theaters near you.

Notes

1   Mather is quoted in F.O. Matthissen's Review of *Day of Doom and Other Poems*, edited by Murdock. The Harvard libraries own the fol-

lowing editions: 1662, 1666, 1673, 1687, 1701, 1715, 1751, 1777, 1811, 1867, 1929, and 1966. Murdock lists some others: 1711, 1828.

2 Naturally beyond the scope of this chapter is speculation into modern-day millennialism and the dramatic means brought to its illustration, including such bestsellers as Tim LaHaye and Jerry B. Jenkins's *Left Behind* series of novels. Studies of apocalypticism from the Puritans on would begin with David Hall's *Worlds of Wonder: Days of Judgment*, Sacvan Bercovitch's *The American Jeremiad*, and Avihu Zakai's *Exile and Kingdom*. For studies of millennialism across American history see Daniel Wojcik's *The End of the World as We Know It*, Tina Pippin's *Apocalyptic Bodies*, Robbins and Palmer's *Millennium, Messiahs and Mayhem: Contemporary Apocalyptic Movements*, and Frykholm's *Rapture Culture: Left Behind in Evangelical America*.

3 See Lisa Gordis's *Opening Scripture: Bible Reading and Interpretive Authority in Puritan New England* for an analysis of ministerial reading practices.

4 See Ann Kibbey's *The Interpretation of Material Shapes in Puritanism: A Study of Rhetoric, Prejudice and Violence* for interesting analyses of Puritan "meaning," and Lisa Gordis' *Opening Scripture* as well as texts by Toulouse, Delbanco, Schweitzer.

5 Studies of apocalypticism and Gothicism, terror and horror, overlap. One especially informative survey is *Imagining Apocalypse: Studies in Cultural Crisis* edited by David Seed. One especially useful study is *The Bang and the Whimper: Apocalypse and Entropy in American Literature* by Zbigniew Lewicki, which begins with an excellent opening chapter on Puritans and offers a sustained reading of *Day of Doom*. Some others I have found useful are *Nightmare on Main Street* by Edmundson, who uses the term "apocalyptic Gothic" (23–32) to describe gothic written by "pseudo secular moralists" as well as "premillenarian fundamentalists," and *American Horror Fiction* edited by Brian Docherty. Leslie Fiedler anticipated and founded the field in *Love and Death in the American Novel*.

6 As with the topic of Christian apocalypticism, that of hermeneutics and its afterlife in narrative is beyond the scope of this essay. The sources I have found most illuminating are Geoffrey Hartman's "Literature High and Low: The Case of the Mystery Story" which focuses on mystery's hermeneutic allure and Frank Kermode's *The Genesis of Secrecy*. A good survey of this protean genre is to be found in *American*

Mystery and Detective Novels: A Reference Guide by Larry Landrum. The most celebrated discussion, occasioning a sub-industry of poststructural debate, began with Lacan's "Seminar on The Purloined Letter," mediations on and elaborations of which are to be found, among other places, in John Irwin's provocative although labyrinthine *The Mystery to a Solution*.

7 Brown's Protestant "opening" of scripture stands, not incidentally, against Catholic secrecy: as in Protestant agitprop from the Reformation on, Brown's Church sustains itself through freakish tortures, tyrannical chains of command, and ill-gotten gains.

8 See Dixon, Seed, and Edmundson on spectacles of urban destruction in American film.

9 See Jenny Franchot's magisterial *Roads to Rome: The Antebellum Protestant Encounter with Catholicism*, especially chapters one and eight for fascinating treatments of the Gothicization of Catholic culture. See also David Reynolds' *Beneath the American Renaissance*.

10 Edward J. Ingesbretsen's *Maps of Heaven, Maps of Hell* surveys precisely this territory, giving attention to faux Christian (often New England) landscapes from the Puritans to the present day.

11 Nearly every scholarly treatment of Poe addresses his famous accusation of Longfellow as plagiarist for which scholars have manifold explanations. For a concise chronological account of Poe's "campaign" see Sidney P. Moss's *Poe's Literary Battles*.

12 Critics have tended to evaluate the interest of Poe's *Eureka* based on the saliency or non-saliency to them of his cosmological, and even Christian, vision. Perry Miller, who gave Poe's *Eureka* real attention in an essay called "End of the World," argued that Poe "perceived the true location of the concept of the end of the world in perfection of plot" (*Errand* 188), while Yvor Winters argued that though there is "remarkable agreement between his theory and practice, he is exceptionally bad at both" (Budd and Cady 55); Daniel Hoffman strikes a middle position, calling the text an example of "Hoaxiepoe" (Hoffman 29) while also finding analogue for it in Yeats' "A Vision." Such critics of the next generation (1960s) as Wagenecht and Davidson, arguing for Poe's familiarity with the Millerites and his quite contemporary brand of apocalypticism and drawing from his explicitly Millerite fantasy, represent Poe as a man of his day. For a background in the ante-bellum context of millennial speculation to which Poe was exposed, especially to the revivalism of William Miller, see

James H. Moorehead's "Between Progress and Apocalypse: A Reassessment of Milleniallism in American Thought 1800–1880" and Gary Scharnhorst's "Images of the Millerites in American Literature." More general studies treating Miller in the 1840s include Stephen D. O'Leary's *Arguing the Apocalypse: A Theory of Millenial Rhetoric* and Jon Butler's *Awash in a Sea of Faith*.

One critic who tries to align formalistic and apocalyptic endings is Paul John Eakins. As Eakins writes, "Whether Poe's endings take the hero to the brink of the abyss or plunge him into the gulf beyond, they all confirm that Poe and his heroes believe in a significant universe: they believe in its buried treasure and they dream of the man who could find it and cry 'Eureka!' to an astonished world" (Budd and Cady 170).

13 My favorite essay on *Eureka*, and from which I have learned a great deal, is Joan Dayan's "The Analytic of the Dash" in Carlson's *Critical Essays on Edgar Allan Poe* (171–186). Dayan argues that what Poe does in *Eureka* is to create poetic effects of sufficient continuity and drive to mimic or, rather, enter the orbit of divine Unity. The dash is, she argues, his chief device in this endeavor. See also Hoffman's excellent chapter in *Poe Poe Poe Poe Poe Poe Poe Poe*, "The Mind of God" (278–299). Hoffman's wonderful title, which makes an ellipsis of Poe's name, is the graphic equivalent of Dayan's dash.

References

Bercovitch, Sacvan, ed. *The American Jeremiad*. Madison: University of Wisconsin Press, 1978.

Budd, Louis, and Edwin Cady, eds. *On Poe: The Best From American Literature*. Durham: Duke University Press, 1993.

Butler, Jon. *Awash in a Sea of Faith: Christianizing the American People*. Cambridge, MA: Harvard University Press, 1992.

Carlson, Eric. W., ed. *Critical Essays on Edgar Allan Poe*. Boston: GK Hall, 1986.

Davidson, Edward H. *Poe: A Critical Study*. Cambridge, MA: Harvard University Press, 1957.

Delbanco, Andrew. *The Puritan Ordeal*. Cambridge, MA: Harvard University Press, 1989.

Dixon, Wheeler Winston. *Visions of the Apocalypse: Spectacles of Destruction in the American Cinema*. New York: Wallflower Press, 2003.

Doherty, Brian. *American Horror Fiction: From Brockden Brown to Stephen King*. Basingstoke: MacMillan, 1990.

Edmundson, Mark. *Nightmare on Main Street: Angels, Sadomasochism and the Culture of Gothic*. Cambridge, MA: Harvard University Press, 1997.

Fiedler, Leslie. *Love and Death in the American Novel*. Harmondsworth: Penguin, 1984.

Franchot, Jenny. *Roads to Rome: The Antebellum Protestant Encounter with Catholicism*. Berkeley: University of California Press, 1994.

Frykholm, Amy Johnson. *Rapture Culture: Left Behind in Evangelical America*. New York: Oxford University Press, 2004.

Gordis, Lisa. *Opening Scripture: Bible Reading and Interpretive Authority in Puritan New England*. Chicago: University of Chicago Press, 2003.

Hall, David. *World's of Wonder, Days of Judgment*. New York: Knowf, 1989.

Hartman, Geoffrey. *The Geoffrey Hartman Reader*. London: Edinburgh University Press, 2004.

Hoffman, Daniel. *Poe Poe Poe Poe Poe Poe Poe*. Garden City: Doubleday, 1972.

Ingesbretsen, Edward. *Maps of Heaven, Maps of Hell: Religious Terror as Memory from the Puritans to Steven King*. Armonk, NY: M.E. Sharpe, 1996.

Irwin, John. *The Mystery to a Solution: Poe, Borges and the Analytic Detective Story*. Baltimore: Johns Hopkins University Press, 1994.

Kermode, Frank. *The Genesis of Secrecy: On the Interpretation of Narrative*. Cambridge, MA: Harvard University Press, 1980.

Kibbey, Ann. *The Interpretation of Material Shapes in Puritanism: A Study of Rhetoric, Prejudice and Violence*. Cambridge: Cambridge University Press, 1986.

LaHaye, Tim, and Jenkins, Jerry B. *The Left Behind series of novels*. Carol Stream, IL: Tyndale House, 1995–2007.

Landrum, Larry. *American Mystery and Detective Novels: A Reference Guide*. Westport, CT: Greenwood Press, 1999.

Lewicki, Zbigniew. *The Bang and the Whimper: Apocalypse and Entropy in American Literature*. Westport, CT: Greenwood, 1984.

Matthiessen, F.O. *American Renaissance: Art and Expression in the Age of Emerson and Whitman*. New York: Oxford University Press, 1941.

Miller, Perry. *Errand into the Wilderness*. Cambridge: Belknap Press of Harvard University Press, 1956.

Miller, Perry. *Jonathan Edwards*. New York: Sloane, 1949.

Moorhead, James H. "Between Progress and Apocalypse: A Reassessment of Millennialism in American Religious Thought: 1800–1880." *Journal of American History* 71:3 (1984): 524–542.

Moss, Sidney P. *Poe's Literary Battles: The Critic in the Context of His Literary Milieu.* Carbondale: Southern Illinois University Press, 1969.

O'Leary, Stephen. *Arguing the Apocalypse.* Oxford: Oxford University Press, 1994.

Pippin, Tina. *Apocalyptic Bodies.* New York: Routledge, 1999.

Poe, Edgar Allan. *Complete Stories and Poems of Edgar Allan Poe.* New York: Doubleday, 1984.

Reynolds, David. *Beneath the American Renaissance: The Subversive Imagination in the Age of Emerson and Melville.* New York: Knopf, 1988.

Robbins, Thomas, and Susan J. Palmer. *Millennium, Messiah's and Mayhem: Contemporary Apocalyptic Movements.* New York: Routledge, 1997.

Scharnhorst, Gary. "Images of the Millerites in American Literature." *American Quarterly* 32.1 (1980): 19–36.

Schweitzer, Ivy. *The Work of Self Representation: Lyric Poetry in Colonial New England.* Chapel Hill: University of North Carolina Press, 1991.

Seed, David, ed. *Imagining Apocalypse.* Basingstoke: MacMillan Press, 2000.

Toulouse, Theresa. *The Art of Prophesying: The New England Sermon and the Shaping of Belief.* Athens: University of Georgia Press, 1987.

Wagenecht, Edward. *Edgar Allan Poe: The Man behind the Legend.* New York: Oxford University Press, 1963.

Warner, Michael, ed. *American Sermons: The Pilgrims to Martin Luther King, Jr.* New York: Library of America, 1999.

Wigglesworth, Michael. *The Day of Doom: Or a Poetical Description of the Great and Last Judgment.* Ed. and intro. by Kenneth Murdock. New York: The Spiral Press, 1929.

Wojcik, Daniel. *The End of the World as We Know It: Faith, Fatalism and Apocalypse in America.* New York: New York University Press, 1997.

Zakai, Avihu. *Exile and Kingdom: History and Apocalypse in the Puritan Migration to America.* Cambridge: Cambridge University Press, 1992.

Further Reading

Bosco, Ronald. *The Poems of Michael Wisgglesworth.* Lanham, MD: University Press of America, 1984.

Conforti, Joseph. *Jonathan Edwards, Religious Tradition and American Culture.* Chapel Hill: University of North Carolina Press, 1995.

Gura, Philip F. *Jonathan Edwards: America's Evangelical.* New York: Hill and Wang, 2005.

Marsden, George. *Jonathan Edwards, A Life.* New Haven, CT: Yale University Press, 2003.

4

"I Take—No Less than Skies—"
Dickinson's Flights

> Exhilaration is the Breeze
> That lifts us from the Ground
> And leaves us in another place
> Whose statement is not found—
>
> Returns us not, but after time
> We soberly descend
> A little newer for the term
> Upon Enchanted Ground—
>   (Emily Dickinson)

In the poetry of Emily Dickinson, weather is to geography as Spirit is to Letter.

Poetry, a species of verbal weather, moves across language's literalism, lifting and lending dimension to the prosaic. Poetry's fronts, relieving lexical inertia, produce meaning by changing, raising the music out of, and thereby "en-chanting" prosaic ground. The inclined wind, the sunlight refracted through moisture and clouds, the season's effulgencies and denudations, the tidal ebb and flow – for

New England Beyond Criticism: In Defense of America's First Literature, First Edition. Elisa New.
© 2014 Elisa New. Published 2014 by John Wiley & Sons, Ltd.

Dickinson, these forces, counterparts or even agents to the spirit and, via feelings, to the soul, continue the work of Creation, and allow poetry itself to become a medium for delivering Creation's force.

In the poetry of Emily Dickinson, weather has poetry's – and God's – slant on things.

But weather plays a more than incidental role in Dickinson, for in her work ground is lower than sky – baser, beneath it. Sky correlates with motion of the spirit; land, with a merely physical selfsameness. Like a bodied self, a fixed identity, or printed book, bounded, proprietary land just lies there. Settled within its various fences, boasting the dimensions of its own extent, land epitomizes the flatness and banality Dickinson associates with prose and embodies the spiritual inertia she contrasts with poetry's "possibility." Like her forebears, transmogrifying their theology into a poetics, Dickinson lives in this world, but would not be "of" it. To be too rooted in village, burrow, warren, or barn, too tied to landmark, too defined by nation, burg, or property is to mistake the contingencies and conveniences of living in and on the earth for the far ampler – if also more unstable and fugitive – benefits of knowing one's true home is above. Dickinson may dispense with the narrower applications of Calvinist orthodoxy, but we do not have an American poet who cared more about Heaven, broadly understood.[1] Thus "acre," "plot," "house," "town," "land," "roofs," "doors," "walls," "property," "sod" are all words in Dickinson's lexicon for that settled state we find soon enough in the graveyard. "I often passed the village," Dickinson writes in an early poem, "When going home from school—/ And wondered what they did there— / And why it was so still" (Poem #51). The poet affects a child's naïveté here, feigning innocence about what kind of village the cemetery might be. Later poems, however, will make clear just how moribund the "village" is in its own right. In her work, the here, the owned, home, terra firma, are mired all in stasis and identity.

As we saw in Chapter 2, for Dickinson, as for Cotton, Taylor, and Edwards, the effect of the Spirit is to complicate, turn, and expose new facets of a world we think we know, introducing and revealing its fuller

76

reality. Excesses of adaptation and familiarity, complacency in belonging, are, by contrast, obvious; they are redundant, vaunting, and vain. An excellent illustration of this principle may be found in poem #975, "The Mountain sat upon the Plain / In his tremendous Chair." Disposing all of its bulk "upon" and then adding to this mass the trisyllabic surplus of his "tre-men-dous" chair, the mountain projects and extends claims in every direction. Not only is its base massive, but above this base, "His observation omnifold." the mountain's wrinkled brow of rock broadcasts seigniorial inquisition. Dickinson lets the Latinate syllables pile up to mock the grandeur of this furrowed eminence enthroned so obtrusively. And then, to suggest yet more excess, she gives it probing sightlines: "His inquest, everywhere—." Further still, to this physical bulk Dickinson then superadds another kind of crude priority, antiquity: "The Seasons played around his knees / Like Children round a sire— / Grandfather of the Days is He / Of Dawn, the Ancestor—." What else, we realize, would a mountain be but a "Grandfather," the honorific of ancestral precedence blazoned in capitals? By the poem's end, this Mountain in his tremendous chair seems obvious and clichéd. Like a caricature of divine immensity, he is big but unprofound.

Size, whether largeness or smallness, confines objects within shells of familiar identity, proximity prejudices perception in favor of limited views, and culture reigns over things that stand still, even impounding the sky. Dickinson comes to seek higher, less mimetic, and more dynamic skies than those above, wilder skies whose movement may wreak change and so deliver knowledge of "Where the Meanings, are" (Poem #258). Higher than the land they engulf, their origins elusive and their ends deferred, these skies ruffle and disturb the earth below. So much wind blows through Dickinson's work, it is as though the whole oeuvre is unsettled by it. Ever turning, ever troping, this wind stands in Dickinson's work for the force poems can discharge, the force true Spirit fills with breath. These skies liberate the objects they carry from their more static relations. They loosen the "here" to the refreshment of "there," today to yesterday or way back when. They free the known, the inert, to find correction and redemption in the unknown.

The Wind didn't come from the Orchard—today—
Further than that—
Nor stop to play with the Hay—
Nor joggle a Hat—
He's a transitive fellow—very—
Rely on that—

(Poem #316)

In reading these lines, we might think back to Chapter 2 and to the winsome, coaxing tones of Edward Taylor's "Preface." There, associations between the created world and God's fashioning Hands instructed immature faith in the ABCs of Awe, while subsequent lines in Taylor's "Preface" rendered more abstract – and thus more powerful – the force of God's Agency. Here, a similar evolution occurs. In the first stanza, the poem humors the innocence that must localize to perceive, that traces wind to the likeliest, most proximate source: the moving boughs of the nearby orchard. How credulous are such chains of cause and effect, how simple the dot-to-dots we knit between objects! And how object-centered or, rather, subject-centric and lopsided are our instruments of measurement and description! Capitalized, "Orchard," "Hay," and "Hat" are mere collateral phenomena promoted to principals. They claim a force larger than discrete effects, one larger too than mere selfhood or agency. There is absurdity in describing wind by saying, "He's a transitive fellow—very— / Rely on that." Something so transitive must withhold "that's," just as something so transitive repels familiarities. The sheer silliness of making wind a "fellow" is rendered yet more risible by the assurance that this "transitive" fellow is also one on whom one might "Rely."

In the next stanza, then, Dickinson begins to buffet and reroute all the hard objects wind carries, then mystifies and multiplies the wind's ineffable turns:

If He leave a Bur at the door
We know He has climbed a Fir—
But the Fir is Where—Declare—
Were you ever there?

78

If He brings Odors of Clovers
And that is His business—not Ours—
Then He has been with the Mowers—
Whetting away the Hours
To sweet pauses of Hay—
His Way—of a June Day—

(316)

The first connotative level of the lines above asserts the wind's roundabout ways, especially beginning in stanza two. But more than that, these lines confute identities and linear links between objects and the wind that carries them at deeper levels of sound and typographic resemblance. The splayed and softened endings of slant and half rhymes, in combination with the mutation of sound clusters internal to lines, begin to smear relations. For instance, the "Bur at the door" (that presumably came from a fir) begins in a sort of typographic mimicry, nearly pictographic: the protuberances and prongs or the "B" and the "r" subtly imitate the bur itself, while the thinner bristles of the f, i, and r have the visually vertical look of the fir. At the same time, these rhymes begin to lose exactitude, deprived of visual bite through subtly mismatched vowels: the B[u]r we have found by the "d[oo]r" may indeed have come from the "f[i]r" the wind climbed, but the wind has carried it through other zones too, zones whose variety is suggested through the visual disturbance of the mutating vowels.

Thus in this poem we have precisely the opposite – a correction – of what one can see in a poem like "I'll tell you how the Sun rose— / A Ribbon at a time," where color and rhyme stay within defined bands, inventoried by a speaker in ribbons of unspooling verse. As the rhymes of bur, fir, and door are scrambled by visual variation, the lengthened vowel sounds and blunted fricatives of "There" and "Where" also swell and inflate the poem's vista beyond orchard or fir or door. Indeed, the fertile congress of vowel sounds promoted in stanza two now extends to consonants, as v's and z's and r's and s's begin to hum and vibrate in all directions. Astounding internal rhymes (business/been with), homonyms (Ours/Hours), and chiastic resonances (of Holy—/His way) give a tacking texture to the stanza, as, thematically, the movement of wind mingles rather than disaggregates.

Sonic mixings of this kind help the poet to conjure sensory ripenings – of smell, of temporal durée; of faintness and fadingness, of potency and sparcity – not readily conveyed in the black and white of print. If the Odors the wind bears are from Clovers, they are also more complexly decanted – of fields being mown, grass cut in sunshine and drying to hay, of days and weeks of scent stirred through a season's ripening. Time itself is distended and then compacted by wind, one moment made a quintessence by this force that gathers sight, sound, and smell. If temporal duress as well as spatial distance ("whetting of hours"; "sweet pauses of hay") contribute to the scent, both place and time keep the odor, the essence, of the many "wheres" that comprise any "where." Like poetry, weather's turns breed variety within identity.

We have seen that in Dickinson's verse, "where" we truly live is as much – or ought be as much – in the atmosphere as on the ground. In Dickinson's work, terrestrial life solicits the rousing transformation by the mobile sky, whose changefulness makes things happen.

Dickinson's earliest editors may have missed a great deal about her verse, but their attentiveness to meteorological Dickinson earns them more respect than we accord them. Weather – "The Far Theatricals of Day" – was an organizing topos of Mabel Loomis Todd and Millicent Todd Bingham's 1945 *Bolts of Melody*, and the mother and daughter editorial team were correct in surmising how crucial to Dickinson, how firm an organizing, even first, principle were the intersecting movements of light and moisture, temperature and tide. A poem, as Todd and Todd Bingham understood, was an event or occurrence of transmogrifying power.

Indeed, to attend to the meteorological and climatological organization of Dickinson's imagination is to begin to see the firm-featured earth demoted from scene of action to platform or stage, taking and displaying the sky's effects. Mountains may rear up, projecting that "observation omnifold" we saw in "The Mountain sat

upon the Plain," but it is the movement of the sun and its planets
that gives the mountains their royal qualities:

> The Mountains—grow unnoticed—
> Their Purple figures rise
> Without attempt—Exhaustion—
> Assistance—or Applause—
>
> (Poem #757)

Mountains do not, of course, "grow"; their own locked sinews never
budge. Rather, they are daily revealed: as Dickinson shows, the royal
purple of the mountains' majesty is an effect of the rising sun, whose
movement purples them. Just as firm, just as vividly placed, are the
colors of the sky:

> Whole Gulfs—of Red, and Fleets—of Red—
> And Crews—of solid Blood—
> Did place about the West—Tonight—
> As 'twere specific Ground—
>
> (658)

In these lines, mobile banks of color, superimposed, mass together to
make evening a destination. By docking there, Dickinson marvels,
color achieves a locality as definite as any landmark, as any "specific
ground."

In another poem, Dickinson gives more scope to light and color,
which again define place; and here, as in other poems, sky wins the
contest with earth:

> "Red Sea," indeed! Talk not to me
> Of purple Pharaoh—
> I have a Navy in the West
> Would pierce his Columns thro'—
> Guileless, yet of such Glory fine
> That all along the Line
> Is it, or is it not, Marine—
> Is it, or not, divine—
>
> (1642)

Navy and Marine, terms for ships under earthly command, have nothing, this poem proposes, on the inky saturated blues of the deepening sky. These hues, dropping on, drink the rose of dusk into night's navy, and as the pink goes, so does the very horizon's line. This stealthy flotilla of the sky's "Navy," its powers "Marine," overwhelm and commandeer earthly empires, however lofty, just as sunlight presided over the growth of mountains.

Other poems go even further to unsettle the conventionality of the lateral. It is, Dickinson shows, a flatfooted sensibility that imagines that the world expands flatly outward from where we stand, that primary movements are all horizontal. To pay more mind to weather is to see the line between earth and sky made fluid, the stacked planes of the terrestrial and aerial confuted every minute by the vertical risings of heat and the falling moisture, by evaporation and condensation.

Other, non-human animals run on this up–down axis that connects earth to sky, and these instruct the poet. Waking by a bedroom window, the poet reports, "By my Window have I for Scenery / Just a Sea—with a Stem— / If the Bird and the Farmer—deem it a "Pine"— / The Opinion will serve—for them—" (Poem #797). Feet on the ground, we are all "farmers," with limited, landlocked view; we mistakenly believe that trees are rooted in the earth. But trees, as this poem reminds us, are rooted just as much in the sky: trees drink in water and light, and their branches are root systems expanding upward and outward, casting off into the deep blue. The simplest change of orientation – from standing up to lying prone, where there is no glimpse of ground beneath her feet to distract her – gives the speaker the pine's more expansive view upward, frees her from pedestrian earthliness. From this angle, the pine steers its green prow into the deep blue, its advancing wedge a "Line" for the "Jays" – the squirrels, and the speaker too, now out on a "giddy Peninsula."

Similar upendings, rotations of ground and horizon, recur in other poems. In poem #1649, for instance, Dickenson writes, "A Chill came up as from a shaft / Our noon became a well." Elsewhere, in the poem that begins, "I think that the Root of the Wind

82

is Water," Dickinson reminds us that wind does not come from the "Orchard" or the "Fir" at all, but from much further away: its "root" is in the turbulent ocean. Wind's side-to-side, she suggests, the horizontal east–west strokes of its passing, are less consequential than its deeper motions:

> I think that the Root of the Wind is Water—
> It would not sound so deep
> Were it a Firmamental Product—
> Airs no Oceans keep—
> Mediterranean intonations—
> To a Current's Ear—
> There is a maritime conviction
> In the Atmosphere—
>
> (1302)

In the lines above, in the doubled oo's of that first "root," and then the subsequent doublings and diphthongs of the internal vowel clusters, "silent" sounds lend volume by letting us see sound: visual variety lends aural texture. Read aloud, the audibles trump inaudibles. On the page, though, the a, o, and e are next to, or rather below, more apparent tones: the words in which they appear enchamber deeper sounds. "Mediterranean Intonations / To a Current's Ear" discovers registers, deeper spectra of sound, that one must see to "hear," the remote sense informing the proximate one. The poem's ostensible theme – wind's root in water – turns out to be itself rooted in an account of internal diversity as it deepens all being.

That the deepest meaning will require the hearing of hearing, or distance sufficient to register in order to catch the message borne our way, is a theme Dickinson develops further. "The Spirit is the Conscious Ear," she writes, we "actually Hear," so naming spirit as hearing heard, hearing that hearkens. Such hearing is, Dickinson puns, "admitted—Here." If, "For other Services—as Sound— / There hangs a smaller Ear," this one "only—Hear" (Poem #733). Sound, like vision, must be borne to us, or carried by something else. Only thus, from a distance or through metaphor, is the world thoroughly "sounded." The familiar depends on the far and comes from afar:

> A South Wind—has a pathos
> Of individual Voice—
> As One detects on Landings
> An Emigrant's address.
> (Poem #719)

Some might allegorize and call this a poem hinting at Southern fugitives, or Atlantic immigrants, with Dickinson bestowing subtle sympathy on those making their way North. To do so, however, would be to swap the poem's tenor (wind) for its possible vehicles (migrants) in a way that the poem's second stanza discourages. Neither place nor origin, nor even traceable vector, the south wind is a conductor, an invisible current whose nature is to preserve or carry transition and flight. In the next stanza it becomes clear that pathos needs distance:

> A Hint of Ports and Peoples—
> And much not understood—
> The fairer—for the farness—
> And for the foreignhood.
> (719)

A hint is all a wind can carry, not information but suggestion, an invitation to apprehend, to enter a deeper chamber. The last two lines – with their sprouting punning homophones (fair, far-n, foreign) and their exaggerated and tacked-on suffixes of intensification (fair-*er* , far-*ness*, foreign*hood*) are, we might say, "far fetched." This is their power. These lines defend the proposition that the best here is a there, the fullest possession the one that is fetched from far away. Poetry, for Dickinson, is not merely a way of sounding the world but also of carrying sound.

Increasingly, in Dickinson, meaning is borne in from elsewhere, from distant climes, or is itself a distant clime. If poetry is produced by the shift of meanings from tenor to vehicle, meaning in Dickinson is made of attractions, apprehensions, conveyances – the vehicular. We

84

might say – and it is this proposition the last section of this chapter illustrates – that poetry, for Emily Dickinson, is not merely a way of seeing far-off things but of seeing distance itself.

For Dickinson has further reasons for transferring attention from ground to air. "The Wind didn't come from the Orchard—today" makes a windy day deliver a mixed bouquet of sensate experience, complicating cruder divisions of earth and sky, and in Dickinson's poems of heavenly spectacle she upends horizons, confutes liquid and solid, gives color broad powers, promotes squirrels above farmers – all to loosen the clay from prosaic experience, to broaden the literally pedestrian ranges of perception. Historical sophistication and spiritual rigor also encourage her to write poems that decouple spirit from land mass. Dickinson works hard to disrupt truisms about the settlement of the North American landmass and its providential rightness. In many of her poems, old correlations between spiritual elevation and North American geography – correlations dear to her Calvinist forebears – are raised to question.

If, after their Cities on Hills, her forebears called their settlements godly plantations, Dickinson reminds us that spirit is a dynamic, mobile force, one that breathes. In the poem below, genuine spirit is that afflatus stirring the tent flaps but departing from any particular encampment:

> I've known a Heaven, like a Tent—
> To wrap its shining Yards—
> Pluck up its stakes, and disappear—
> Without the sound of Boards
> Or Rip of Nail—Or Carpenter—
> But just the miles of Stare—
> That signalize a Show's Retreat—
> In North America—
>
> (Poem #243)

The "Tent" might, at first, seem mere conceit for the shifting of weather fronts, for weather's literally migratory character. But soon enough, one hears in this tent other tents of meaning: the Spirit of Revival sweeping the farmlands. Dickinson allows the "tent" to accommodate the full range of religio-cultural possibilities, but especially to gesture toward those camp meetings and revivals indigenous to western New England. In the plucking up of "stakes" the reader may additionally hear intimations of homesteading and the push west, of Manifest Destiny staking its claims and all the windiness of stump politics. Hints toward that most sorrowful circus of all – the excruciating pageant of board and nails devised for one carpenter's suffering – are present in the poem, and hints, too, toward those mobs or masses, crowds or congregations whose sheer number leave them insensible to stirring Spirit. "Miles of Stare" lets Spirit pass right by, and the gaping crowd is too avid for any spectacle to be moved. Ballooning with all these possibilities, the tent is Dickinson's image for the spirit's more parochial dwelling places.

As "I've known a Heaven, like a Tent" would show, the coincidence of Heaven and a particular geography is just that: coincidence. Divinity may apparently be captured on a flapping bill of advertisement or find illustration in vernacular pageantry, but the spirit cannot be engrossed by any one region any more than wind is confined by a tent. Now gracing a camp meeting, now a circus, now a spell of prairie weather, now the light off a bird's wing, the spirit is not to be confused with the booster's, the bumpkin's, or the post-chaise driver's "North America":

> No Trace—no Figment of the Thing
> That dazzled, Yesterday,
> No Ring—no Marvel—
> Men, and Feats—
> Dissolved as utterly—
> As Bird's far Navigation
> Discloses just a Hue—
> A plash of Oars, a Gaity—
> Then swallowed up, of View.
>
> (Poem #243)

More fugitive even than the birds, wind's "far Navigation," complexly vectored, abstracts and multiplies planes of visibility. Rowing through sky, the sound of its currents cutting a visible furrow, the wind at this poem's end stands for the transport the poet calls, elsewhere, "Exhilaration."

In the 1850s, Dickinson's Amherst was still West, and this West not yet forgetful of the great migrations. Gusty with the revivals, Dickinson's Massachusetts had seen legions of journeyers calling themselves Israelites. For Dickinson, however, westward migration and the Christian march across the landscape were Spirit's temporary vehicles. Expedient forms without lasting relevance, the rituals and social formations of American spirituality were best regarded – and their value best protected – when no undeserved prestige accrued to the pilgrim or the land he settled. Pilgrimage preserved a population's internal dynamism, but settlement dampened spirit. In a poem reflecting back on journeyers westward, "The lonesome for they know not What," Dickinson is at pains to preserve the travelers from certainty of cause, coherency of peoplehood, and status of locale. She honors the immigrant and the nation in its still unfinished, still progressive state of itinerancy. The spiritual buoyancy that preserves the lonesome is not self-assertion but a capacity to be moved.

> The lonesome for they know not What—
> The Eastern Exiles—be—
> Who strayed beyond the Amber line
> Some madder Holiday—
>
> (Poem #262)

The immigrants remembered in these lines have faith and urgency adequate to carry them ahead of the "amber line," the western sky's horizon. Nameless and not limited to one generation, these are not emigrants who "were" but Exiles who "—be—." The weirdly atemporal verse tense is allowed to correspond to the miraculous suspension of these same pilgrims in air, the risk and the giddy anomaly of their venture holding them up where lateral crosscurrents and up- and down-drafts press in.

> And ever since—the purple Moat—
> They strive to climb—in vain—
> As Birds—that tumble from the clouds
> Do fumble at the strain—
>
> (262)

It is, Dickinson suggests, a providential blessing that saves humans from solid ground and firm attainments. Unlike the birds whose wingspan turns the wind's buffetings to poise, human beings pursue linear goals, fasten their sights on unworthy attainments, and mythologize the ardor of their quests. But, in the end, it is not these quests, not Holy Land nor Destiny nor Castle in the Air that gives firmness to their strivings. What upholds them best is the sheerest exhilaration, the casting off from terra firma itself, their "loneliness for they know not What," more valuable than certainty. It is something higher than justification, something more glorious than a merely manifest Destiny that

> The Blessed Ether—taught them—
> Some Transatlantic Morn—
> When Heaven—was too common—to miss—
> Too sure—to dote upon!
>
> (262)

With Spirit de-coupled from particular locales and divided too from sacralized mythic journeys, it follows that New England's superiority to Old England – the oldest New England conviction – would also go by the wayside. Dickinson's most regionally specific poems treat regional attachments as second-order, even flimsy. These poems evince skepticism about how local customs define cherished norms. Take the one that begins "The Robin's my Criterion for Tune":

> The Robin's my Criterion for Tune—
> Because I grow—where Robins do—
> But, were I Cuckoo born—
> I'd swear by him—
> The ode familiar—rules the Noon—
> The Buttercup's, my Whim for Bloom—
> Because, we're Orchard sprung—
> But, were I Britain born,
> I'd Daisies Spurn—
>
> (Poem #285)

Winsome, skeptical, the poem shows the connective tissue between a region and any of its meanings to be entirely contingent. To make the robin one's "criterion" for tune is, Dickinson suggests, to elevate convention, custom, and the comfort of animal belonging above possibilities not so tamed by familiarity. Although this is the poem where Dickinson makes the famous admission that she sees "New Englandly," she makes it clear that such sight, educated narrowly, has limited vision. Dickinson's dubiety of patriotic allegiances and of such oaths as natives love to make becomes clear when she writes, "were I Cuckoo born— / I'd swear by him." Enclosed worlds are, this poem suggests, made yet smaller by those too invested in them, who extrapolate from narrowest experience (robins) to criteria more general (criteria for tunes). Far from actually seeing "New Englandly," the poet lets the awkwardly tacked-on adverbial ending distance her real vision from such blinkered sight. The robin in his local tree, the sovereign in her kingdom – indeed, all creatures in their habitats – may erroneously call their little domains a world. As Dickinson writes, "The Queen, discerns like me— / Provincially—" (285).

"Location's narrow way is for Ourselves," Dickinson insists in poem #489, and these pages have gathered evidence for the case that locales, landmarks, points on maps, and North America itself have a place-filling status in Dickinson. Her perspective on the chauvinism of any locality makes her chary of local pride, skeptical of regional boasting. Settled opinions, like settled life, have an obviousness that argues against their spiritual consequence. Against the values and verities of land and ground, Dickinson's poetry bids us regard the changing spectacle of the ever-moving skies, which unsettle ground and bestir stolidity of soul.

What remains to be discussed is the bearing Dickinson's aerial view had on the scenes of reading and, in particular, on such reading Dickinson imagined her oeuvre would sustain. Such scenes – events of world-altering moment – can be found on nearly every page of Dickinson's enormous body of work, where poetry becomes climatological, its fronts turning and straining the fibers of mere words. Page after page, day after day, poetry – and especially metaphor – operates in Dickinson to freshen and redeem language.

To return again to the argument offered in "Variety as Religious Experience," Chapter 2, the Calvinist discourse Dickinson inherited and developed abounded in terms for incidents of spiritual expansion. Word was the bearer of Spirit, and proper reading or listening to scripture had the power to aid revelation and conversion. The Word could make mere mortal existence into life: the chariot of the Word lifted existence off the ground and filled it, tent-like, with buoyant spirit. The slow absorption and incorporation of transcendental-romantic elements into the Congregational plain style Dickinson inherited seems only to have enhanced her sense of meaning's hidden situation in the world and its transformative movement through it. Meaning was, as William James would later say, not to be confined or discovered in substantives; for Dickinson, as for James, meaning *happened*.

Thus Dickinson's famous question to Thomas Wentworth Higginson whether her verses "breathed," and thus her image of volcanic eruption, irresistible and explosive, to describe a genuine poem's effects: "If I feel physically as if the top of my head were taken off, I know that is poetry." Not satisfied with the merely figurative claim that poems offer "escape" and "adventure," Dickinson constructed her own verses to register, and be changed by, the subtlest stirrings. Indeed, she sought to emancipate the book itself from binding, page, and ink, to give the book the quickness of life itself:

> There is no Frigate like a Book
> To take us Lands away
> Nor any Coursers like a Page
> Of prancing Poetry—
> This Traverse may the poorest take
> Without oppress of Toll—
> How frugal is the Chariot
> That bears the Human soul.
> (Poem #1263)

Given such poems, one should not be surprised that Dickinson's mode of publication (her "letters to the world") preserved lightsome characteristics more consonant with transport than with publication. Those lucky enough to have held Dickinson's manuscripts in their hands or looked at selected pages from the fascicles in Harvard's

Houghton Library know the uncannily aerated quality of these documents. "So much breath," Harvard's Peter Sacks has beautifully put it, "between the graphite and the page." And as critics such as Sharon Cameron, Susan Howe, and Martha Nell Smith – all helped by Ralph Franklin's reconstruction of the fascicles – have concurred, Dickinson's method of binding and bookmaking was also apparently devised to unbind poetry from the two-dimensional space of the page, liberating meaning from strict location in the book.[2]

Some of these ideas bear further expansion. While the "slant" dimensions of Dickinson's world are, perhaps, better seen in the origami of her fascicles than a book, it is, after all, good to remember that even ordinary books live in light's weather. All books are more mobile and multiplanar than we notice, even though we read them every day. We may think of books as rectangular oblongs, their orientation as more or less flat. But the frigates and coursers that Dickinson describes in poem #1263 break through this inaccurate assumed geometry. These lines remind us how books sit in the angle of the hand as in saddle, how the pages furl and tack with reading's movement. To call books frigates or chariots is to see the page as a bellied sail, stirred and flexing up from its lashings. Or a vane, swung and pivoted by winds and pressures. Or a pane: through which the changing diorama of the day filters the changing light.

Neither eye nor mind is ever fixed in the act of reading. Eyes skim left to right along a page and back again, moving in a sweeping tidal fashion. Meanwhile, especially as we absorb a poem, the mind pursues a more jagged course – working up and down along the crucial right-hand margin to note rhymes or absence of rhymes, daring diagonals to note internal rhymes, associations, repetitions, and tracing switchbacks down the page. Even before the eye commences to sweep the page, the mere act of turning the page changes its face, pulling, opening and then shutting wings of light and shadow over and across the book's surface. Open a book and you spill brightness out from the vertebral crack. Close it, and you gather shadows in the gutter. Glimpses of other pages – their corners, their page numbers, the partial shapes of stanzas and paragraphs – slip in and out of view as pages turn. And binding matters: if the book is a hand-sewn affair, loose at the left hand side, as Dickinson's were, light seeps through the pierced crack of the binding, and the turning pages shift louvers of light from crease to the outward edge. A book of this kind, a fascicle, draws the eye transversely off the horizontal and vertical axis and into new lozenges the changing light apportions. Thus does the Dickinsonian page "choose," in Sharon Cameron's terms, not to be a page – choose, we might say, the turnings between pages. This "turn" is also a trope.

Without a stable "here," a Dickinsonian fascicle boasts superior faculties of "there," for the transfer and translation of proximate into more approximate meanings, of identity into change. Nowhere is this power of approximation more powerfully illustrated, at least for me, than in the deservedly famous poem that begins, "There's a certain Slant of light." Written in 1861, from what we now call Fascicle 13, the four-stanza poem is from the period when Dickinson wrote a poem a day, from a period, that is, when the sheer number of poems produced would have made her waking hours a veritable tempest of versification. The poem, familiar to virtually anyone who has ever read even a little Dickinson, transfers the pang of one moment across time and space. It begins by delivering the effects of winter's onset in a place – a poem – far from winter's chill:

> There's a certain Slant of light,
> Winter Afternoons—
> That oppresses, like the Heft
> Of Cathedral Tunes—
>
> Heavenly Hurt, it gives us—
> We can find no scar,
> But internal difference,
> Where the Meanings, are—
>
> None may teach it—Any—
> 'Tis the Seal Despair—
> An imperial affliction
> Sent us of the Air—
>
> (Poem #258)

Now, the actual moment to which the poem refers is a powerfully fraught one. When, on midwinter afternoons, night begins to come on at roughly four o'clock, who is not susceptible to just the feelings Dickinson invokes? In a church, especially a cold church, who is not a little depressed? And yet it is not really the experience of being in a wintry place, or even the apprehension of winter's onset, or even the experience of sitting in a chilly pew that this poem so powerfully invokes, though it summons all these. Rather, its power comes from turning each of these into a figure for one, or more, of the others. The "Meanings" it conjures and summons do not belong to any substantive experience but to the refraction of that experience into and across others: it is about diffusion rather than concentration. Nothing substantive, nothing palpable or placed can stir the kind of profound feelings that uncertainty can; nothing met head on has the power to unsettle the feelings the way sensations catching us unawares do. Insinuated sidewise, leaking through the louvers, slant meanings weigh heavier.

Dickinson uses all the formal means in her repertoire to tell this truth about slantness, about oblique meanings and their power to move us.

Strong trochaic meter, hard-stressed from the left and leaning firmly right, is Dickinson's first sonic device of decoupling meaning from stable identity principles and commending it to realms more mysterious. Observe how the first line of the poem introduces three trochees in row – "Thére's a / cértain / Slánt of light" – layering over a riddling diction ("There's a": where's a? "Certain: which?), a meter likewise oblique. Eventually, this unremitting trochaic rhythm of the opening lines ("There's a," "Winter") will press the weak iambs before them until, at "Heavenly," iambic regularity, still unestablished, literally gives up its footing. Then, the top-heavy dactyls – "None may teach," "'Tis the Seal" "Sent us of," echoing and shadowing the also dactylic "Slant of light" – will press in from the left, slowly tilting and then tipping the uprights of the hymn stanza till they lean.

And if persistently trochaic rhythm were not enough, subtle effects of chiasmus and multiple internal and half rhymes press

93

deeper, gouging obliquities of grain into the upright of the stanza. "Slant of" dully echoes in "After"; "That opp" and "Of Cath" make a little oblique knot on the page, while "heft" gathers in all those throbbing shadowy f's and th's and gives them pressure to bruise.

Now it can be no accident that the specific "here" the light apparently passes through has qualities of a "Cathedral." The word brings to mind stone pews, drafty architecture, and even a musical instrument that fills the dim space with waves of sound, so that the "light" the poem begins by invoking is not only dark or bright, direct or diffuse, but also deep-booming and tufted, as if pumped out by a pedal, extruding volume and projecting drafts. Sonically invoked by the word "Winter," wind now circulates through the poem in the image of the pipe organ pressing, pumping out its frigid drafts. The heavy architecture, the solidity and the evocation of sounds and lights with weight and volume all begin to draw more organized forms of faith into the poem. The human craving for things solid and iconic, the human faith in holy ground and sacred halls wants, Dickinson shows us, to kneel where prayer (as Eliot would say) has been valid. There is no denying how this "Cathedral" rears up at the end of the stanza, suggesting (and not subtly) the Certain Slant as equivalent to that revelatory Christian light. Certainly the increasingly churchly lexicon of the poem (Heavenly Hurt, the Seal Despair, Imperial Affliction) allows more than disallows orthodox associations. The middle two stanzas of the poem seem to trace the slant of light straight up to God, to follow the light like Jacob's ladder up from the Cathedral into the winter air. Up, up from the steepled Church, up, up through the steely sky, up from earth to the Calvinist source of divine rebuke – (Heavenly Hurt it gives us / We Can find no Scar / But Internal Difference / Where the Meanings, Are) Dickinson's poem allows us a straight line from the Divine wrath to the breast of man, pierced by his monitory light.

And yet for all their evocative power, by the last stanza of the poem all the Christian iconography has more or less evanesced. Heaven, Hell, and the whole Christian ensemble of those scarred by light (Cain, Jacob, Moses, Christ) have been exposed as but changes rung on that still-mysterious "Certain slant" of feeling. Types, their shades and shadows, were not permanent any more than the immense cathedral of the first stanza was. There never were, in fact, any church walls, pews, stained glass filtering winter light in the first stanza of the poem; these were merely qualities indwelling for a time. Neither, Dickinson goes on, can experiences of genuine meaning prove themselves through talismanic marks (they leave no "scar"); nor are creeds and catechisms predictive, in the end, of their having occurred ("None may teach it—Any—"). Rather, meaning opens in transactions from and between one and the other, in enlargements of sender and sent, wrought as each admits the other. Variety, which soul and psyche register in inflections of "internal difference," is not merely a poetic but a religious experience.

Thus, finally, it is that the movements of light through landscape, like those of a soul moved, are signs of that "Certain" changefulness that makes the present different from the past, and makes Creation an ongoing motion. Land, mind, and poem are soul's tabernacle. The tidal coming and going, the climatic fronts of "Meanings" ebb and flow, are what guarantees it. Here light's transparency, its impermanence, has the motion and facility to wash and change what merely "Is." Light's sheerness, its easy stroking back and forth over the solid ground, keeps meaning alive.

> When It comes, the Landscape listens—
> Shadows—hold their breath—
> When it goes, 'tis like the Distance
> On the look of Death—
>
> (258)

In these lines, light's movement is conveyed in sound's expression. Light's pages turn, and as they turn even the most inert of things, the capitalized "Landscape," is unbound from its tie to earth and "listens." What seemed unchangeably solid, abstract, and visible turns out to be, in fact, aural. More easily than expected, ebbing light is transposed to sheerest respiratory sound: h's and s's, softened frictive t's again brush the earth.

In "There's a Certain Slant of Light," Meaning instructs the world of lumpen substance how to take in, how to internalize the fullness and the spirit of expectancy. Like poetry itself, and dwelling within it, Meaning is an intimation of truth's mobility. Consciousness stuck in the provinces of identity has, in a way, no view. But consciousness more loosely bound is like a fascicle: its slant light opens the antique volume, exposing all soul's surfaces.

Spirit turns the page.

Notes

1   My *The Regenerate Lyric* and *The Line's Eye* may guide interested readers to the critical literature on Dickinson's verse. Twenty-first-century contributions to the Dickinson critical archive include some superb edited volumes gathering newer work by the most distinguished, established Dickinson critics: Martin, Pollak, Erkkila, Juhasz, Wolosky, Sewall, Stoneham and Miller, among many others. See *The Cambridge Companion to Emily Dickinson* and *The Cambridge Introduction to Emily Dickinson* (the first edited and the second written by Wendy Martin), *A Companion to Emily Dickinson* (edited by Martha Nell Smith and Mary Loeffelholz), and the *Emily Dickinson Handbook* (edited by Grabher, Hagenbüchle, and Miller).

Also auguring well for the health of Dickinson criticism is the recent publication of some excellent books by younger Dickinson scholars putting Dickinson in fresh transatlantic, environmental, and theoretical contexts. A stimulating compendium of the newer transatlantic criticism is *The Traffic in Poems*, edited by Meredith McGill. Dickinson affords Virginia Jackson the opportunity to offer a "theory of lyric reading" in her challenging *Dickinson's Misery*, while Jim von der Heydt's *At the Brink of Infinity* returns to, but refreshes, theological readings of Dickinson by drawing the theological and the environmental into dialogue. Finally, readers of contemporary Dickinson criticism would do well to refer to the revitalized *Emily Dickinson Journal*, now under Cristanne Miller's imaginative editorship. Representative of its excellence is Katie Peterson's "Surround Sound: Dickinson's Self and the Hearable (Fall 2005).

2   A note on editing and criticism: The most active and interesting debates in Dickinson scholarship of the last twenty years have concerned editing and, specifically, the representation of the little booklets Dickinson assembled (the so-called "fascicles") in print. Contemporary Dickinson scholars are united in judging Ralph W. Franklin's editions of Emily Dickinson's verse superior to those of Thomas Johnson and earlier editors for their meticulous reconstruction of the fascicle books, their more faithful transcription of Dickinson's variants, and, especially in *The Manuscript Books*, Franklin's scrupulous efforts (enabled by Harvard University Press) to represent the material aspects of the Dickinsonian page.

The Manuscript Books really does preserve – as much as a handsome, cloth-bound, tightly stitched bound book could – the "unbound" quality of Dickinson's packets as well as their visual impact. Treating the fascicles as physical artifacts, indeed almost as works of visual art, Franklin's work is an exemplary contribution to the history of the book. He names varieties, dimensions, and qualities of papers used (whether ruled or not, embossed or not, watermarked or stained by other means) and stipulates when Dickinson used pen, as she usually does, or pencil. He photo-replicates each manuscript page so that one can see that some were copied onto stationery opaque or "lightly ruled," while other pages were translucent enough to show, in faint ghostly shadow, the poem on the obverse side. The volumes make it easy to observe not only how Dickinson's handwriting over the course of her life loosens and grows larger (a development doubtless influenced by her eye troubles) but also the great variability in her spacing, in the slant and size of her letters and, of course, in her capitals. Sometimes these seem so exaggerated as to mimic printer's conventions of capitalization imported from the dictionary, the hymnal, and other decorative books. Puncture marks, disintegrations at the edge of any page are faithfully reproduced, and along with the full-sized fair copies, Franklin has even had bound into the spine the smaller scraps or "slips" Dickinson sometimes pinned to longer poems. Along with all the foregoing, Franklin includes tables that endeavor to show the historic organizations and reorganizations from the time of Dickinson's death through the late twentieth century. For all these reasons, I too find Franklin indispensable: his *Manuscript of Emily Dickinson* always sits next to the one-volume *The Poems of Emily Dickinson* on my shelf, I regularly use Franklin's texts in the classroom, and they are consulted whenever I write about Dickinson.

And yet candor requires me to say that, for a reader's edition, I think we ought not retire Johnson too soon. My own work in Dickinson has very deep roots in the fat, gray paperback Johnson edition, authoritative for generations, with its longer dashes, its wider layout and larger margins, and which, for the purposes of the argument made in these pages, I often prefer. I have doubtless been influenced in this preference by years of familiarity and with the opportunities I have had, precious ones, to see how the manuscripts themselves so change over the years of their production as to make any editor's choice of typeface, punctuation, or style only accurate to a degree. It is also relevant that Johnson's edition remains the source for such major classroom anthologies as *The Oxford Book of American Poetry* (edited by David Lehman) and *Nineteenth Century American Poetry* (edited by William Spengemann), both of which use the Johnson without comment. Franklin published *The Manuscript Books of Emily Dickinson* in 1981, and his editorial practices began to influence the field rapidly: by the mid-1990s, some scholars had begun to criticize Johnson's practices as patriarchal and print-centric; others going so far as to call any print version of the fascicles a violation of Dickinson's handmade mode of production. Meanwhile, however, other readers and critics were reluctant to allow Johnson's dating and, in particular, Johnson's use of the longer em dash to disappear. For instance, the editors of *The Norton Anthology of American Literature* and *The Norton Anthology of Women's Literature* take until the Eighth (present) edition and Third (present) Edition, respectively, to replace the Johnson em dash with the Franklin hyphen, splitting the difference for twenty years by explaining in bibliographic notes that Franklin's *Poems of Emily Dickinson: Variorum Edition* (1998) "will supersede" the Johnson edition while continuing to represent the poems Johnson fashion until 2012. If these classroom editions remain the ordinary reader's – and all of my own students' – Dickinson, I think it is not simply laziness or cost that keeps Johnson in circulation and cherished by readers. Franklin's most consequential decision (one justified, to be sure, by many, many of the manuscripts) was to use a shorter dash, a sort of pin tuck of a punctuation mark. These briefer dashes give us a Dickinson who seems tighter than Johnson's poet; they capture something more pierced and spastic about Dickinson's affect, a battened down but also a latent and explosive quality. These dashes seem tension marks, and they give us a poet who is always psychological. Johnson's dashes, on the other hand, were always more expansive. They seem to allow the poet out of the poem, and out of herself, affording her an elasticity and extemporaneity that Franklin does not. Johnson's edition gives us a less meticulous but also a more risk-taking, open-chested poet, one who could, when occasion required, let "horizon's swell in her vest," one who even let poems look "dashed" off. More lightly "bound to earth" (to borrow Robert Frost's words of "The Silken Tent"), Johnson's Dickinson is freer, and so it is perhaps logical that in this chapter about an airborne Dickinson, I should have been loathe to part with Johnson.

Meanwhile, candor also requires the admission that, in the course of writing this essay, I also found more than I'd have thought to love in the generally discredited and discarded volume that preceded Johnson's of 1950: namely, the thematically and, yes, lovingly organized *Bolts of Melody*, compiled by Mabel Loomis Todd and completed by her daughter Millicent Todd Bingham and published in 1945. Despite the now dated, unscholarly, and twee practice of referring to the poet as "Emily," despite an admittedly marked prejudice in favor of the finished, the unitary, and even the pretty (as opposed to our age's preference for the fragmentary, dis-integrated, and rough), Todd and Bingham's volume has much to recommend it. The decision to sort Dickinson's poems according to climatic taxonomy, making places secondary to seasons and emphasizing changefulness, preserves a certain turbulence and dimensionality of the fascicles that scholarly uniformity flattens. Todd and Bingham also reproduce Dickinson's handwriting, and I think that they let her calligraphy influence them: its swept, streaked, stroked look, as if the very slants of the handwriting were the effects of some force, allows them to represent themselves, and the poet, as moved, and thus the poetry itself as movement or turning. There is an aerated, changeful quality to *Bolts of Melody* that makes it worth keeping on our shelves. And finally, the informality of this volume (as opposed to the authoritative quality of both Johnson and Franklin) is not without merit. Authoritativeness has its hardening effects, weighting down the experience of reading poems with obligations of correctness and fixing each poem under the (museum-quality) glass of the scholarly imprint. There is a "significance effect," a "career effect" that, even lacking a two-inch brick of spine, chains a volume of poems to a library table.

In sum – and as I argued in my introduction – while one must welcome the contributions of Franklin, we may be too hasty in letting his, or any volume, supersede others, just as we might be more cautious in letting the critical contributions, however worthy, of the current generation supersede those of earlier moments.

References

Baym, Nina, gen. ed. *The Norton Anthology of American Literature*, 8th ed. New York: W. W. Norton, 2012.

Cameron, Sharon. *Lyric Time: Dickinson and the Limits of Genre*. Baltimore: Johns Hopkins University Press, 1979.

Dickinson, Emily. *Bolts of Melody*. Ed. Mabel Loomis Todd and Millicent Todd Bingham. New York: Harper & Brothers, 1945.

Dickinson, Emily. *The Complete Poems of Emily Dickinson*. Ed. Thomas H. Johnson. London: Faber and Faber, 1970.

Dickinson, Emily. *The Manuscript Books of Emily Dickinson*. Ed. R. W. Franklin. Cambridge, MA: Belknap Press, 1981.

Dickinson, Emily. *The Poems of Emily Dickinson: Variorum Edition*. Ed. R. W. Franklin. Cambridge, MA: Belknap Press, 1998.

Dickinson, Emily. *The Poems of Emily Dickinson: Reading Edition*. Ed. R. W. Franklin. Cambridge, MA: Belknap Press, 2005.

Grabher, Gudrun, Roland Hagenbüchle, and Cristanne Miller. *The Emily Dickinson Handbook*. Amherst: University of Massachusetts Press, 1998.

Gilbert, Sandra M., and Gubar, Susan, eds. *The Norton Anthology of Literature by Women: The Traditions in English*, 3rd ed. New York: W. W. Norton, 2007.

Jackson, Virginia. *Dickinson's Misery: a Theory of Lyric Reading*. Princeton, NJ: Princeton University Press, 2005.

Martin, John Frederick. *Profits in the Wilderness: Entrepreneurship and the Founding of New England Towns in the Seventeenth Century*. Chapel Hill: University of North Carolina Press, 1991.

Martin, Wendy, ed. *The Cambridge Companion to Emily Dickinson*. New York: Cambridge University Press, 2002.

Martin, Wendy. *The Cambridge Introduction to Emily Dickinson*. New York: Cambridge University Press, 2007.

New, Elisa. *The Line's Eye: Poetic Experience, American Sight*. Cambridge, MA: Harvard University Press, 1998.

New, Elisa. *The Regenerate Lyric: Theology and Innovation in American Poetry.* New York: Cambridge University Press, 1993.

Peterson, Katie. "Surround Sound: Dickinson's Self and the Hearable." *Emily Dickinson Journal* 14.2 (2005): 76–88.

Smith, Martha Nell, and Mary Loeffelholz, eds. *A Companion to Emily Dickinson.* Oxford: Wiley Blackwell, 2008.

von der Heydt, James E. *At the Brink of Infinity: Poetic Humility in Boundless American Space.* Iowa City: University of Iowa Press, 2008.

Further Reading

Dickinson, Emily. *Selected Letters.* Ed. Thomas H. Johnson. Cambridge, MA: Belknap Press, 1971.

Gardner, Thomas. *A Door Ajar: Contemporary Writers and Emily Dickinson.* New York: Oxford University Press, 2006.

Part II

Congregations:
Rites of Assembly

5

Lost in the Woods Again

Coming Home to Wilderness in Bradford, Thoreau, Frost, and Bishop

Is it lack of imagination that makes us come
to imagined places, not just stay at home?
Or could Pascal have been not entirely right
about just sitting quietly in one's room?

Continent, city, country, society:
the choice is never wide and never free.
And here, or there . . . No. Should we have stayed at home,
wherever that may be?

(Elizabeth Bishop)

1. Scholar in the Wilderness

The story is told by one of his students that when, in the early
1960s, the legendary Harvard scholar Perry Miller stepped up to
the podium to begin his famous course, English 70, he would open
his lecture with a reading from William Bradford's *Of Plimouth
Plantation*.

New England Beyond Criticism: In Defense of America's First Literature, First Edition. Elisa New.
© 2014 Elisa New. Published 2014 by John Wiley & Sons, Ltd.

Begun around 1630, Bradford's history of the people we now call Pilgrims is a far cry from elementary school hallway accounts of the Mayflower landing. Our earliest, and certainly most eloquent, history of a New England settlement, Bradford's is a text that aims a long searchlight both backward and forward, looking back to the pre-history of pilgrim settlement and forward to its future prospect. These do not encourage him. By the time Bradford completes the *Plantation* in 1647, he is already witnessing the dispersal of his community, individual homesteaders drifting away from the godly settlements clustering the eastern coast of North America. Their piety flagging, their sins piling up, Bradford's pilgrims are only thirty years – a mere one-and-a-half generations – past their landing at Plimouth, but he cannot describe his flock as very different than they'd been in Holland, where, as disheartened English fugitives scrabbling for their livings, they'd feared to lose their children's souls to bourgeois Dutch pleasures. The sailing to America (a project decided upon finally for the children's sake) had exacted terrible costs, but it had not kept these children from straying. God's Providence might be great but it was not, at least in Bradford's account, addressed to guaranteeing America's future.

Bradford's *Of Plimouth Plantation* provided so perfect a prooftext for Perry Miller's influential "declension theory," adumbrated in *The New England Mind: The Seventeenth Century*, and the sins of Miller's own time so perfect a prooftext for Bradford's Calvinist darkness, that even the most powerful account to rebut it – Sacvan Bercovitch's, in *The American Jeremiad* – had to reckon with the tragic aspects of both. The crux of Miller's thesis was that New England Puritanism was, from its inception, already in decline – the simple reason an intrinsic and perennial human sinfulness no society could overcome. First published during the Depression, as World War II, Holocaust, and Hiroshima followed, Miller's theory only gained traction, gaining even more saliency as America's midcentury struggle with totalitarianisms kept ideas of sin and evil to the fore. On the other hand, by the time he began to take up early American rhetoric in the late 1960s, Bercovitch could see how accounts of dire sinfulness could breed far more optimistic, triumphant – and triumphalist – rhetorics of American progress, and he traced these to the very rhetorical form that had epitomized declension for Miller: the jeremiad. A thunderous sermon against Puritan backsliding, a genre flourishing from the 1660s to the 1690s, the jeremiad made wandering in the wilderness the incubator of triumph, and the sensation of being lost, the very ground of America's exceptional progress. Even as the jeremiads announced communal wrack and ruin, Bercovitch demonstrated that they also augured certain triumph over that ruin, so paving the way for later accounts of American unsinkability – accounts that remain with us to this day.

Bradford's distinctly untriumphant narrative gets in the way of such triumph.

To make his case, therefore, Bercovitch had to cut Bradford loose; and so he did, showing how the Providence Bradford's Pilgrims may have enjoyed was ordinary, not "extraordinary": that is to say, bestowed by a God who might pity, but had certainly not chosen them. Distinguishing Bradford's pilgrims, and his *Plimouth Plantation*, from later accounts by later Massachusetts Bay migrants, Bercovitch showed how Bradford's account of wanderings in the woods was powerfully motivating for writers more eager for their American Destiny. If Bradford's woods had been mere woods, theirs would have to be more like testing grounds, crucibles out of which would emerge Israel, and then America, triumphant.

This account, however, still left to Miller's Bradford – and to Miller – plenty of civilizational angst and, more importantly, plenty of lonely individualism to be tested in the crucible of wilderness. And this other strand of the wilderness account is also with us to this day. Its crux is that the wilderness *mise-en-scène* inaugurated a strain of American self-reliance, the woods functioning as a natural chapel of what Luther called the soul's "lonely church of one" (Pelikan 174). The association of wilderness as the crucible of character has become so engrained in national mythology that we tend to forget its origins. But in fact Miller and his generation had much to do with codifying the idea that errands into the wilderness are heroic and character building. Late twentieth-century analysts have mustered sharp critiques against this idea, noting how much exceptionalist swagger and national mischief this wilderness account has inspired, and how much arrogant disparagement of collective life it has fostered.

In this, however, they may be wrong, for Miller's account of declension was always, in fact, if not deeply communitarian, then lonely for such. The coming pages trace a line of argument that may have been present in Miller all along. Here we shall observe instances where the wilderness ordeal secures precisely the reverse of individual definition, where migration leads not to solitary individualism but into profounder varieties of filiation and affiliation. As much as wilderness comes to represent existential isolation and individualist mettle, it also comes to stand for "relation" in all its senses: as proximity, as kinship, and, of course, as narration – the establishment, through telling, of a culture's closeness to itself. The moving out and away into wilderness, the casting off from civilization is figured as a kind of homing, a return that resituates the isolated self on the manifold grounds of its many dependencies.

The casting off, the getting lost, the reduction to the level of the animal or the instinctual, the migration or errand into salutary disorientation – these, and versions of these, comprise a set of New England learned literary responses whose power derives equally from the reflexive and the transmitted: from, on the one hand, experiences of isolation in the inhuman world and, on the other, from narratives of such experience drawn close to us in myth and as memory. It might perhaps be expected that the sojourn in the woods would deliver the sensation of isolation and existential aloneness – the shock of the unknown. Less to have been expected, and yet entirely common in the texts that shall occupy me in this chapter, is how getting lost in the woods actually bestows the comfort of the *known*: the wilderness episode confers familiar and even familial nearness.

There is a long tradition of seventeenth- through twentieth-century poetic and prose texts – Bradford's "Of Their Voyage and How They Passed the Sea," Thoreau's "The Village," Frost's "Desert Places," and, finally, Elizabeth Bishop's "Brazil, January 1, 1502" and "The Moose" – in which the venture into "howling wilderness" is also a return to what Whitman called the "cradle endlessly rocking" of our deeper nativity. The errand into wilderness proves an errand into a set of inherited and communally recorded experiences of the emergence from wilderness into sociality – and, thus, into humanness itself. In these terms, the errand into wilderness is, and is from the beginning, an integration and re-incorporation of the individual into relations (instinctual, cognitive, physiological, genealogical, ecological, historical) and forms of contact more manifold than any individual self, any discrete historical epoch, or any expressive modality can comprehend.

Truly secure abidance, or "settlement," might seem to originate in the establishment of civil society and depend on rudimentary features of the village, with its culture, organization, laws, etc.[1] In fact, as these writers discover, settlement has a much earlier genesis: in the sensation of unsettlement and in the psyche's propriceptive gropings to set down mental stakes. The adaptive setting of a threshold – what Thoreau calls "housewarming" – begins not with sticks or brick, but with the familiar, breathless sensation of being lost.

2. "Of Plimouth Plantation"

It was on, and from, his podium – lost there, we might say – that Miller enunciated this other, more needy, and more humane vision of wilderness and its lessons.

Miller's student (who was my own teacher, Ann Douglas) conjures memories of Miller opening English 70 looking bereft – and I can affirm that it can be lonely up there, and scary to begin this story without a backdrop, to offer a narrative without a pre-narrative. That is one reason why when I teach my own American literature surveys, I like to begin exactly where Miller was said to have begun, with the chapter called "Of Their Voyage, and How They Passed the Sea and of Their Safe Arrival at Cape Cod," and also to begin by conjuring memories of Miller himself, and by relating these memories as borne to me by his student, Ann Douglas. Douglas recalls that Miller began the class abruptly by reading aloud from William Bradford's description of Cape Cod . . . His auditors were plunged *in medias res*. Ponderously and unforgettably, though with no explication, Miller rested on Bradford's homely eloquent phrase: "All things stand upon them with a weather-beaten face." This line, he implied, *mattered* to Americans in ways that reverberated and ramified endlessly, and he issued to the class a summons to its significance ("The Mind" 26).

Miller assumed for her, Douglas explains, a "narrative presence, almost Biblical in its density." Her account, in turn, which I first read in 1982 (the year also happened to be my first year in graduate school), has become part of the narrative I inherit and bestow. Thus I also make sure to utter the sentence "All things stand upon them with a weather-beaten face" in all its starkness, bidding my students, as Miller did, and as Douglas did for me, to heed the moment when Bradford himself steps outside the story in which he is character to become instead its narrator, explicator, and posterity's teacher: "But here I cannot but stay and make a pause, and stand half amazed at this poor people's present condition" (Bradford 61).

Miller wanted, I think, for his students to absorb the cultural import of the historian – Bradford and then Miller – moved to such naked reflection; to absorb, that is, the great and homely relief of narrative, addressed by one person to others, unseen and unknown. Miller would have been concerned to emphasize this state of "amazement" I have been describing, to draw attention to the orientation-deprivation, the condition of abiding near nothing but oneself. But I think, too, that he may well have been letting his own isolation on the podium, his own readiness to "stay and make pause," signal the fertility of living within a narrative inheritance, to signal the sense of belonging we accrue by living within a tradition of narrative. Thus I make pause before my classes – and here – in order to live with Miller in that same tissue, within the fabric of New England memory that has to be woven, and is woven, generation by generation.

For when Bradford halts to note and urge empathy for "this poor people's" plight, it is not their lack of dry clothes, shelter, or even vulnerability to savages, but the more terrible situation of being in a place so unfamiliar, cast off from that perspectivizing vision

110

bestowed by forebears, by a past. To have lost one's sense of descent from a place or a purpose is to be a poor people indeed, for it is to experience one's personhood as tenuous. Worse than hunger or cold is to see the world with nothing but one's own eyes.

> Neither could they, as it were, go up to the top of Pisgah to view from this wilderness a more goodly country to feed their hopes; for which way soever they turned their eyes (save upward to the heavens) they could have little solace or content in respect of any outward objects. For summer being done, all things stand upon them with a weather-beaten face, and the whole country, full of woods and thickets, represented a wild and savage hue. If they looked behind them, there was the mighty ocean which they had passed and was now as a main bar and gulf to separate them from all the civil parts of the world. (Bradford 62)[2]

In Bradford, what deprives the land of "solace" is the curiously untouched, unhandled quality of all phenomena – the way discrete objects, without the sanctification of the "civil" on them, seem unknit both from one another and from those beholding them. Bradford's woods (as Frost's later will be) are most terrible for having "no expression, nothing to express," for being outward objects bare of prior description. It really matters, in other words, that the spatial "bar" and "gulf" that separate the migrants geographically from the "civil" parts of the world suspend them temporally as well. All history behind them, no history before, Bradford's amazed pilgrims suffer from an extreme form of presentness – a condition that turns out to be the opposite of "civil." Whether they are to find habitation, shelter, or food, the comfort of some prior history proves just as essential to existence.

And so, in Bradford, and in the American wilderness narrative his history founds, it is. Notice how Bradford's very next paragraph finds his stranded emigrants reunited with kith and kin by means of the genealogy they declare. With no one else to do it, they must. As progenitors, if not inheritors, these pilgrims lost in a maze must join the civilizational procession by fiat and force.

111

> May not and ought not the children of these fathers rightly say:
> "Our fathers were Englishmen which came over this great ocean,
> and were ready to perish in this wilderness; but they cried unto
> the Lord, and He heard their voice and looked on their adversity,"
> etc. (63)

Why did these Englishmen come to America; why suffer rigors of
woods, of animals; why cross space? The Scripture text Bradford
invokes here had adjured the Hebrews to retell the story of wilderness in every generation, to set on each generation the obligation
to imagine it is they themselves who came out of Egypt. Bradford's
families wander the woods so that the wandering might bind them
to those who come after, and that those who come after might feel
kinship forged through the mnemonic of the telling. The wilderness
tale becomes the narrative seed of the whole cultural inheritance,
remanding generations to mutual solicitude and recognizance.

For Bradford, and then for those who follow, the migration from
home is also a journey into narrative, the cradle of a certain kind
of civilization.

3. "The Village"

Every man, Thoreau explains in the chapter in *Walden* called "The
Village,"

> has to learn the points of compass again as often as he awakes,
> whether from sleep or any abstraction. Not till we are lost, in other
> words, not till we have lost the world, do we begin to find ourselves,
> and realize where we are and the infinite extent of our relations.
> (171)

The more confident a reader is in Henry David Thoreau's unso-
cial agenda, the more surprised she may be on rereading "The
Village." Although largely about the woods, this chapter from *Walden*
advances the paradox, foundational in Thoreau and in much of the
literature of New England, that nothing connects a person to

human community like a spell of isolation; and, that nothing so efficiently detects the "infinite extent of our relations" as a tale of the howling wild. To found a village in the literature of New England takes a wilderness.

Thoreau famously argues in the early pages of *Walden* that he leaves town in order to "front" the facts of his experience. It may be fair to ask why Thoreau thinks he'll find more in the way of frontage alone, in the woods, a mile from any house or store or neighbor. It turns out that the self, even alone, is thronged about with such facts that "fronting" the facts of existence consists in realizing how many, many fronts of relation there actually are: nothing stands discrete, every physical object, every act of consciousness is phalanxed with neighbors. To be lost in a place like the dark woods, a place confuting all facile recognition, is to be thrown upon, confronted with, deeper forms of re-cognition. To be equal to such an environment requires abandoning all abstraction, letting the mind encounter edges perception defines.[3] It means letting the very hands – in which one's fate lies – curl prehensile. It means submitting vision to the eyes, relying on the "faint track" the feet have laid down:

> I frequently had to look up at the opening between the trees above the path in order to learn my route, and, where there was no cart-path, to feel with my feet the faint track which I had worn, or steer by the known relation of particular trees which I felt with my hands, passing between two pines for instance, not more than eighteen inches apart, in the midst of the woods, invariably, in the darkest night. (*Walden* 169–170)

The passage above finds its speaker experiencing a radical contraction of the world, back from longer sight lines to consciousness's own situation within the body's competencies.[4] The sensation of being lost in the woods in Thoreau is a lesson not only in one's own most proximate faculties, but in the adjacency of all phenomena. Even in the remotest woods, tree neighbors tree: one is never not near something. Getting lost, a state of literal amazement, untethers the agent from his vision while it sharpens sight; it contracts his very reality to proximate obstacles, felicitous breaks. Wilderness as experienced by one lost in it has none of the yawning remoteness we may associate with "wilderness" taken metaphorically. Instead, there is the closeness of trunk to trunk. Everything is next to something in the woods, breath tucked up into breath, and agency's thrust retracted back into perception.

The woods are intimate; in the woods we come near what is: we front facts. Far different is this manner of being lost from the usual daily manner! In the woods, all things neighbor each other, and the soul lost in the woods may near himself. Not so, however, the one too certain of his way. The blithe confidence that "knows" the way does not know its own feet, is startled by its own door, lives with all its faculties scattered. Routine, which abstracts facts, strips the world of all frontage.

> Sometimes, after coming home thus late in a dark and muggy night, when my feet felt the path which my eyes could not see, dreaming and absent-minded all the way, until I was aroused by having to raise my hand to lift the latch, I have not been able to recall a single step of my walk, and I have thought that perhaps my body would find its way home if its master should forsake it, as the hand finds its way to the mouth without assistance. (*Walden* 170)

How did it happen? Pursuit *of* a way somehow paves the way to competent vacuity and self-forsakenness. Habit may guide the way through darkness, but habit is its own form of darkness, a waking sleep that actual darkness illuminates.[5] Mind's safe passage in, as it were, the body's hands is sometimes reduced to repetitive motion, to the literal hand to mouth. When we recall that the larger project of *Walden* is to question action that drains, rather than sustains, value, such reversion to the hand to mouth shows the peril of becoming too much at home in the active, individualist self pursuing its linear path. Competence reverts to incompetence, efficiency into automatism. A culture with its keys, its mastery, dangling casually in hand has gone astray.

Such a chapter as "The Village" shows Thoreau far more wary of progress, less self-reliant than we are accustomed to seeing him. As in Emerson, unmindful repetition blunts the edges, weakens the pressure points, obscures the prints and fronts and ranges of living, all of which Thoreau would regain when he sets out to live "deliberately." And yet such deliberation, though it may sound a-historic, oriented to the future and even to self-reliance, is actually as backward- as forward-looking. Accountability to what truly is and has been turns out to be crucial to Thoreau's version of deliberateness. Renouncing cruder burdens of inheritance (money, habituation, routine) frees Thoreau to perceive the past's more textured and topographic ranges. A restored sense of closeness with one's own experience, a renewed sense of local sensation now waken other voices: not only this moment's crunch of foot through snow, of leaf on ruffled leaf, but the epochs of rustlings and crunchings in the ever-sounding woods – a sedimented, historical place. It is a fresh but also recursive stance that Thoreau cultivates: unoriginal in order to be legible; unrefined, the better to achieve full "extent of relations."

Thus Thoreau's identification with Puritan forebears in the Concord woods does not so much simplify and evacuate as complexify and populate wilderness, leaving the forest, we might say, in order to enter the trees. Compared to the wilderness of the Village, to arrive in the woods is a "housewarming," a return and a redemption. The North American woods' thickets and outcroppings, its tangled paths and clearings had long been, as Thoreau's prose recalls, a terrain of rich fact, of redemptive occasions for a return to fundamentals. The departure Thoreau performs in the "The Village" from town life and its toxins and corruptions is analogized to a sea journey, a "voyage." Like his Protestant forebears, he undergoes an emigration from Old World Babylon back into a more vital consciousness of being. The soul making its way into the howling wilderness pursued just the right itinerary: out of facile confidence in village fires, out of abstracted comfort, and back into the woods, where one had neighbors.[6]

In the inaugural chapter of *Walden*, "Economy," Thoreau had contrasted both Indians' and earliest settlers' rudimentary but efficient technologies of keeping warm and dry with those of contemporary Christians, shivering in their overheated bungalows.[7] The irony he directs against settled contemporary Christians ("I have heard of many going astray even in the village streets") gains point as he evokes the original settlers' perhaps crude, but snug winter quarters and the snugness of the human congregation (170). The rugged settlement of these first pioneers is precedent for his own.[8] Thoreau's final encomium, with its expansive perspective and ultimate contextualization of the individual "I" within the larger "we" ("Not till we are lost, in other words, not till we have lost the world, do we begin to find ourselves, and realize where we are and the infinite extent of our relations") asserts the saliency of getting lost in the woods, a harshly orienting but also profoundly socializing experience (171).

To know oneself thoroughly lost is an education in how to settle; to root oneself in a world of phenomena. As hand, mouth, legs, arm, and sight are neighbors – and interdependent as neighbors often are – so too, Thoreau shows, do village and wilderness front one another. It is in wilderness that the writer of *Walden* finds the common thoroughfare.

4. "Desert Places"

Frost's "Desert Places" takes up the same reciprocity of disorientation and deep belonging that other writers before him, especially Thoreau, had also found in the woods.

The poem's first two lines, in registering shock at winter's onset, delivers us into the known by way of the unknown. We progress no further than the initial couplet before recognizing surprise itself (expressed here in the experience of wilderness vulnerability) as utterly familiar:

> Snow falling and night falling fast, oh, fast
> In a field I looked into going past,
>
> (296)

Winter may be shocking, but it is not novel. "The onset" of winter that occurs in this poem (as in Frost's earlier poem of that title) has occurred before, and the body knows this before the mind does. The metrical fibrillation of the phrase "fast, oh, fast," like the atrial raciness it mimes, is part of an old condition: "fast, oh, fast" is not a fresh response, but a recollected reflex. Perhaps the poem's speaker had been idling, scarcely thinking at all, when snow began to fall in "a field [he] looked into going past." But now, his own uptake of breath, his body's sharp involuntary stop, triggers the memory of other such sudden onsets. "Fast" is, as always before, the way snow falls, and "fast," too, is the way night's and dread's frigid mantle falls. Nearly as fast is the speaker's recall of all precedents, of all the times before he had walked into danger "unawares."

Ground mum, sky blank, sound smothered, the landscape's physical features are correlates of the speaker's muffled or negligent senses, of the habits that have led him along a blank way no less engulfing than that which traps "[a]ll animals . . . smothered in their lairs" (296). The line "I am too absent-spirited to count" suggests the habituated mind's tenuous hold on its own existence, its deafness to its own counting and so to its own separate agency. All the deliberative capacities – tracking, measuring, pacing that make a trail survivable and that give, too, a poem its form – are at risk here, as the voice is now governed by deeper rhythms. Transfixing and insidious, the lines that follow suspend the speaker in a rhythmic automatism where pattern loses cultural moorings and music reverts to the tidal noise of blood or breath:

> And lonely as it is, that loneliness
> Will be more lonely ere it will be less –
> A blanker whiteness of benighted snow
> With no expression, nothing to express.
>
> (296)

Semantic foothold is confuted by sonic rhythm. Perception given over to such motions cannot execute choice or intention. The state of abstracted reverie is of the kind where all lines, all beginnings

117

and endings, blur, and where the recognizably human is liable to lose its place.

At this frightening pass – lost in the woods in winter, lost where nature's processes blur or engulf human continuity – it is then that the poem's speaker will let forth a cry from the very cradle of humanness. Like the reconnaissance of birds, or dogs on a scent, the enjambment of the lines above seeks exit from the drift and accumulation of the speaker's maunderings. Primal might not be too strong a word for this cry, except perhaps that it misses the history of "expression" the cry recapitulates. Articulation, human language, begins with a speaker at "home" locating himself in a "here I am." Let us call the cry, then, primary.

> They cannot scare me with their empty spaces
> Between stars – on stars where no human race is.
> I have it in me so much nearer home
> To scare myself with my own desert places.
>
> (296)

A sort of shibboleth, "human race is" has a childish, solecistic sound, but it also summons forth the whole history of human language. Its very awkwardness, the very syntactic crudity of that stressed "is" claims an existential, or what I am calling primary, power – the power, say, of the scriptural subject (Adamic, Abrahamic) who may be picked out, found somewhere: in a garden, on a mountain, stark, outlined against inchoate wilderness. "Human race is" comprehends and mobilizes consciousness to erect shelter and demarcate the human from the non-human. The speaker's capacity to assert himself against a "they" rouses him from his state of absence to consciousness that he must, after all, count. Warmer, more vernacular tones now exist to confirm that where declarative statement is, the "human race is" found too. The more secure self that says "I have it in me so much nearer home / To scare myself" is, with this utterance, evolved into sociality. In "Desert Places," a self's intimacy with its own vulnerability, closeness of the human to the human, sets a threshold in the wilderness.

118

5. "Of Plimouth Plantation" and "Brazil, January 1, 1502"

In one of her many poems of New World encounter, "Brazil, January 1, 1502," Elizabeth Bishop writes: "Nature greets our eyes / exactly as she must have greeted theirs" (91). Beginning with a pathetic fallacy (does Nature greet us, or is it merely that we, in our hubris, imagine such greeting?), the long first verse paragraph of the poem unrolls in one vivid and densely worked panel whose front and back sides, like perception and image, fuse and blur. Projection is one of the ways – sometimes the most perilous, certainly the most pleasurable – we humans have of making ourselves at home in wilderness.

"Are they assigned, or can the countries pick their colors?" Bishop had thus asked, mock ingenuously, in the first poem of her first published volume, *North and South* (3). From the very first poem, "The Map," Bishop let her poetry suggest the way the conqueror, via ideology, lends his own tint to whatever he finds. Bishop herself had ample opportunity to consider the moment of wilderness encounter. Raised in Massachusetts and Canada, and then spending years in Brazil, she garnered a set of personal experiences at the geographical pressure points of European penetration into the Americas. Tracing one's finger up and down the *Table of Contents* of Bishop's *Collected Poems* down is a little like that history as Bishop leaves her poetic calling card down the whole long eastern edge of the Americas where Europeans first made landfall. And she shows particular interest in that early modern epoch when Europeans journeyed West – to Brazil and Florida, to Maryland and Virginia, up from Cape Cod along the rocky lands north of Boston to the coast of Maine and thence up more, to New Brunswick, Nova Scotia, and finally Newfoundland.

In the end, there is no denying that the urge to discovery is kin to, if not one with, other urges quite primal and violent. Reading, naming, cartography, and narrative all retain similarities to occupation. But, to put it another way – and it is this insight that Bishop, Thoreau, and Frost all contribute to our understanding of the earliest wilderness narrative – occupation is kin to pleasure of place, that sense of congruity Bishop bids us consider in "The Map" when she lets the printer who engraves it "experienc[e] the same excitement / as when emotion too far exceeds its cause" (3). Bishop locates its global expression in the way "peninsulas take the water between thumb and finger" and in the more local: "women feeling for the smoothness of yard-goods." The defenselessness of the globe's bright skin, its broad rondure and infinity of textures, quickens curiosity and rouses the grasping instincts ("We can stroke these lovely bays, / under a glass as if they were expected to blossom," Bishop writes in "The Map"). With a surface so fecund, something human in us cannot resist sticking the needle in.

It is remarkable, indeed, how many of Bishop's poems are, in fact, versions in verse of what literary and cultural critics now call the "contact narrative" – the narrative of first European encounters with the wilderness. She takes as her purview the same landscape to which literary critics and historians of the last generation have addressed themselves, and with consistently enlightening results.[9] Thus, however far removed William Bradford and Elizabeth Bishop may be on our map of literary studies as currently organized, it is Bishop I am always sure to read before teaching Bradford, and Bradford I am sure to review before reading Bishop. For in both, the wilderness is a remembered, misremembered place.[10] Bishop takes always for granted that destiny is not manifest till some interest, some ideology, declares and represents it so: the barest outline once traced in, then power may sit back and admire its own progress. Thus as she puts it, so mordantly, in "View of the Capitol from the Library of Congress": "The gathered brasses want to go / *boom – boom*" (69). In just two lines the poet exposes the power that so loves to toot its own horn it might as well be a horn; and, voilà (in "brasses"), it is. Whether Spanish or Portuguese, English or French, whether twentieth or seventeenth century, power weaves itself into the foliage, hums itself into the sound of a place. Power turns threatening woods and jungles into illustrated atlases of its own making.

This is why I like to let Bishop's poem "Brazil, January 1, 1502" have commerce with Bradford's accounts of European/Indian encounter. Who better than Bishop to help us see the full irony of Bradford's giving the name "First Encounter" to a place where the Mayflower pilgrims first experience a "surprise" attack by Indian arrows? Readers of Bradford's *Plimouth Plantation*'s earlier chapters already know that the Indian attack labeled "First" has, in fact, been so long anticipated, already so embroidered into the texture of New World experience, that when the historian relates how he and his fellows find that "sundry of their coats, which hung up in the barricado, were shot through and through," the episode has a familiar ring (Bradford 70). "[F]alling into such thickets as were ready to tear their clothes and armor in pieces," the scouts wandering Cape Cod find precisely what they had imagined (65). For well before the "First Encounter," back in Holland, where the migration story had begun, Bradford and his community had scared themselves with tales of a "savage people who are cruel, barbarous and most treacherous," who delight in "flaying some alive with the shells of fishes" (26), the same whom he will retrospectively call "readier to fill their sides with arrows than otherwise" (62).

With what subtlety, with what insight, Bishop incises exploration's triumphalisms and idée fixes: ". . . humming perhaps / *L'Homme armé* or some such tune, / they ripped away into the hanging fabric, / each out to catch an Indian for himself" ("Brazil, January 1, 1502" 92). Thus she shows through what motifs, by what styles, and with the aid of what cultural frames – chivalric adventure, Golden Age conjurings, traditions of Christian allegory, the literature of maritime adventure, transoceanic cartography, aristocratic pornography, styles of paint handling, of book design, of stitchery – Europeans transposed one world onto another, familiarizing as they went. Further still, with what economy, yet amplitude, Bishop conveys the limited sympathies, narrow notions of land use; the ignorance as to other modes of dress, food, family, celebration; the constricted range of imagination that makes exploration, ultimately, provincial. Finding a disorienting chaos of "foliage – / big leaves, little leaves, and giant leaves, / blue, blue-green, and olive,"

121

explorers deploy the conventions they knew to press back the riot and clear space for the "big symbolic birds" (91). They use vanishing-point perspective to define a background such that "in the foreground there is Sin" (91). Bishop's spondees, "Christians," "glinting," thrust forward their brave fronts as, meanwhile, she lets the cliché "hard as nails" suggest the persistent unoriginality of all aggressors: "Just so the Christians, hard as nails, / tiny as nails, and glinting, / in creaking armor, came and found it all, / not unfamiliar" (92). Such conflation of imagined with actual dangers turns the early chapters of *Of Plimouth Plantation* into a thicket of sharp missiles and pierced coats, and the colonial encounter into a veritable tapestry of violent piercings. As in Bishop's "Brazil, January 1, 1502," Bradford's wanderers relieve their bewilderment by weaving this same fear, this sense of claustrophobic suffocation, into a landscape rank and prickling with their own terror: "every square inch filling in with foliage" (Bishop 91). And as in Bishop's poem, where the date in the title is factitious, any date for the colonial encounter is stitched out of other days remembered, anticipated.

Written more than two decades after the landing near Pamet Bay, and after a full twenty-four years of peace with local natives, Bradford's record of the landing on Cape Cod incident shows compressions and telescoping of temporal horizons as he treats now specific days, now longer periods – weeks, months, seasons, even generations. Just as in Bishop's "Brazil, January 1, 1502," the urge to find ourselves at home in the most alien of places leads inexorably to projections, sometimes violent ones. History loomed on a Christian timeline – history creased by typology's deferrals and fulfillments, history torqued by the urge to explain and justify, history slubby with additions and excisions – is unreliable.

It is our way, Bishop suggests, as Miller suggested of Bradford, of going up to Pisgah.

6. "The Moose"

Traveling in her last book, *Geography III*, to her own Canadian roots, back to the Novia Scotia landmass that is ambiguously America and not America, Elizabeth Bishop plots "The Moose" as a journey westward, forward, and also backward into genealogical time.

That is, she inserts her own family's migration into a timeline whose history is the whole history of man. She does this from the volume's homemade cover (daubed with Bishop's own watercolors) to its Canadian flatness and quaint locutions. *Geography III* provides the poems of old age with the latitude to settle into second childhood, to find in anachronism an art form of great charm, but also to discover within the distantly remembered an even deeper substrate of experience.

Even as the poem "The Moose" moves forward, plotting a bus trip westward from Eastern Canadian provinces "all the way to Boston," it is drawn back into the deeper history of North American contact: back into the history of European (and before that Indian, and before that warm-blooded, and before that cold-blooded) inhabitation of a geography itself historical and shifting (171). This poem that would "discover America," that retraces the hard route west from those Canadian inlets where Europeans first made landfall, hazards geographical features so changeable, boundaries so unclear as to vex landing and orientation. The poem's "progress," if one can call it that, is impeded by ocean tides, stoniness of coast, and the belt of watery, foggy, fickle-winded, densely thicketed land between Nova Scotia and Boston. Forward movement is stroked back and back into the thick perceptual sensorium of the wilderness encounter, and only there does the self find its settledness, its nestedness.[11] As we have earlier seen in Frost, Thoreau, and Bradford, in Bishop's late great poem, "The Moose," the shock of the wild is the shock of the known. What we hear in the trees and the brush are not wild sounds but our own sounds: "Grandparents' voices / uninterruptedly / talking, in Eternity" (171). The great elderly female moose who appears in the thickest woods is civility's unlikely, but most tender, guardian.

Can we ever leave the "narrow provinces" from which we come? Or rather, as is the case with the poet's own favored sestinas, does every pulsive movement forward draw one back? Certainly, from this poem's first stanza, the tides are against leaving. Getting out of the provinces is not so simple.

> From narrow provinces
> of fish and bread and tea,
> home of the long tides
> where the bay leaves the sea
> twice a day and takes
> the herrings long rides,
>
> where if the river
> enters or retreats
> in a wall of brown foam
> depends on if it meets
> the bay coming in,
> the bay not at home;
> ("The Moose" 169)

The poem's stanzas each roll out serviceably, accessibly, lumbering out of the poem's initial "From" as from a depot in a stolid caravan. The poem is set in the simple present tense, but whether it tracks one bus trip over an itinerary of equidistant stops (stanza breaks marked on the page in pneumatic puffs of white space, like a door swinging open), or, rather, one route, bus after bus, over a month of typical journeys – this remains unclear. In any case, little distinguishes the route's passengers from the herrings who have taken "long rides" and are then received back into the bay. All trips are round-trips. Indeed, the indigenous tradition that calls this point of departure "Home of the Long Tides" looks beyond the departure to the return. Its sagacity as to eventual regress knows every vehicle of change – even a bus – to participate in a slow and recursive process whose cycles bank history, even as they pierce time. The very sun, passing east to west, reflects this same process, this same round-trip. Its arc is beached in surface area. Its mobile transparency is splayed in substance, in color, and as heat.

> where, silted red,
> sometimes the sun sets

124

facing a red sea,
and others, vein the flats'
lavender, rich mud
in burning rivulets;

(169)

The lines echo, but also condense, the beautifully slow revelations of Bishop's earlier poem, "The Fish," where the victorious haul, the conquest, turns out to hold not only fish, but fisher too, on the line, gasping for her life. The wonder of the fish was twofold. The poem evoked amazement that the fish could be constructed so artfully, so cunningly, his body with its "dramatic" patterns and antique trim eliciting the admiration one tenders a couture gown or a well-preserved tunic of museum quality. And yet the ornamental look and appearance of the fish is deceptive, for its depths are its surface and its surface depths – the fish's "brown skin [hanging] in strips / like ancient wallpaper," its fish's body "speckled with barnacles, / fine rosettes of lime" (42).

In this later poem reflection dredges such depths out of flatness that not even these literal flats can remain flat. Vascular, they instead dimensionalize to hold more colors in the spectrum. It is a beautiful sight, this lavender mud, brown pinked to violet, which the slow wave of sunset flushes and crazes in its course: red flashing off a blue fender, which then flushes pink. Drenched in the spectrum – a version of the Rainbow appearing so often in Bishop – these flats *remember* every hue the light ever bestowed.

Just so, in the poem's coming lines, are impressions of today and yesterday, image and images kin to it, banked in memory. Stanza by stanza, as the bus breasts the thick dusk, objects solicit attention: each as percept, and, then, as percept nested in the memory of the percept. Thus the double take – "Five Islands, Five Houses, / where a woman shakes a tablecloth / out after supper" – and, then, not one but "[t]wo rubber boots" that present themselves "illuminated, solemn" (170–171). Is anything ever to be left behind in its insignificance? Not even the verbs, much less the nouns, in this poem manage to be transitive. Instead of kissing, a journeyer "gives / kisses and embraces / to seven relatives / and a collie supervises" (170).

125

In the last of the light even "the sweet peas cling / to their wet white string" (170). All phenomena are distended, affiliated, every thing comprised of itself, its apprehension and its softer image vouchsafed to memory, like the poem's own collie guarding the home fires. This penumbral thickness – of dusk, but also of strangeness made familiar – is precisely the opposite of Bradford's "savage hues," his account of objects without "solace." Here each thought is nested in provenances and remembrances. Cognition itself has genealogy. Penetrating wilderness, we penetrate the world's "civil parts."

To this point, "The Moose" has been proceeding so slowly through the woods, it cannot be surprising when all motion stalls on the unmarked boundary where Canada becomes Maine. Dense and thick, "hairy, scratchy, splintery," the geographic terrain is so confusing the very mist catches in the brambles "like lamb's wool" (171). Arrival across distance is vexed by terrain and weather, by that ineluctable obscurity and remoteness of the close-at-hand that makes them say in Maine, "You can't get there from here."

Is, was, Maine a place at all? An American place? Part of New England? The terrain the poem begins now to penetrate is legendarily remote, and Bishop, who had been a schoolchild both in Massachusetts and in Canada, would have had ample occasions to learn the region's particular history. Originally occupied by Algonquins, what is now Maine had been originally claimed by French Protestants as well as by the Plymouth Company. Through the eighteenth century, a great variety of occupants – Micmac squatters, opportunistic militia, Halifax belles, Acadians, American loyalists, beef-and-potatoes Surrey transplants – all mingled promiscuously in this frontier, their common bond: fear of the woods.[12] The British fought insurgent Americans for this land during the Revolution, and Massachusetts claimed the spoils after the Revolution, but the Northern reaches of the terrain were so forbidding that Maine remained part of Massachusetts until the Compromise of 1820, when it was carved out as a free state to balance the admission of Texas into the Union as a slave state. As the schoolbooks Bishop imitates in her homemade cover of *Geography III* would have taught her, the wrangling did not end until 1828, when two governors, both named Lincoln, fought over who would draw the boundary line between the two states.

Notwithstanding 1828's settlement of the question, as Bishop finishes her poem one hundred and fifty years later, the matter of just where precisely one enters the United States from Canada remains foggy. Extreme climatic instability combined with the dense and pathless woodlands make the Maine/Canada border forbiddingly unnavigable.

The revelation Bishop's poem thus begins to summon, or better, to scent, is that meaning is not to be found, as Marianne Moore had put it, in any one locality, nor even in the most thorough analysis of that locality's history – except, that is, as this meaning admits this "all": the whole embodied, accented genealogy of relations and attachments massed behind singular apprehension of the new. Flashes of insight, like bridges crossed in a second, like miles marked off, print the retina and disappear. Sometimes these flashes are formalized: here Maine protects her flanks with a landmark (the Canada/Maine border); there, explorers pronounce an epochal day, "Brazil, January 1, 1502." But a more redolent and dimensional history travels with us. Not to be hunted out, it finds us nevertheless. Overtaking from the back of the bus, it engulfs the voracious present with its circadian rhythm, its accent and odor.

Now the poem's music seems to shift warmly on its springs, the phrases rock from side to side, settling into the vague cradle carved out by a voice unseen:

> In the creakings and noises,
> an old conversation
> – not concerning us,
> but recognizable, somewhere,
> back in the bus:
> Grandparents voices
>
> uninterruptedly
> talking, in Eternity:

> names being mentioned,
> things cleared up finally;
> what he said, what she said,
> who got pensioned;
> (171)

Meanings emerging out of the more evanescent and invested forms of human expression – storytelling, gossip, platitude, cliché, social murmurings – scarcely leave their mark, for they are more like breathing or circulation, more like the body's motions than cognition's sharper modes. The "gentle, auditory, / slow hallucination" (171) that takes over at this stage of the poem is inimical to epiphany, lulled as it is by the comforts of conventional wisdom, and dependent, too, on received and reflexive strains. It is not progress or articulation Bishop strives for here, but the linguistic equivalent of passing go, rounding the bases of the familiar. The vernacular broadness, the flatness of "who got pensioned" barely musters any music, any poetry, at all (the rhyme like a wooden spoon clapping the prosaic "names being mentioned"). The same unconcise, woolgathering awkwardness of the adverbial "finally" (itself rhymed against the adverbial "uninterruptedly") puts abstract Eternity in its place. Human time as it passes smells of bosom, age, and bedding. In light of the animal closeness of the body's settling, such abstractions as Eternity shall have to squeeze into such pews or bus seats as they find – say, between freckled aunts.

Poems like "The Moose" of Bishop's last volume give considerably more weight to meaning's ancestral sources, to tacit registers rooted in reciprocities, than her earlier work had done. Once, Bishop had been concerned to show how elemental the difference between human knowledge and an ontological order of Being is – much too cold, too icily "free," for us to fathom. The absurd credulity of those who saw in a stand of firs "a million Christmas trees . . . waiting for Christmas" or the comfort enjoyed by a speaker telling herself that dolphins were "like [her] a believer in total immersion" did not, Bishop reminded, make cold truth any less cold ("At the Fishhouses" 65). Our whistlings in the dark (singing, say, to these same dolphins, "A Mighty Fortress is our God") could not alter the fact that knowledge is separate from us, born of another mother: "dark, salt, clear, moving, utterly free / drawn from the cold hard mouth / of the world, derived from the rocky breasts / forever" (66).

Now, however, in these poems finished in Bishop's own last years, Eternity flowing from the "cold mouth" of some remote origin seems oddly stiff and unsympathetic. The aging process drives us back, rather, into the rangy freckled frames from which we emerged. In the process, it discovers in us, finds at home in us, deeper understanding. Rhyme is sonic means of tying befores to afters, intimations to realizations, kin across lines, and so it should not surprise that rhyme pervades these lines. The ancestral, atavistic, and finally animal origins once pushed back in the mind, to the back of the bus, now return. Rhyme is the "yes" of reciprocity and assent, of breath following breath:

> "Yes . . ." that peculiar
> affirmative. "Yes . . ."
> A sharp, indrawn breath,
> half groan, half acceptance,
> that means "Life's like that.
> We know *it* (also death)."
>
> Talking the way they talked
> in the old featherbed,
> peacefully, on and on,
> dim lamplight in the hall,
> down in the kitchen, the dog
> tucked in her shawl.
> ("The Moose" 172)

So vague is this species of meaning, to be sure, so instinctual, so creaturely, its voicings made of the same breath as snoring ("it's all right now / even to fall asleep") that when a moose appears in the road it is not interruption, but confirmation (172). It is as when the lights go out in the old feather bed and one sinks more deeply into body's nearness to itself. That a certain animal vulnerability is

129

the only real indigeneity: this is the moose's office to announce.
Our kin, fellow denizen of evolution's long tides, the moose too is
"provincial."

> – Suddenly the bus driver
> stops with a jolt,
> turns off his lights.
>
> A moose has come out of
> the impenetrable wood
> and stands there, looms, rather,
> in the middle of the road.
> It approaches; it sniffs at
> the bus's hot hood.
>
> (172)

Moose and bus are bedmates for each other, but their impulses
harmonize. They are clearly twins in some sense, both vehicles
exhaling warmly in the woods. Note the rhymes Bishop chooses:
sound nesting in sound, each stanza turned into its own intimate
vestibule. Yes solicits yes; breath accepts death, the dog down the
hall in its shawl augurs the moose from the wood who sniffs at the
bus's hood, one heat-seeking beast to another. In this moose ("high
as a church, / homely as a house / (or, safe as houses)"), Bishop
finds the same homing instinct that sleeps under our seeking, our
sniffing curiosity (173). Like the herring, the dog, and all the freckled grandmothers with their shopping bags, Bishop lets the moose
on the macadam stand for the uncanny, complexly evolved and
persistent grandeur of the lifecycle: the, if you will, perennially
repeated Great Migration from the Home of the Long Tide that
underlies all more linear, more prodigal journeys.

Thus, if the prosaic, colloquial, homely gift of animal belonging
describes a force of unison exceedingly (to use a word from an
earlier poem) "unlikely," even more unlikely is the human capacity
to utter feeling in so many ways. The speaker's question, "Why, why
do we feel / (we all feel) this sweet / sensation of joy," marvels at
the common energy that propels human beings forward into civil

expression, that quickens in them the language instinct (173). The last expression, emitted by the "quiet driver," opens mere observation up in phrases pithy with wonder – accented, addressed to others, transforming raw energy to complex expressions:

> "Curious creatures,"
> says our quiet driver,
> rollng his *r*'s
> "Look at that, would you."
> Then he shifts gears.
>
> (173)

No less curious than the moose are the other, antlerless creatures, the curious persons with their capacity to shift gears, to gesture through language at shared understanding, to feel and to express "all." Indigenes of the same primordium as the moose and of Frost's and Bradford's wanderers lost in the woods, Elizabeth Bishop's "The Moose" discovers not the New World only, but the narrow province of the human every pilgrim calls home.

Notes

1   In his *Authorizing Experience*, Jim Egan argues that, for a Christian, "exile becomes the paradigmatic experience" insofar as exile tears away illusions of belonging in the world or the body (87). Egan's book is exemplary, and also representative, of a critical trend that assumes Puritans to be largely negligent of material reality and thus liable to refusals, denials, and repressions of bodily experience and vulnerability. Indeed, from William Carlos Williams's screed against the Puritans in *In the American Grain*, to Richard Slotkin's magisterial treatment of bodily experience redeemed in and through sacrificial violence in *Regeneration Through Violence*, to John Canup's *Out of the Wilderness*, with its emphasis on the "disafforestation" of the mind (forest itself a threat to the transplanted "English vine"), and on through Egan's more recent argument for the "Insignificance of Experience" (82), especially bodily experience, Puritan anti-materiality has been an article of critical faith. This chapter would introduce some qualifications of that account.

2 This Pisgah passage is deservedly famous, and many critics since Miller have cut their teeth on it. I am happy to join the cavalcade. Most recently, Larry Buell writes: "Bradford deliteralizes the vista in order to reinvent it diasporically and biblically . . . The point is not that the new world is a nowhere. But the actual 'where' is *felt* only in terms of where one had come from: tribally, intellectually, spiritually" (Dimock and Buell 236). I would add, and am arguing here, that this "where" is felt also in kinship with human beings, and with humanness itself, with a surmising of one's humanness essentially "sounded" lyrically. For a fuller discussion of place as a "subjective horizon," see Buell's powerful central chapter in *The Future of Environmental Criticism*, "Space, Place and Imagination from Global to Local."

3 For a stimulating recent treatment of what it means to be lost in the woods in Thoreau, see Van Noy's *Surveying the Interior*. I have profited from Van Noy's concept of "intelligence of place" in Thoreau, and especially from his description of bodily intelligence as it refines cartographic survey. Jeffrey Myers explores a similar contrast between bodily intelligence and reason in his *Converging Stories*.

4 The argument I develop here owes a lot to ideas introduced by Stanley Cavell in his beautiful *The Senses of Walden*. There, Cavell argued that any American's withdrawal from experience is also, at some deep level, a means of near approach. He showed, too, that identification with the Great Migration can signify more than our desire for the Puritan's distance. Through such identification we may test our own mettle, while also experiencing those rigors of body and psyche that bred need of abstraction. The scene in the woods is for Thoreau, as Cavell sees it, a symbolic topos of the *a priori*, of that bareness excluding the human until the human settles it. To be next to oneself, to "neighbor" oneself is, Cavell teaches, to achieve a very subtle, very delicate kind of philosophical poise. See note 6 of this chapter as well.

5 As William James describes in *Habit*, "A path once traversed by a nerve-current might be expected to follow the law of most of the paths we know, and to be scooped out and made more permeable than before; and this ought to be repeated with each new passage of the current. Whatever obstructions may have kept it at first from being a path should then, little by little, and more and more, be swept out of the way, until at last it might become a natural drainage-

channel. This is what happens where either solids or liquids pass over a path; there seems no reason why it should not happen where the thing that passes is a mere wave of rearrangement in matter that does not displace itself, but merely changes chemically or turns itself round in place, or vibrates across the line" (14). See my *The Line's Eye* for a more detailed description of the perceiving self and of "sight" versus vision.

6   Thus the unforgettable last chapter of Mary Rowlandson's *Narrative of the Captivity* finds her wide-awake, weeping in her bed "when others are sleeping" (51). Rowlandson knew her Christian "estate" was more secure for the woods she brought nearer home, as Frost would discover his "nearer home" in a woodland scene smothered by snow, and Thoreau would find his bearings by losing them. All three know, too, the wider applicability of such recognition, the urgency of bearing wilderness lessons back to the town.

7   Frederick Garber develops in *Thoreau's Redemptive Imagination* an argument about "housewarming" that is kin to that offered by Cavell. In effect, these pages reflect a synthesis of what I have learned from Garber about "warmth" in Thoreau and what I have learned from about nearness, nextness, and neighboring from Cavell's *The Senses of Walden*.

8   Cavell explains, "To say that the writer re-enacts the Great Migration and the inhabitation of this continent by its first settlers is not to suggest that we are to read him for literal alignments between the history of the events in his woods and in theirs. That would miss the significance of both, because the literal events of the Puritan colonization were from the beginning overshadowed by their meaning: it was itself a transcendental act, an attempt to live the idea . . . The more deeply he searches for independence from the Puritans, the more deeply, in every step and every word, he identifies with them" (10). Cavell sees Thoreau trying to find his own place, to acknowledge, touch, and re-establish closeness with his own forebears, all the while mindful of how the historicizing move itself estranges epochs one from another. Cavell shows Thoreau implicated in and by the history of those who over-historicized, insulating and estranging themselves from the sharpness that all historicizing and all reflection can blur. In attempt to redress, to front the facts of his own experience by fronting the facts of theirs, Cavell draws attention to how Thoreau "quotes at some length from two accounts, one

133

contemporary and one nearly contemporary, of the first shelters the colonists made for themselves to get them through the first winter in the world which for them was new" (8). Thoreau's historical method, a sort of rubbing of two sticks together, allows one epoch to spark another. In other words: housewarming.

9   Most scholarship of the last generation has, and with good reason, endeavored to restore the material/geographic/topographic contexts that Miller's errand effaced, showing how wilderness was and was not a "fact" but always an idea. Transformed in the 1980s by *Albion's Seed* (David Hackett Fisher) and *Changes in the Land* (William Cronon), investigations into the facts and fictions of "New England" – and especially its wilderness – proliferated. See the Notes to my *The Line's Eye* (1999) for the most influential texts of the 1980s and 1990s. Among treatments of wilderness and encounter published since, I have profited from reading Joseph Conforti's *Imagining New England*; Robert Blair St George's *Conversing by Signs: Poetics of Implication in Colonial New England Culture*; Christopher Lenney's *Sightseeing*; Don Scheese's *Nature Writing: The Pastoral Impulse in America*; John Gatta's *Making Nature Sacred*; John Frederick Martin's *Profits in the Wilderness*; the stimulating and methodologically diverse essays in Ayers, Limerick, Nissenbaum, and Onuf's *All Over the Map*; Foster's *Thoreau's Country*; Robert Thorson's *Stone by Stone*; Karen Ordahl Kupperman's *Indians and English*; Dana Phillips's *The Truth of Ecology*; Matt Cohen's *The Networked Wilderness*; and Lisa Tanya Brooks' *The Common Pot*. A truly superb, one-volume guide to the field, including rich materials on New England culture, geography, history, politics, and pithy bibliographic citations besides, is Feintuch, Watters, and Hall's *The Encyclopedia of New England*.

10   Our canons of critical procedure make it not only proper but even necessary to note the early modern confusion of Christian religion and imperial prerogative. Indeed, from the very royal patent authorizing the journey, the mixed agenda is clear: "Having undertaken, for the Glory of God and advancement of the Christian Faith and Honor of our King and Country, a Voyage to plant the First Colony in the Northern Parts of Virginia" (Bradford 76). One wants then to let Bishop's sustained and pithy observations on the experiences of landfall find application beyond the purview of poetry studies – and that is precisely my experiment here, one I am aware may occasion objection. With Bradford, cordoned off in early American studies, and

134

Bishop in twentieth-century poetry, we deem his texts susceptible to inquiries in regional, religious, and literary intellectual history, and hers to inquiries launched out of poetics, aesthetics, and the theory of representation. Bradford's work is assumed to invite, and support, historical questions, while Bishop's questions are formal; Bradford, rhetorical, and Bishop, epistemological and perceptual. Of Bradford but not Bishop it is considered proper to ask what map, mental or material, subjunctive, textual, or spiritual, guides his narrative through the thickets of Cape Cod.

11 What Theodore Bozeman calls the "primordium" – that place before cultural civility, not to mention nations, made landfall – has a place of honor in Bishop's work, as it does in Frost's (think of his "old stone savage") and Thoreau's as well, with all three writers positing against the "world of 'Chaos and Ancient Night'" the ineluctably human settlements inherited from ancestors. The extreme edge of backward-looking lookingness, whether in reflexes of generation consciousness, filiopiety, primitivism, noble savagery, or regression, is one of the richest veins of Puritan scholarship. (See Bozeman's *To Live Ancient Lives*.) With its interest in a long land crossing, its inception in Home of the Long Tides and its reliance on oral modes of transmission, Bishop's poem situates itself in a terrain where white and Indian cross. (See Kenneth Lincoln's *Native American Renaissance*, especially the chapter "Ancestral Voices in Oral Traditions," which describes how tribal bonds are based on "a mutual past and present.") Bishop's recursive loops in the poem connect the telling of stories and the exchange of human meaning with the pre-intentional sounds of sleep and further back to the movement of tides. Voices in this poem are "ancestral" as they are in Native American literature, where "[w]ords do not come after or apart from what naturally is, but are themselves natural genes, tribal history in the bodies of the people . . . Singers chant songs, drawing tonally on the voice as an interpretive human instrument for words living in the mouth and body" (Lincoln 47).

12 One week in the Boston Athanaeum I lost myself in the basement stacks reading nineteenth-century pamphlet histories of the Maine – Massachusetts border dispute. Educated in Worcester and then in Nova Scotia, it is safe to say that Bishop would have learned from both sides details of the 1827 dispute waged between the governors of Maine and New Brunswick. Such histories of Maine and Canada

all concern themselves with the period, a few months between November of 1827 and February of 1828, when interest and tempers flared over the Maine/Canada boundary. Massachusetts's governor Levi Lincoln wrote to the Secretary of State of the United States, urging clear demarcation of "the frontier line of National boundary" (which delineation, Lincoln hastened to assure the secretary, Massachusetts militia would be more than happy to accomplish). Maine's governor responded with his own words of cartographic punctilio. The archives record Maine's defender bestirring himself to vow that though "politically peninsulated," Maine would defend its prerogatives despite "non-occurrence between British and American Commissioners of fixing that boundary." For more on the Northeast boundary disputes, see Linklater's *The Fabric of America.*

References

Ayers, Edward L., Patricia Nelson Limerick, Stephen Nissenbaum, and Peter S. Onuf. *All over the Map: Rethinking American Regions.* Baltimore: Johns Hopkins University Press, 1996.

Bercovitch, Sacvan, ed. *The American Jeremiad.* Madison: University of Wisconsin Press, 1978.

Bishop, Elizabeth. *The Complete Poems 1927–1979.* New York: Farrar, 1983.

Bozeman, Theodore Dwight. *To Live Ancient Lives: The Primitivist Dimension in Puritanism.* Chapel Hill: University of North Carolina Press, 1988.

Bradford, William. *Of Plymouth Plantation, 1620–1647.* Ed. Samuel Eliot Morison. New York: Alfred A. Knopf, 1952.

Brooks, Lisa. *The Common Pot: The Recovery of Native Space in the Northeast.* Minneapolis: University of Minnesota Press, 2008.

Buell, Lawrence. *The Future of Environmental Criticism: Environmental Crisis and Literary Imagination.* Oxford: Blackwell, 2005.

Canup, John. *Out of the Wilderness.* Middletown, CT: Wesleyan University Press, 1990.

Cavell, Stanley. *The Senses of Walden.* New York: Viking, 1972.

Cohen, Matt. *The Networked Wilderness: Communicating in Early New England.* Minneapolis: University of Minnesota Press, 2010.

Conforti, Joseph. *Imagining New England: Explorations of Regional Identity from the Pilgrims to the Mid-Twentieth Century.* Chapel Hill: University of North Carolina Press, 2001.

Cronon, William. *Changes in the Land: Indians, Colonists, and the Ecology of New England*. New York: Hill and Wang, 1985.

Dimock, Wai Chee, and Lawrence Buell. *Shades of the Planet: American Literature as World Literature*. Princeton, NJ: Princeton University Press, 2007.

Douglas, Ann. *The Feminization of American Culture*. New York: Anchor, 1977.

Douglas, Ann. "The Mind of Perry Miller" *The New Republic*, Feb. 3, 1982.

Egan, Jim. *Authorizing Experience: Refigurations of the Body Politic in Seventeenth-Century New England Writing*. Princeton, NJ: Princeton University Press, 1999.

Feintuch, Burt, and David H. Watters. *The Encyclopedia of New England: The Culture and History of an American Region*. Foreword by Donald Hall. New Haven, CT: Yale University Press, 2005.

Fischer, David Hackett. *Albion's Seed: Four British Folkways in America*. New York: Oxford University Press, 1989.

Foster, David R. *Thoreau's Country: Journey Through a Transformed Landscape*. Cambridge, MA: Harvard University Press, 1999.

Frost, Robert. *The Poetry of Robert Frost: The Collected Poems, Complete and Unabridged*. Ed. Edward Connery Lathem. New York: Henry Holt and Company, 1969.

Garber, Frederick. *Thoreau's Redemptive Imagination*. New York: New York University Press, 1977.

Gatta, John. *Making Nature Sacred: Literature, Religion, and Environment in America from the Puritans to the Present*. New York: Oxford University Press, 2004.

James, William. *Habit*. New York: Henry Holt and Company, 1914.

Kupperman, Karen Ordahl. *Indians and English: Facing Off in Early America*. Ithaca, NY: Cornell University Press, 2000.

Lenney, Christopher J. *Sightseeking: Clues to the Landscape History of New England*. Hanover, NH: University Press of New England, 2003.

Lincoln, Kenneth. *Native American Renaissance*. Berkeley: University of California Press, 1983.

Linklater, Andro. *The Fabric of America: How Our Borders and Boundaries Shaped the Country and Forged Our National Identity*. New York: Walker & Co., 2007.

Martin, John Frederick. *Profits in the Wilderness: Entrepreneurship and the Founding of New England Towns in the Seventeenth Century*. Chapel Hill: University of North Carolina Press, 1991.

Miller, Perry. *Errand into the Wilderness*. Cambridge, MA: Belknap Press of Harvard University Press, 1956.

Miller, Perry. *The New England Mind: The Seventeenth Century*. Cambridge, MA: Harvard University Press, 1954.

Myers, Jeffrey. *Converging Stories: Race, Ecology, and Environmental Justice in American Literature*. Athens: University of Georgia Press, 2005.

New, Elisa. *The Line's Eye: Poetic Experience, American Sight*. Cambridge, MA: Harvard University Press, 1998.

Pelikan, Jaroslav. *Reformation of Church and Dogma (1300–1700)*. Chicago: Chicago University Press, 1984.

Phillips, Dana. *The Truth of Ecology: Nature, Culture, and Literature in America*. New York: Oxford University Press, 2003.

Rowlandson, Mary. *Narrative of the Captivity, Sufferings, and Removes of Mary Rowlandson, Who Was Taken Prisoner by the Indians at the Destruction of Lancaster in 1675*. Clinton: Ballard & Bynner, 1853.

Scheese, Don. *Nature Writing: The Pastoral Impulse in America*. New York: Twayne Publishers, 1996.

Slotkin, Richard. *Regeneration Through Violence*. Middletown, CT: Wesleyan University Press, 1973.

St. George, Robert Blair. *Conversing by Signs: Poetics of Implication in Colonial New England Culture*. Chapel Hill: University of North Carolina Press, 1998.

Thorson, Robert M. *Stone by Stone: The Magnificent History in New England's Stone Walls*. New York: Walker & Company, 2002.

Thoreau, Henry David. *Walden*. Ed. J. Lyndon Shanley. Princeton, NJ: Princeton University Press, 2004.

Van Noy, Rick. *Surveying the Interior: Literary Cartographers and the Sense of Space*. Reno: University of Nevada Press, 2003.

Williams, William Carlos. *In the American Grain*. New York: New Directions Publishing, 2009 (Original work published 1925).

Further Reading

Bercovitch, Sacvan, ed. *The Puritan Origins of the American Self*. New Haven, CT: Yale University Press, 1975.

Bercovitch, Sacvan, ed. *Reconstructing American Literary History*. Cambridge, MA: Harvard University Press, 1986.

Bercovitch, Sacvan, ed. *The Rites of Assent: Transformations in the Symbolic Construction of America*. New York: Routledge, 1993.

Bercovitch, Sacvan, ed. *Cambridge History of American Literature. Volume 7: Prose Writing, 1940–1990*. New York: Cambridge University Press, 1994–2005.

Costello, Bonnie. *Elizabeth Bishop: Questions of Mastery*. Cambridge, MA: Harvard University Press, 1991.

Documents Relating to the Northeastern Boundary of the State of Maine. Boston: Dutton and Wentworth – Printers to the State, 1828.

Kalstone, David. *Becoming a Poet: Elizabeth Bishop with Marianne Moore and Robert Lowell*. Ed. Robert Hemenway, Afterward James Merrill. New York: Farrar, 1989.

Millier, Brett C. *Elizabeth Bishop: Life and the Memory of It*. Berkeley: University of California Press, 1993.

Moore, Marianne. *The Complete Poems of Marianne Moore*. New York: Penguin, 1981.

Moorsom, W. *Letters from Nova Scotia: Comprising Sketches of a Young Country. By Captain W Moorsom, 52 Light Infantry*. London: Henry Colburne and Richard Bentley, New Burlington Street, 1830.

6

Growing Up a Goodman
Hawthorne's Way

"Deep as Dante." Thus Herman Melville described Hawthorne in his famous essay of 1847, "Hawthorne and his Mosses" (Wineapple 75). Attributing Hawthorne's genius to his "strong New-England roots," Melville marveled at this writer who "expands and deepens down, the more I contemplate him" (224).

Later generations of admirers have agreed that Hawthorne was, whatever else, profound. Robert Lowell's 1964 cameo of Hawthorne, written from his new post at Harvard, echoes Melville's judgment of Hawthorne as a writer equally gifted as afflicted with the moodiness Melville called "the hypos." "[H]ead / bent down, brooding, brooding," Hawthorne's intensity not only augurs Lowell's own seriousness but that of all New England literature, whose force, as Melville suggested, derived "from its appeals to that Calvinistic sense of Innate Depravity and Original Sin" (Wineapple 225). Obsessions are deep-rooted in Hawthorne and consequences are invariably profound. Local, apparently ephemeral episodes turn out to have their origins in the national or cultural past, and every

New England Beyond Criticism: In Defense of America's First Literature, First Edition. Elisa New.
© 2014 Elisa New. Published 2014 by John Wiley & Sons, Ltd.

material object, every color, every breath of wind or rain may bear a clue. Live with Hawthorne for long enough, and one comes to crave what he offers, to return again and again to re-experience the pull of mystery, moral obligation, and hard interpretive exercise that his fiction tutors.

The narrator of Hawthorne's greatest work demonstrates the method when, picking up a scrap of faded red cloth and placing it against his chest, he reports to feeling "a sensation not altogether physical, yet almost so, as of burning heat, and as if the letter were not of red cloth, but red-hot iron" (*Scarlet Letter* xxvi). The throb is crucial, for it alerts us to the "deep meaning . . . most worthy of interpretation . . . subtly communicating itself to my sensibilities." This same meaning, however, "evad[es] the analysis of [his] mind" (xxv). The reader who imagines that this "A" the interpreter holds in his hand stands for something simple (like adultery) will be risking a reduction not only obtuse, but nearly unconscionable. As if the alphabet of human feeling could ever be reduced to one stigmatizing letter! As if the contents of a heart could ever be made visible on a bodice! Truth's fullness exceeds its inflamed and merely proximate sign. Thus the "scarlet letter" is not only Hester's public (and her lover Arthur's secret) brand. Nor is it just America's and Art's and Allegory's, either. It is Adam's − from whose fall, Hawthorne admits, we sinned all, but from whose expulsion from Eden, Eve by his side, we also learn tenderness, devotion, and care. The office of the A, and of Hawthorne's own allegorical method, is to indicate the depths of our common imperfection, and so to alert us to that sacred "inmost me" we are morally bound to protect in each other.

There is scarcely a tale in the *oeuvre* that does not show multi-layered depths and this kind of scouring moral comprehensiveness. Take, for instance, the story of the young bridegroom, Aylmer, of "The Birthmark." An ambitious young scientist, Aylmer one day finds himself unable to abide the birthmark on his wife Georgiana's cheek. His quest to complete his wife's perfection by removing this mark leads to her eventual murder. Pursuing an absolute, trading life for truth, Aylmer is Hawthorne's version of the Faustian knower,

141

a figure of fresh saliency in the nineteenth-century age of science. Once a fallen angel or unregenerate Adam, Hawthorne's Faust is a now also a myopic Frankenstein, his intellectual pride and linear drive carrying him past mere sin into active evil.

Yet Aylmer is more than just another Faust: he becomes a case study in ambition's single-mindedness and the impact of its disordering and dis-integralizing power on others. Ideally, love and work can balance, can counterpoise, each other, but Aylmer's workaholism throws off the give-and-take of a working marriage. His pursuit of one transcendent goal makes all life adjunct to the self. Indeed, what is most uncanny about Alymer is his precocious but unmistakably American "individualism." Machinelike of will, he is capable, in Flannery O'Connor's phrase, of "forward and reverse," but of nothing tender. This same single-mindedness makes him progenitor to the whole array of hyper-masculine types who come to populate subsequent American fiction: Henry James's priapic Goodwood, Henry Adams's Dynamo, Faulkner's brutal Sutpen and all the dull stiffs, strutters, and ruthless titans and tyros since. Such man-machines have, rather than strength, force.

Such force, Hawthorne uses Aylmer to show, is inveterately at odds with beauty, that fresh and delicate thing that is not exclusively but so often the property of women. Henry James, following in Hawthorne's footsteps, will call this thing Isabel, May, Daisy. Adams calls it Virgin; Nabokov, Lolita; Whitman, Calamus; Williams, simply, Beautiful Thing. Melville lets Ahab breathe deep of its fragrant, human essence before he drags his floating oilrig down to death. Tales like "The Birthmark," "Artist of the Beautiful," "Wakefield," and "Rappacini's Daughter" show Hawthorne as one of the first to make this beauty an outward sign of the "inmost me." He is also first at using fiction to instruct pity and solicitude for those wearing this beauty abroad where it is bound to be marred. And first, too, in suggesting how the very institutions established to protect our inmost selves (marriage, religion, the halls of justice) instead turn against them. Hawthorne offers pity to the beautiful above all.

Which is to say: pity to us all. But especially for women and wives. For if Alymer is a sort of Frankenstein, he is also a very bad husband. His drive to change his wife, or to kill what he does not like in her, illustrates that species of male narcissism that loves its own desire more than the beloved. Theorists of pornography could do worse than study the toxic erotics of this husband who, in order to "cure" his wife, has her installed in a perfumed boudoir where he may "study" her compelling, obsession-making "ugliness." Moreover, as Georgiana's birthmark appears in the shape of a tiny hand, a sign of birth itself, Aylmer's war on the birthmark shows itself to be an intellectual assault on female reproductive power. His quest for beauty is a form of homicide and infanticide which, in its attempt to capture the perfection of the future, kills it.

Lest one think the foregoing quite enough for one tale to accomplish, there is yet more. Hawthorne's story also tracks the evacuation of Georgiana's pride and self-esteem, her growing dependence on Alymer's (and only Alymer's!) approval, and her masochistic internalization of her husband's disgust. Meanwhile, as Georgiana is sacrificed to her husband's career, Hawthorne explores too how little protection the institution of bourgeois marriage affords. The insularity of the marriage bond, its claustrophobic idealism, makes marriage a perfect laboratory for exploitive cruelty and, the allegory hints, a bit of a mad experiment. Here and in other tales, Hawthorne leads us to question a world where even the primary institution of human relationship, marriage, cannot protect relationships, and so to grow more mindful of the human connections we have. Intimate relations to others, along with our responsibilities to the social systems that protect us all, are, Hawthorne adjures, simply what keep us from being "no longer worthy of a position in the universe" (*Mosses* 169). The man who thinks first and feels later is consigned to end, as Aylmer does, an Adam in free fall, an "Outcast of the Universe" (*Twice Told Tales* 105).

With stories like "The Birthmark" to remind us of his method, it is no use gainsaying Hawthorne's depth or questioning the essentially Calvinist and New England materials on which he draws. The sea was Melville's Harvard and Yale. Innate Depravity and Original Sin were Hawthorne's.

At the same time, Hawthorne knew depth's limitations. Sentry of surfaces, of present history and of the day-to-day, he was wary of anything drastic and suspicious of the manifold forms of self-regard that New Englanders confused with care of the soul. Melville was not wrong when he said that "the rich and rare distilment" of Hawthorne's "spicy and slowly-oozing heart" was ineluctably moral (Wineapple 224). Still, Melville may not have been the best judge of Hawthorne's complexity, in particular of Hawthorne's disinclination to the fire-eating and social alienation to which Melville himself was all too susceptible. Just how ill at ease with his own profundity, how much of two minds about the darkness business, and how solidly and even ploddingly devoted to moderation Hawthorne really was Melville could not fathom.

His choice of a best friend is one illustration. More comfortable among mediocrities than geniuses, Hawthorne chose not the passionate Herman Melville, or the gentle Longfellow, but rather shallow, loyal, potato-faced Franklin Pierce. Hawthorne liked the cozily married, the gainfully employed, and, when possible, the advantageously connected. The society he selected excluded (or at least limited the access of) the lonely and lightning-struck. He made a few notable exceptions for those who called themselves Transcendental, but the actual "school of Hawthorne," in Richard Brodhead's wonderful phrase, mixed select New Englanders with various prodigals and Democrats, and even a few New Yorkers. The motley assortment of Hawthorne's intimates were united most by a certain resistance to New England pieties, New England proprietarinesses, and New England politics.

Once one realizes that Hawthorne was no transcendentalist and lacked patience for genius, it is bracing to find so saturnine and satiric a writer waiting inside the vestibule. There is scarcely a tale or a sketch in which moral urgency is not somewhere outed for a feint of overactive sensibility, or where the ostensibly purest of human motives doesn't crack along some obvious line of fracture. Hawthorne lets the ironic, caustic, and sometimes reactive currents of his personality ripple, and sometimes rip, across his style, showing a stubborn resistance to prevailing pieties and a temperament especially reactive where humbug – especially contemporary humbug – is concerned.

Take, for instance, the attitude he maintained toward the New England Abolitionist community. Hawthorne frequently found his neighbors absurd. But around the issue of abolition, and later war, their weakness for and defense of absolute measures disgusted him. The tolerance of violence that Whitter, Thoreau, Melville, eventually Lincoln himself endorsed, Hawthorne stubbornly refused. Emerson might breathe piously on the eve of John Brown's execution that John Brown "will make the gallows as glorious as the cross"; such endorsement of a man who had butchered innocents in cold blood seemed to Hawthorne evidence of how companionably bad faith could live with good causes. Hawthorne's own flat reaction to Brown's execution was that "nobody was more justly hanged." His further admission to taking "intellectual satisfaction . . . in requital of [Brown's] preposterous miscalculation" sums up his conviction that overreaching is always dangerous, and the pursuit of principle before persons frequently criminal. For from Hawthorne's point of view, in life and in his fictions, the "preposterous miscalculation of possibilities" – the moral hazard afflicting all men since Adam – is the true serpent in the garden (Wineapple 333). Certainty breeds sin, and too much faith in ultimate depths (as opposed to delicate surfaces) can sharpen belief to a dangerous edge, making it a weapon.

No conviction is insusceptible to being overdone. Remorse taken too far eats at the social fabric ("It gnaws me! It gnaws me!" says the morbid sufferer of "The Bosom Serpent," setting loose his neurosis on an unsuspecting world). Too much patriotic independence becomes mob cruelty (as innocent Robin sees, beholding his tarred and feathered kinsman, Major Molineux). Too much love of children renders them vulnerable hothouse specimens (such is the fate of Rappacinni's daughter, killed as much by the poison of paternal overprotectiveness as by the poison of a suitor's lust). Routinely, Hawthorne forces the singular passions, the idée fixes, and the deepest convictions of all of his characters into contact with the everyday, the trivial, and the transient. Those who respond well to his lessons in moderation he repays with long, uneven, and compromised lives.

145

These are allowed, as Milton's Adam and Eve did, "to choose / Their place of rest, and Providence their guide. / They . . . Through Eden took their solitary way." The rest he lets go to the Devil.

Worldliness, rather than depth; history, rather than time; the exigent rather than the transcendent – these were as much a part of Hawthorne's moral repertoire as the taxonomy of fall, sin, love, and salvation that was his New England inheritance. It can be disillusioning, after one's high school romance with this author, to see how much dispassion he packs around passion, how delightedly he dispenses disenchantment. As one grows acquainted with, and indeed ages with, Hawthorne, one realizes that he does not soften, but, rather, cruelly subtilizes justice by making it poetic. Why else is Reuben Bourne's eldest born but to die for his father's guilt, Bourne for Bourne? What other reason for the good Reverend Hooper becoming a freak in a veil but to become a better minister? When the priggish Hilda marries the cold Kenyon in *The Marble Faun*, or when Goodman Brown leaves his clinging wife, Faith (in pink ribbons, no less!), to keep an assignation with Satan, Hawthorne is disinclined to wring his hands. What, after all, can one expect of a Goodman?

Lucky, then, for this Goodman that though he dispatches himself to the Devil, he has his Faith and his town to return to. That cosmic damnation can, in the provincial setting (marriage being the most provincial setting of all), sometimes get spun as damned foolery is to the credit of the community. Communities guard the fallible from ultimate danger – though not from the laughter that plays a key role in many of Hawthorne's darkest tales. Thus, one use Hawthorne makes of the "sketch" (as opposed to the tale) is to administer the reality check of humor to his more self-absorbed characters. The distance between the lonely sufferer and his salvation is often that between the dark woods and the work-a-day town. In the town, if he is lucky, someone might laugh at him. With excess running so high in New England's dark woods, it is best, Hawthorne reckoned, to have a town around. It takes, as Hawthorne recognized early, a village.

Indeed, so much of the grist for Hawthorne's skeptical mill was provincially grown that the artist Melville called "deep as Dante" took a very dim view of those too beautiful for their own good. Illogical as it may seem, the preciousness and inutility of artists, like that of political purists and purists of all kinds, got on Hawthorne's nerves, and he regularly satirized them, regularly exposed the smug woolgathering privilege of those holed up in Old Manses or before cozy reading tables by cozier fires. The same archness, for instance, that Hawthorne adopts when he writes in the "Custom House Sketch" of the most out-there Transcendentalist, "Even the Old Inspector was desirable, as a change of appetite, to a man who had known Alcott," colors his portrait of the artist Owen Warland (too "beautiful" for his own good) and his many self-cameos (23).

Hawthorne was, if not outright anti-social, entirely ready to lift his handsome eyebrows at the parochial sanctimony of this New England worthy or that. Contemporaries remember him as expert at disappearance, ever poised to duck into a doorway, or a brown study, or up a gangplank to escape some raffish, churchly denizen of the Cambridge/Concord/Berkshire elite. The chronic humorlessness of reforming Boston, persistent through generations, made Hawthorne's gorge rise, yet his habitual reserve and his mien (perhaps cultivated) of introverted domesticity helped him to modulate himself and control his reactions. Meanwhile, as he shunned or took in measured doses contact with those too rarified, he preserved steady, fulfilling relationships with persons others found enervating or shallow or both. Flamboyance, wit, and pragmatic worldliness were qualities many of Hawthorne's favorite people, Sophia among them, possessed.

In a letter from Brook Farm (its subject the cow kept by frequent visitor, Margaret Fuller) Hawthorne remarks to his darling, Sophia, that the "transcendental heifer" was as "apt to kick over the milk pail" as its owner (Wineapple 153). An unmistakable touch of malice curdles Hawthorne's sketch of the flamboyant and rather ample Fuller – an intellectual whose "Conversations" to women she played for maximum effect with theatrical velvets, raised chairs and such.

Yet he also clearly esteems Fuller who, like her bovine namesake, gave as good as she got.

Another favorite was James Fields, the ebullient publisher and *saloniste* who, along with younger wife Annie, published Hawthorne's books "a-la-Steam Engine" (Wineapple 229). Buoying Hawthorne's spirits with his "uncorked faith" while seconding his distrust of "damned female scribblers," Fields repressed moping in Hawthorne's company but was sensibly miffed on Hawthorne's behalf that "the writer of *Uncle Tom's Cabin* is getting to be a millionaire" (Wineapple 255). Poor, infatuated Melville gushed with too much love for the restrained Hawthorne ever to requite it. Both Emerson and Thoreau lacked the irony, and sometimes even cynicism, Hawthorne liked in friends. Hawthorne also had a knack, if not for double-dealing, then at least, let us say, for contingency planning, that allowed him to roll the financial dice and go in with George Ripley at Brook Farm. He had, if not a capacity for opportunism, then at least an alertness to opportunity, that allowed him to live for cheap at Emerson's Old Manse, all the while regarding his Concord neighbors as "bores of a very intense water" (Wineapple 170). The mordancy of his imagination, a mordancy that led Melville to call his world "ten times black," was in fact a little tinged with other humors (224). It took a temperament inured to unenchantedness, a bilious bent averse to pieties, to choose to ride shotgun for Franklin Pierce. This Hawthorne did unreservedly.

Hawthorne's saturnity, I think, explains much about the matter that most discomfited his New England colleagues: namely, his politics. Hawthorne joined the Democratic Party in college, at Bowdoin, when it appealed to all sorts of boys impatient of New England's whiggish, seigniorial mien. Melville, Whitman, and others were moved, too, by this party in which young men could find common cause. Through the Young America movement, they struck hands and united their ambitions to those of youthful 48'ers worldwide. Democrats like young Hawthorne took the rough Jackson over the refined Adams any day. They preferred the moral scrubbing of a spirited editorial over that New England staple, Sunday's homiletics served up fresh on newsprint. They liked New York City b'hoys over the landed upstaters remaking Albany into a kind of Boston (sans Congregationalism, and with furs the product for export instead of cod). Eventually this was the same party, its spokesman the brilliant but quixotic John O'Sullivan, that called expansion west our Manifest Destiny, free soil a white man's sacred right, and States' Rights a working man's protection from the patrician North.

When others chose, however, to transfer their political loyalties, Hawthorne did not. It was not all expediency that kept Hawthorne a Democrat, but neither was it spotless principle. Hawthorne's friendship with Pierce, including his dependence on party sinecures for livelihood, went hand in hand with tastes that ran so deep as to imitate principles. Membership in the Democratic Party provided a perch for an oppositionalism of temperament that craved an alternative to the Cambridge/Concord/Berkshire axis of dreamy cerebralism and parochial smugness. Democratic partisanship was a symptom of Hawthorne's allergy to his native New England. No one could find much good to say about Franklin Pierce's dim record as president. Hawthorne tried to give it his all, contending that "Pierce had fully risen to what the office demanded," while perforce admitting, "True, Pierce had not risen beyond what the office demanded" (Wineapple 315).

More than loyalty obscured for Hawthorne the trifling faults of his "dearest beloved," Sophia Hawthorne, *née* Peabody. To be sure, Sophia's sexual enthusiasm, her staunch devotion, and her preference for a cozy night at home over the grandstandings of her sister and other females of their set would naturally have suited the retiring, if ardent, Nathaniel. Still, others saw how much art Sophia poured into being adorable. Before ever meeting Hawthorne, the pubescent Sophia had figured out that a gift for sick headaches could protect her from the various bohemian employments her earnest sisters so relished. Having used her teen years perfecting graceful self-arrangement on a divan, she was most fetchingly arranged when, in 1849, Hawthorne first glimpsed her. Whatever Sophia's deviations from perfect frankness, the marriage that followed was remarkable for loyalty and compatibility. The devotion of the couple did not diminish as middle age cut down the frequent episodes of intercourse Hawthorne called, in letters to Sophia, their "blissful interviews."

In short, evidence suggests that the timeless and immortal Hawthorne – Melville's Dante – was very much a man circa 1850. Since he was personally averse to those of overly beautiful sensibility, his art was, finally, more anti-transcendent than transcendent. It is thus a mistake to let Hawthorne's depths distract his readers from his essential worldliness. Hawthorne's fictions plant their feet on the earth and in neighborly converse with Hawthorne's densely human, inveterately historical existence.

That compromise is human, extremity malign; that a mortal's place is between and hell; and that earth is, as Frost later put it "the right place for love" – these were the articles of Hawthorne's faith in human life. Here, Hawthorne surmised, fiction could help, for fiction is a zone of temperate relations. Placed between a reader and a writer, between hard facts and what imagination wrought, fiction might school us in relations less drastic, more flexible, than either our misguided passions or our social obligations might suggest:

> it may be pardonable to imagine that a friend, a kind and apprehensive, though not the closest friend, is listening to our talk; and then, a native reserve being thawed by this genial consciousness, we may prate of the circumstances that lie around us, and even of ourself, but still keep the inmost Me behind its veil. To this extent and within these limits, an author, methinks, may be autobiographical, without violating either the reader's rights or his own. (*Scarlet Letter* 7–8)

This passage, coming at the very beginning of the prosy "Custom House Sketch," sheds light not only on this particular book's, but also the institution of literature's best offices. Literature is not exempt from the critique Hawthorne renders all other institutions in history. Its agents, authors, will bear those obligations to readers necessary in an imperfect world, beginning with the obligation to present themselves, their own circumstances, candidly. The prosiness, discursiveness, and comedy of the "sketch," its very sketchiness, works to chip away or muss the perfection of *The Scarlet Letter*, just as the dubious career of its author turned civic timeserver raises all careers to question. Military heroes and ministerial cynosures, like mere authors, come to repose in the dusty Custom House. Coming just before Hester and Arthur's classic ordeal (a double epic of twenty-four chapters; a drama in three eight-chapter acts, diamond-cut by three scaffold scenes), the sketch provides precisely the distance from absolutes Hester and Arthur's society will not countenance. So skip the "Sketch" at your peril, dear Reader. You may not know it, but its pratings protect you, too – far more than your most passionate allegiances and identifications with the romance's doomed principals.

For, of course, when we first read *The Scarlet Letter* in school, we tend to over-identify or under-identify with two protagonists. Thus we repeat, if well-meaningly, the sin of those who will not let the sinner veil her face for shame. Adolescents, when they first read *The Scarlet Letter*, tend to cheer Hester's bare-knuckled resistance to the Puritan oligarchy, her disciplined, cerebral radicalism, her passionate readiness to chuck it all, flee, to leave America for Europe, sickly lover in tow. Run away! Fight the power! To thine ownself be true! The Hester of the opening chapters, that Hester brandishing her resplendent A, flouting her middle-aged critics, is our perfect heroine of the Id, the consummate role model of the heart's untrammeled freedom. Dimmesdale, in this version, is the worst kind of establishment Adult, counter to Hester, a sellout and a shill. What excuse has Hester's lover, we ask, but hypocrisy, ambition, and a weak-willed need to please to transmute his private trespasses into public sin? What right has he, we ask, to imagine that public service can ever substitute for naked confession on the public scaffold?

Precisely the right, Hawthorne's book counsels, of any fallen mortal. The fact of our common imperfection seals our obligation to each other as well as guarantees our fundamental equality, extends to every person the right to keep some matters private but also the obligation to translate personal disappointment into some service to the public weal.

The community has no right to our individual sins, for what can it do with them that we could not, ourselves, do better? Exposing transgressions to the common gaze may fix, petrify, and objectify what the heart might prompt to new, warm growth. A case in point is that Hester's own daughter, Pearl, made a freakish, stunted emblem of her mother's long ago mistake: Pearl cannot grow until she is restored to the family, the proper sphere of moral nurturance and privacy's defending institution. Likewise, Arthur, Pearl's father, and Hester, Pearl's mother, are also impeded by their sin's exposure to the gaze of others. Hester hardens herself to escape the pricking of her stigma, while Arthur leaves his wounds open until, penetrated by another, they become gruesome stigmata. Far better for their souls' renovation is the social life that allows them to toil at some human service while their wounds heal in private. If nothing can reverse amputating loss (any more than anything can reverse the Fall), then sewing and nursing, oratory and ministry – all the institutions of work with which Hester and Arthur fill their time – at least allow private anguish the outlet and penitence of public service. Thus sufferers may be, little by little, rehabilitated to the world.

It is thus that the real role of the Custom House sketch, its salutary office, is revealed. The eagle of the Republic over the Salem Custom House enfolds Hester and Arthur's trauma (and Hawthorne's own, as sacked employee) under its institutional wing, as the living community enfolds all traumas in an ambiguity, a social veil and web of social relations that protects innermost selves. Not mirrors for our identification but dense expressive vehicles, the Eagle, the Alphabet, the Pulpit – metonyms for the civic, communicative, and spiritual systems they represent – offer to individuals general, impartial, and thus highly civilized protections. Further, in their very ambiguity and iridescence of weave, these media preserve a world that is interpretable and so amenable to diversity of viewpoint. Full of options, this world is fallen, but it is free. Which is also, finally, to say that while Hawthorne's Democratic politics may have been, in some ways, rather small, the claims he makes for the artist in democracy are large. In his work, art and the artist assume highly responsible regulatory functions within the civic sphere: they exemplify the friendly neutral functions that may be performed by well-designed social institutions. Art, like a functioning civic sphere, teaches us that there is something deeper than our deepest desires. Beware, his fiction shows, of getting what you want.

It was a sound philosophy for Hawthorne to hold, given the frustration that so often attended his own high hopes. The author of the most perfect of American books had plenty of practice with compromise and making do.

In the aftermath of his dismissal from the Custom House and the year following the publication of his masterpiece, 1851 found Hawthorne alarmingly poor and living with his family in a gussied-up shanty in the Berkshires. *The House of the Seven Gables*, Hawthorne's study of the rigors of the American economy, was written in these straitened circumstances. "Thou didst much amiss to marry a husband who cannot keep thee like a lady," Hawthorne admitted to his wife as she laid carpet over rough boards.

Shame and the bizarre reaction formations that attend it had, of course, been longstanding staples in Hawthorne's repertoire. But the earlier short fiction and *The Scarlet Letter* had focused more on the psychological and psychosocial setbacks of the young, on those experiences of embarrassment that occur in youth and, later, harden the character. *The House of the Seven Gables* now treated the humiliations, especially the economic ones, that are the special province of the elderly, while also hinting at those anxieties that come to live with the middle aged when they realize that "[i]n this republican country . . . someone is always at the drowning point" (Wineapple 233).

What is there to save anyone from starvation in individualist America? On the morning on which the book opens, one Hepzibah Pyncheon, scraggly old hen of a woman, has finally given up on gentility and brought herself to the excruciating step of opening a "cent shop." In the course of the romance, Hepzibah will be rescued from starvation, along with faded brother Clifford, by the appearance of two young guests. Her lovely cousin, Phoebe, will come to plant vegetables in the garden and take over the cent shop counter. Her tenant Holgrave, daguerreotypist and radical, will come to fall in love with Phoebe, marry her, and be domesticated into economic competency and meliorist politics. Young America, in essence, rides to the rescue.

Yet even as Hawthorne shows tenderness for these pinched and pitiable throwbacks of New England's Saving Remnant, he does not stint to expose the values of Hepzibah and Clifford as distinctly unbeautiful. Democratically speaking, from the perspective of Young America, their values are repugnant. Hepzibah despises the vulgar ascendance of individualist ambition. And yet the prerogatives she clings to were always the fruit of ill-gotten gains: her hereditary privilege was no less avaricious for having worn silvery noblesse. Nor has that feeble aristocratic wreck, her unhinged brother Clifford, covered himself with glory. His patrimony stolen from him by fast dealing, he has lost his youth rotting in jail for another's crimes, and yet he remains a useless figure. Emerging from prison, Clifford preserves the antique manners and expectations of his cosseted youth. And with fresh Phoebe and Holgrave on hand, he makes the present step lively to keep his illusions in polish. In *The House of the Seven Gables*, the New England Way is a high-maintenance elder relation who makes Democracy subordinate.

And yet what can one really expect of any Hepzibah or Clifford, clinging to their home, their past, and all the provenances and perquisites they have ever known? Since Adam, Hawthorne suggests, it has been human nature to repeat the past, to cling to precedent. Who, Hawthorne inquires, truly leaves his "dwelling place," that hereditary Salem of the timid, backward-glancing heart? No one ever left by choice. Not even, as Hawthorne's next work shows, he who flees for Eden itself.

The Blithedale Romance, an exposé of Eden and Hawthorne's third great romance, is most famous for drawing on the "most romantic episode" of Hawthorne's own life: an eighteen-month sojourn at Brook Farm. But its power derives from the questions of renewal Hawthorne had asked in his previous two romances and which Emerson put thus: "Why should we not also enjoy an original relation to the Universe?" Why, to put it another way, should not every generation discover its own America?

The price of oats in Massachusetts, for one thing. The Panic of 1838 for another. Vast class and cultural differences between those who pursue agriculture and those who revere nature. The clash of young men's ambitions. Urban alienation. Temptations to mendacity. Mechanization. The weather. But most of all: the disordering power of sex.

The Blithedale Romance, Hawthorne's most dynamic (and most untidy) romance, is so full of social and historical texture it strains Hawthorne's own definition of Romance. The title notwithstanding, *Blithedale* depicts a New England whose farm economy no longer supports even families – much less communities of intellectuals. If the idealists of Blithedale fancy they've found Arcadia, their pastoral retreat is actually just an exurb of Boston, their utopia an escape from modernity without originality. On sabbatical from city day jobs, they hold onto what are – there is no mistaking them! – city apartments, and they hold fast too to the complex urban lives and attachments that go with their walk-ups. On weekends, these utopians return to the city where seamstresses from the country risk prostitution, where old men turn to drink, where operators, hucksters, and actors of all kinds purvey stimulants, escapes, forgetful dreams. Blithedale's characters are all actors playing double parts and leading secret lives. Hyper-sophisticated in their pursuit of innocence, they refurbish the very trees in the woods into *pieds-à-terre* so as to better watch themselves disport at innocence.

And disport they do! The transformation of a family-based to an entrepreneurial economy makes the young free agents of their own economic fulfillment. It also liberates their libidos and gives them unsupervised time and space for dalliances. Everything in this book is tinged with sex. Of course, Hawthorne's own sojourn at Brook Farm had coincided with the period when – "Swollen with pent-up love," as he wrote to his betrothed – he thought Brook Farm might feather a love nest (Wineapple 130). In exchange for baling dung and pulling potatoes the impecunious author might nevertheless procure for his Dove a cottage. Hawthorne's bachelor narrator, Coverdale, endures erotic stimulations so potent they literally fell him. The effect of just one night at Blithedale, its cast of

155

warm-cheeked young unmarrieds gathered round a fire, proves sufficiently debilitating that by morning Coverdale has come down with the something-or-other. Confined to his bed for the next twelve chapters, he then receives burnt porridge and daily renewals of the malady from the alluring Zenobia (a.k.a. the Dark Lady). Zenobia's bared shoulder and hothouse flower at the temple make clear that she is "no folded petal, no latent dew drop" and that she "has lived, and loved!" (*Blithedale* 47). With Zenobia available, Coverdale is relieved of the guilt of exploiting the more innocent Priscilla (Fair Lady) as fantasy object. If every young man could launch a career in bed and still be fed by sultry nurses, wouldn't he? If all farmers could hoe half time and spin verse the other, wouldn't they? What babes they are, these utopians, who while away an evening torching up costly kindling while dreaming up names for their "pretty farm"!

Hawthorne's own skepticism squeezes the "romance" of his book into highly compromised corners. And yet if *Blithedale* has its fierce partisans, and I am one, it is probably because even as its author mocks the callowness, the pretenses, and self-deception of his young characters, he lets us feel all the giddy charm of their situation, all while making the most of his genre, the "romance." Hawthorne's *Blithedale* draws from the same well of youthful vigor and amorous joy that powers romances from Shakespeare's *Midsummer's Night's Dream* to Hemingway's *A Moveable Feast* (and even such modern versions as our own TV "Friends" or "The Real World"). Who are Hawthorne's Blithedalers but sundry twenty-somethings of mixed abilities, mixed attractiveness, and mixed motives, all out for sex and glory, life companions, and great careers? They are silly and, in some cases, tragically wrong about themselves. But they are also hard to resist as, on the breezy hillsides and sunburned hayricks of their idealist utopia, they work out who they are.

After *The Blithedale Romance*, published in 1852, it took Hawthorne eight years to finish and publish his next romance. Shortly after finishing *Blithedale*, Hawthorne obtained, courtesy of Pierce and the party, the post of Consul to Liverpool. The employment gave him modest financial security as well as opportunities to meet

English authors, to travel, to enjoy Sophia and children far from New England's suffocations. Yet it turned out that the sinecure that provided the Hawthornes' other bourgeois livelihood and a measure of peace also deprived him of that proximity to the dwelling place and region which, however vexatious, was the source of his art's greatest power.

There are those who find *The Marble Faun*, Hawthorne's last completed romance, not inert. However, I would rather stamp passports in Liverpool, or hazard malaria in Rome, than ever read this book again, and Hawthorne, apparently, had similar sentiments. The materials out of which Hawthorne fashioned this romance were not unpromising; its themes had congealed to good effect before. *The Marble Faun* features a dark and beautiful heroine with a secret (like Hester). It explores tensions between the moldering past and the brisk and ruthless present (like the saga of the Pyncheons). It has an ensemble cast of striving youth in a sexy and unsupervised context (like *Blithedale*). Its subject is art and the artist, now liberated from provincial New England and set down in Rome, a city that is itself a work of art. Nor does the romance neglect those questions of sin, social accountability, and creative self-culture that had always preoccupied the writer as a vexed and self-chastening New Englander. Not casting off from Calvinist obsession so much as returning to its source, Hawthorne might well have fancied that he'd found in Rome the fallen Adam of towns, the Ur-ruin of ruins, the originary setting for the haunting of the New England mind.

Somehow, though, this book walks into a dark gallery, and it never comes out. It is perhaps made a worse reading experience for the fact that its "topics" are manifold and utterly worthy. *The Marble Faun* takes up high art's relationship to vernacular practice; romance as a genre; canonization; culture when it becomes national; nations when they abjure art; art when it abjures nations; inspiration versus imitation; painting's immediacy; and narrative's *durée*. These are estimable themes – and welcome ones, too, from an author who, in *Blithedale*, showed himself not afraid of the novel of ideas. His dislike of abstract thinkers notwithstanding, Hawthorne shows in this novel what will become, in James, the International theme, complete with its host of subcultures, each with their telltale quirks and ideologies. And yet what seemed promising in *Blithedale* becomes tiresome in *The Marble Faun*. Perhaps the most that can be said of the *The Marble Faun* in the end is that, by writing it, Hawthorne turned himself into quite a decent docent. Contemporaries took *The Marble Faun* with them in their trunks, carrying it to Rome as a guidebook.

Returning to America in 1860, Hawthorne lived out the four years after the publication of *The Marble Faun* back in Concord, the country now in the throes of Civil War whose noblest cause, abolition, had always shown Hawthorne its cheapest face. As the conflict approached its bloody close, Hawthorne aged fast, struggling with another unfinished romance, with his failing legs, with gastric agonies, and with the enervating threat of genteel poverty still hanging, as ever, over his family. By age 60 the handsome Hawthorne was portly and bent, his eyebrows, his aquiline nose, and his very hat showing a sag. It was a very disconsolate and spent man who, sent off on a restorative carriage ride with Pierce, finally died. For some time, he had been effectively gone.

Hawthorne had a temperament – delicate, perceptive, and very fine – on which his region and his region's exercised soul daguerreotyped itself. His best work was achieved close to home: at desks turned to the wall to shut out New England's loud sonorities, but in venues no more than a carriage ride from his birthplace, Salem. He was – as Melville recognized, and as those who made New England's mind America's own – deep.

Yet Hawthorne's major works of fiction are all explorations of the Absolute's ineluctability, of the danger of grasping at totality, and of the historical torques and surface tensions that trouble, warp, but also give human face and explicability to truths far beyond human reach. The Custom House was more home to him than self or society: he thought selves and societies both are best kept at some decent remove from themselves, extended but also protected by the symbolic customs and vehicles, veils, and conveyancing instruments that afford safe conduct to sons of Adam. Harbors, borders, houses with their insides and outs; media and metaphors, institutions for the exchange of facts and of fantasy; fictions – such ingenious constructions allow us shelters in our own worlds but also broadening passages into others. Wherever he roamed, Hawthorne's dwelling place was New England. Yet the domicile of his art was not so parochial a place, but rather the liminal zone where the psyche, cast off from its lonely depths, risks growth.

References

Hawthorne, Nathaniel. *The Blithedale Romance*. New York: Penguin Classics, 1986.

Hawthorne, Nathaniel. *Mosses from an Old Manse*. New York: The Modern Library, 2003.

Hawthorne, Nathaniel. *The Scarlet Letter*. Ed. Thomas E. Connolly. New York: Penguin Classics, 2003.

Hawthorne, Nathaniel. *Twice-Told Tales*. New York: The Modern Library, 2001.

Lowell, Robert. *Life Studies and For the Union Dead*. New York: Farrar, Straus and Giroux, 1964.

Wineapple, Brenda. *Hawthorne: A Life*. New York: Random House, 2004.

Further Reading

Brodhead, Richard, ed. *New Essays on Moby-Dick*. New York: Cambridge University Press, 1986.

Cavitch, Max. *The American Elegy: The Poetry of Mourning from the Puritans to Whitman*. Minneapolis: University of Minnesota Press, 2007.

Colacurcio, Michael. "'The Woman's Own Choice': Sex, Metaphor and the Puritan 'Sources' of *The Scarlet Letter*." *New Essays on The Scarlet Letter*. Ed. Michael J. Colacurcio. Cambridge: Cambridge University Press, 1986.

Melville, Herman. *Moby-Dick; or The Whale: A Norton Critical Edition*. Ed. Harrison Hayford and Hershel Parker. New York: W.W. Norton, 1967.

Thompson, Lawrence. *Melville's Quarrel with God*. Princeton, NJ: Princeton University Press, 1952.

7

"Shall Not Perish from the Earth"
The Counting of Souls in Jewett, Du Bois, E.A. Robinson, and Frost

Perhaps it is the great national anniversaries which our country has lately kept, and the soldiers' meetings that take place everywhere, which have made reunions of every sort the fashion. This one, at least, had been very interesting. I fancied that old feuds had been overlooked, and the old saying that blood is thicker than water had again proved itself true . . . (Sarah Orne Jewett, *Country of the Pointed Firs*)

No state can build
A literature that shall at once be sound
And sad on a foundation of well-being.
(Robert Frost, "New Hampshire")

Bisecting the North American continent into North and South, sectional division was, Abraham Lincoln insisted, a peril to America's soul. From its earliest beginnings the United States had been by its very nature free and indivisible, conceived whole and planted on the continent. But, as Lincoln saw in retrospect, tolerance of division and disunion – from the original constitutional compromises of the

New England Beyond Criticism: In Defense of America's First Literature, First Edition. Elisa New.
© 2014 Elisa New. Published 2014 by John Wiley & Sons, Ltd.

1790s to the territorial compromises of the 1850s – had paved the way to a war of cosmic consequence. A nation divided section against section, like a house divided against itself, could not be prevented from perishing from the earth.[1] But a nation outlasting these divisions and repairing their effects might at last achieve in mature sorrow what it had not reaped in preventive wisdom. In sorrow and in patience, with recognition that no nation can escape its history, America might be reborn.

Lincoln used his *Gettysburg Address* to reconsecrate this continent as sacred ground and to commence a necessary tally of living and dead souls. The "field" he indicated was one larger than a bloodied patch of Pennsylvania. It was not just the contained Mason–Dixon landscape but the whole United States beyond – a great indivisible graveyard, the ground sanctified by those beneath it but given meaning by those who would not forget. If Lincoln used the *Address* to call the living – maimed and whole, widows, orphans, and those too young to have endured the struggle themselves – to let the spirit of Union help repair the wounds of disunion, his words also sought to elevate, confer, and secure through meaningful ritual utterance values transcending any one occasion. Lincoln sought, indeed, to call the making *of* meaning requisite to Union. The task he left to those he called (three times) "us" had not just political, but spiritual import, and so this task had artistic consequences too. This task had a gravity for which words "fitting and proper" must needs be found. It was, as Lincoln made clear in the *Address*, the burden of a mature people, those of a never-again New World, to enter history by acknowledging a past. To admit their wrongs, and to carry this past with due solemnity: Lincoln's message, in W.E.B. Du Bois's later terms, was to dispatch the "weary pilgrims" to the long work of returning their country home.

In Lincoln's final great speech, the *Second Inaugural*, he took up this burden himself. Beginning in the passive voice, the orator's voice does not lead so much as listen; it receives. Bowed, moved, impressed, the speaker asserts no gains – territorial or otherwise – but rather acknowledges existential truths, truths "fundamental and astounding." Far more consequential than the clash of regions was, all along, the fact of indivisible, ineluctable guilt. In Lincoln's *Second Inaugural*, the potential recoil of God Himself from liberty's continent judges sectionalism as a collective sin for which political reunion is necessary but insufficient restitution. Spiritual reunion will have to complete what war and politics cannot. And here, too, Lincoln set out in ritual fashion, his elevated rhetoric exceeding its occasion to strum what he had earlier called "mystic chords of memory."

Whether union itself could heal sectional strain, how America would cohere as a polity, how it should reassemble and reconstruct itself, Lincoln left to the efforts of posterity. Its work would be long. But the grief-work, Lincoln's injunction to recognition, to memory, and to sadness itself as the proper element of national reconciliation, would be, had to be, taken up far sooner. At the end of the Civil War, poetry preceded policy. Artists stepped into the breach to claim and consecrate a new American "land of living," one which "we," the people, lived in together.

But who were "we"?

Answers to this question after the Civil War were not long in coming. When they did come, the reassertion of "region" was closely related to Lincoln's sense that space left unsanctified, like time unimproved, was space whose misuse was on the heads of "the people." Put another way, Lincoln's challenge was to the oft-named "us." Now that the static face-off of North and South had passed, could more mindful living on American ground reawaken the nation's soul?[2] Could the continent, once healed of its wounds, the wounds of section, provide true Union's foundation and embodiment?

In the four studies that make up this chapter – on Sarah Orne Jewett, W.E.B. Du Bois, Edwin Arlington Robinson, and Robert Frost – we shall see the consolidation of regionalism as the region came to be understood as the people's, rather than the section's, sanctuary.[3] What this chapter explores in particular is the region as a stronghold of soul, and the post-bellum rededication of the American continent. Throughout, we shall note the forms and representational modes developed to capture this quality of soul. The bloody contest of North and South that made every region a graveyard brought forth, too, a literature appropriate to the melancholy of the survivors and to the deeper stakes of the national project.

There is an unmistakably elegiac and memorial tone to all of the work I look at here. And yet it is worth pressing beyond this obvious point to describe what is less apparent but still fundamental: literature's emergent role as a genre of tallying, of counting, not just individuals but the collective force of their peoplehood. The regionalism described here evinces regard for the stamp of personality that diversifies the typical, at the same time as it is friendly to rhetorics, formalizations, and the stylized rhythms of speech, work, and song. The poetic, as a bearer of spirit, of ceremony, as culture's genre of self-recognition, acquires new saliency and purpose in this period following the Civil War. In the writings of these four New England authors I treat in this chapter, the common language is deliberately elevated to carry the stately music of civilization. In order to assess the country's diminishment, and then to fortify the courage of a decimated people, language itself had need, these four writers concur, of form.

The argument developed here challenges the arguments of those identifying the regional with perniciously nostalgic impulses, and it also runs counter to those who criticize regional pride as a form of chauvinist exceptionalism.[4] It is not that the regional literatures to emerge in the post-bellum period were innocent of parochial and even reactionary reversions to inwardness. Post-bellum population shifts and the sudden industrialization or deindustrialization of regions brought into relief, and stirred, reactionary forms of nostalgia for native "character."[5] Advances in transportation permitting long-distance travel, plus the rise of tourism, anthropology, and the museum, had their effects, too, making possible easy excursions to unfamiliar sites.[6] But the attentions of New England writers that interest me here had aims subtler than nativism, boosterism, or commodifying the landscape. The hypostases of sectionalism had done this too well. Instead, this chapter focuses on the essentially civic purpose to which such writers as Jewett, Du Bois, Robinson, and Frost dedicated themselves: to save and reclaim the souls sectionalism

163

had bled; to journey to the lost places – the *culs de sac* of the land, the hollows and outcroppings, valleys and mounts where weary pilgrims might join together in procession. All the most telling qualities and attributes that characterize the people – their modes of candor and social intercourse; the mores and institutions they find indispensable; their itineraries quotidian and ceremonial – all these come in for close survey by writers committed to what I call spiritual census-taking.

Ultimately, the censuses of souls taken by writers as various as Jewett, Du Bois, Robinson, and Frost have a common end: to resanctify, reconsecrate, and gather together an imperishable nation, a population of the living and dead. For when is it that a new country becomes a lasting one? Perhaps it is when the poet is called to the census of souls, and the nation turns to its poets. Even if no actual persons, no living, breathing figures are discernible in the frieze or engraving the poet completes, what he or she styles is an American procession, now too advanced in history to go any longer unrecognized.[7] Moreover, as the names, the places, the times of death may be lost, the biographies of individual souls gone missing, the poet's medium of memory must be stylized too. It must ring, echo, sound and resound until individuals, part of the procession, walk in time.

In ways that are already apparent, the literature treated in this chapter is sad. But as Frost avers, and as Lincoln's tone of grief augured, soundness derives from this very sadness. In the decades following the Civil War, the soul of America's oldest regions is heavy with bitter humors: sorrow, melancholy, loneliness, anxiety. But the heaviness also supports a new kind of gravity. Sarah Orne Jewett, my first example, retraces native ground in order to discover this gravity. Her aim is not to worship the soil watered by the fathers, nor to apotheosize those gone, but rather to reconsecrate American land through the knitting of human bonds. In Jewett, healing begins with reacquaintance: her first chapter is called "The Return."

Post-bellum America was a country of returnees, persons for whom homecoming also brought experience of rupture. In Jewett, cycles of homecoming restore and heal a social body no longer young or whole but still susceptible and responsive to care. Thus, the cynosure of the Maine locality Sarah Orne Jewett calls Dunnet Landing is the returning visitor, its most welcome guest. The *Country of the Pointed Firs* refers to the fictional place, Dunnet Landing, visited by the book's narrator, but also to the realm visited by readers, and re-readers, of the book. It is a zone where returning is a first chapter, where the shared past is the beginning. To truly become part of a region, Jewett's book shows, does not require that one farm it, win it in battle, or represent it in government – or even to speak its characteristic idiom. To be of a country is to return to it, to assent to the ways of its company, and so to enjoy a membership that goes deeper than technical citizenship: a sense of history. As Jewett's narrator admits, "I felt something take possession of me which ought to communicate itself to the least sympathetic reader of this cold page. It is written for those who have a Dunnet Landing of their own: who either kindly share this with the writer, or possess another" (Jewett 150).

In its largest sense, this "country" the narrator shares with others, both as region and as book, is nonspecific. Its possession is not a matter of embracing a specific geography but of stopping at a "Landing," sojourning there communicatively. To be sure, one gives up a certain originality in this country, and this is an irony. For the book's narrator is a writer, and her original intention is to find at Dunnet Landing a retreat. This wholly eludes her. A place of comings and goings, of island hoppings, meetings and greetings, Dunnet Landing turns out to be a very bad place indeed to find writerly seclusion or to begin anything of one's own. What she finds instead is a place to pick up the thread, to be knit into partnership. Pressed into helpful service, the book's quiet-seeking author becomes receptionist/cashier/publicist for her landlady, a purveyor of herbal cures. All day long the writer answers her landlady's door; her very sleep is interrupted by the sound of her hostess trampling herbs in the garden. This stately footfall is that of the muse, the soul who presides over *Country of the Pointed Firs*, Mrs Almira Todd:

If Mrs. Todd had occasion to step into the far corner of her herb plot, she trod heavily upon thyme, and made its fragrant presence known with all the rest. Being a very large person, her full skirt brushed and bent almost every slender stalk that her feet missed. You could always tell when she was stepping about there, even when you were half awake in the morning, and learned to know, in the course of a few weeks' experience, in exactly which corner of the garden she might be.

At one side of this herb plot were growths of a rustic pharmacopoeia, great treasures and rarities among the commoner herbs. There were some strange and pungent odors that roused a dim sense and remembrance of something in the forgotten past. Some of these might once have belonged to sacred and mystic rites, and have had some occult knowledge handed with them down the centuries; but now they pertained only to humble compounds brewed at intervals with molasses or vinegar or spirits in a small caldron on Mrs. Todd's kitchen stove.[8] (14)

Gatherer of herbs and gatherer of souls, Mrs Todd's movements in her garden are, the reader comes to see, the overtures of acquaintance. Mrs Todd's very tread is fertile, broadcasting essences, making mystery known. Her skill at compounding simples and poisons keeps the past and present in colloquy. Although she draws her living from the ground, it is not the land *per se* that defines Mrs Todd so much as her skill at dispensing what she grows, her robust conversancy with her environment, natural and cultural:

She stood in the centre of a braided rug, and its rings of black and gray seemed to circle about her feet in the dim light. Her height and massiveness in the low room seemed to give her the look of a huge sibyl, while the stranger fragrance of the mysterious herb blew in from the little garden. (17)

Almira Todd's great facility is for drawing circles about her. Familiarity rather than individuality; hospitality as it welcomes into the indoors and embraces out-of-doors, as it domesticates the foreign and encircles the out-of-place – these characterize Mrs Todd's gift.

Scholars of the past twenty years have rightly adduced such passages in rebuking earlier critical condescensions to Jewett as a "local colorist." And yet I want to suggest that Jewett's text claims for Mrs Todd a gravitas and chthonic force scarcely more comprehended by "New England" than the dramas of Aeschylus are by "Greece." Mrs Todd's depiction makes her so comprehensive, and indeed expansive, as to render inadequate, too, those critical categories too attentive to the female or the private.[9] Like the Greek heroines with whom the narrator compares her, Mrs Todd's potency derives from a deep sadness that draws as much on its mortal as its living qualities. Death is Mrs Todd's – like Emily Dickinson's – "flood subject." Made large by grief, Mrs Todd's mortal wisdom permeates her healing practices. She eases the labor of childbirth but also, with pennyroyal, terminates pregnancies. Treading on "thyme," Mrs Todd's very feet bruise and release the essence of mutability she then boils on her stove. The popularity of her decoctions draws equally from her talent at pharmacopeia and her sympathy bred in sorrow, the palliative cure, which she also dispenses. The healing bundles she gathers do good to her community, but of course the "company" she gathers promotes healing too.

One recalls that it is just this healing – of widow and orphan, wounded and bereaved – that Lincoln called for in his *Second Inaugural Address*. And it is the same healing to which Jewett devotes the central chapters of her book, those chapters concerned with the Bowden family reunion, a gathering of survivors where Union itself is restored. A reunion is a motivated, a meaning-making journey. At a reunion, and indeed along the way of a journey to a reunion, personal incidents have a larger spiritual import.

Jewett underscores this in the deliberate way she slows, halts, and gives reflective pause to the three journeyers on the way to the Bowden reunion. Stops are not just pauses, but stations. For instance, as Mrs Todd, her mother, Mrs Blackett, and the narrator pick their way toward the old Bowden homestead, they pass through a "stone-walled burying-ground that stood like a little fort on a knoll overlooking the bay" (88). As they stand in respectful meditation, Mrs Blackett tallies the list of souls gone but not forgotten. Her census includes "plenty of scattered Bowdens who were not laid there, – some lost at sea, and some out West, and some who died in the war" (88). But it is the war and its wounded that especially haunt the reunion. Then, after the graveyard (itself militarized in the image of a "fort on a knoll"), the journeyers reach a barn with a "stockade of carriages" in it (90), and they give themselves over to Sant Bowden, a "soldierly little figure of a man . . . imperative enough, but with a grand military sort of courtesy" (89).

Sant Bowden is a clearly pitiable figure, in whom the Civil War still rages. Organizing the loose and mostly elderly assortment of relatives into a military parade, Sant discharges martial spirit. Indeed he is over-endowed with this spirit, mustering troops for a "march Decoration Day" or some other, even less suitable event (91). A dysfunctional, broken soul, the embodiment of patriotism, Sant epitomizes a certain regional offensiveness – a righteous sectional-ism – that has not yet laid down its arms. Others also show this tendency. Mrs Kaplin's reflexive policing of bloodlines, Mrs Todd's sometime moody prickliness, her brother William's shyness all have self-protective, border-enforcing aspects. All are susceptible to syn-dromes of inwardness. The larger set of bereft or pitiable characters in Jewett's book – the transcendentally befogged Captain Littlepage, the minister-pedant Reverend, the frail net-maker Mr. Tilley, the recluse Joanna, the unpatriated Anglophile, the Queen's Twin, and here, Sant Bowden – all these are captives of locale. Sant illustrates how those immoderately contextualized, those too much identified with places, become misfits *of* place. On the other hand, the osten-sible local, Mrs Todd, offers in her role as innkeeper something better than indigeneity: courteous exchange. Just as the post-bellum coastal economy will not, in Jewett's book, sustain those tied to pre-war trades and dogmas, so the ministerial intellectualism, Euro-pean nostalgia, or unreconstructed Calvinism of old New England will not sustain cultural vitality.[10] The regionalism capable of survival will instead renew itself through cross-fertilization and hospitality – and, indeed, through acts of inspired, non-bookish reading: of faces, of social cues, and sometimes of much-loved texts.

The Bowden reunion, festive and funereal both, lets national trauma find expression in rituals of communion. The marriage bond that mingles Bowdens with Todds, Blacketts, Tilleys, Kaplins; the evidences of geographical mobility that bring new families to offer doughnuts to wayfarers in "dooryard visits" (82); and the compounded soothing unguents or herbal beers of Mrs Todd's homeopathy – like all of these, the grave peripatetic holiday promotes healing. The re-knitting, the healing of local traumas, personal wounds, and provincial frets must, Jewett's novel argues, depend on something other than the coagulant power of "blood" or even "earth." Jewett's regionalism must, like Mrs Todd's herbalism, wander abroad for its healing simples. Admixture and cross-fertilization are recipes for hardiness, not vitiation. While the ingrown wither, those broadening their circles thrive. Those truly "proficient of soul," as Jewett explains, know, though they live on islands, to return to the common ground of hospitable affection. This ground may be found everywhere:

> St. Theresa says that the true proficiency of the soul is not in much thinking, but in much loving, and sometimes I believed that I had never found love in its simplicity as I had found it at Dunnet Landing in the various hearts of Mrs Blackett and Mrs Todd and William. It is only because one came to know them, these three, loving and wise and true, in their own habitations. Their counterparts are in every village in the world, thank heaven, and the gift to one's life is only in its discernment. (151)

It is fitting, then, that a company of intimates, but one including our narrator, should gather to seal and ratify the book's values in its last chapter. "It is difficult to report the great events of New England," writes Jewett in this final chapter of *Country of the Pointed Firs*; "expression is so slight, and those few words which escape us in moments of deep feeling look but meager on the printed page" (150). The great event to which Jewett refers here is in fact nothing more momentous than the long-deferred, quiet wedding of the elderly William to the shepherdess, Esther, delayed until after the funeral of the bride's mother. Without any boisterousness, this union of two faded souls has both the gravity and the delicacy Jewett's novel has cultivated. Included among the select company permitted to pay their respects to the happy couple, the reader relishing this solemn union will have been well tutored in the proper attitude toward such rites. She will understand that sharing such an event at Dunnet Landing is the gift of civilization itself, a gift of far greater significance than mere attendance at such rites, and one requiring a properly elevated attitude.

Violations, maladroitnesses, breaches of tact, crossings of boundaries are always a threat. But by now the reader has been taught and now understands to shudder at the busybody Mari Harris – she who, on the very day of William's wedding, showed such lack of discretion, such indifference to social cues as to meddle into William's intentions: "'He was all dressed up,' insisted Mari – she really had no sense of propriety. 'I didn't know but they was going to be married?'" (154). Mari Harris, like others liable to pompous or self-assertive claims, shows that the insensitivity is, in fact, the writer's own occupational hazard. After all, writers do pry, and are as hazardous as other meddlesome, wordy types who impose themselves where tact would have had them wait to be asked. It is better, in this sense, to be reader than writer. Best of all: to be a writer with the manners of a reader, a guest or sojourner in the *Country*.[11]

In the end, reading is the ultimate form of tact, and Sarah Orne Jewett assigns readers such an important role in her book to make clear that no attachment to a place, a land or region, makes it a "country," but only courteous extension out of the self, capacity for hospitality, and the gift of sharing. Readers, the consummate visitors, comprise a category of non-native locals who acclimate quickly, crossing the boundaries of the "cold page" undeterred.[12] Those qualities good readers develop make them superior even to mere indigenes. In the writings of Sarah Orne Jewett, the test and the promise of national reunion are in the openness of a reader's heart.

In the pages to come, we shall see how Sarah Orne Jewett's regionalism finds analogue in the regional soul-work and census taking of another New England born – and elegiac – writer, W.E.B. Du Bois. Engaged in reconstructive projects with different stakes but similar methods, Jewett and Du Bois discern, track, record, and, in so doing, honor the expressive folkways, the daily rhythms, norms, and institutions of people rich in what they join in calling soul.

Du Bois's challenge was, of course, different than Jewett's, his burden objectively greater, and it was Abraham Lincoln, in his last great speech, who outlined the work Du Bois would shoulder. In the *Second Inaugural*, Lincoln tore the veil off the nation's unspoken sin of allowing slavery. He tore away, too, the fig leaf of Northern innocence, revealing as false and futile the fiction of geographic quarantine, the too easy division of Northern as well as Southern accountability. As Harriet Beecher Stowe's eye saw not just Southerners but Northerners exploiting, killing, and raping slaves in their own houses, Lincoln knew that the North had always lived under the same roof as the South, however convenient it was to deny. The question Lincoln put in his astonishing speech was whether God should or would abide America; whether a nation, having partitioned itself into sections of imputed meaning, into black and white, would now be allowed to wither within the arid boundaries it had drawn for itself. If the shallowest, most soulless occupation of American space had brought the nation to the tragic situation Lincoln's speech described, could the people be reassembled? And if so, where would the people be found?

Du Bois's answer, like Jewett's, asserts stakes for the reunion higher than those of mere political reconstruction. As in Jewett, so in Du Bois: the soul of the country – whether in Massachusetts, Atlanta, or the Black Belt – is vested in its people, in the sympathetic faculties these people develop, and in the reach of their sympathy across boundaries of space and time. In Du Bois's writing, and especially in *The Souls of Black Folk*, soul will be realized in the transmission across the divides of section and color. Soul is communicative. Once implanted, once disseminated, it contributes to and has claim to what Jewett called the "common inheritance" that cannot be owned but only given and received.

171

Your country? How came it yours? Before the Pilgrims landed we were here. Here we have brought our three gifts and mingled them with yours: a gift of story and song – soft, stirring melody in an ill-harmonized and unmelodious land; the gift of sweat and brawn to beat back the wilderness, conquer the soil, and lay the foundations of this vast economic empire two hundred years earlier than your weak hands could have done it; the third, a gift of the Spirit. Around us the history of the land has centered for thrice a hundred years . . . (*Oxford* 238)

Thus, in the last chapter of his masterpiece, *The Souls of Black Folk*, does Du Bois make his claim and defend his people's contribution to the common inheritance, to a "country" still unestablished. Two gifts – story and song; sweat and brawn – go to make up the last, which is spirit, and it is spirit that turns wilderness into a "country." Passing this spirit from blacks to whites and from America to the whole world, Du Bois insists, is America's only hope for true Union, and for a true and lasting redemption of its history. By proclaiming that the sound of the spiritual, of sorrow songs, hums beneath America's entire development, Du Bois identifies America's racial trauma as its deepest wound and sin, which only acquaintance with, and due counting of, its "black folk" can redeem. At the same time, he makes America itself a work forged of black labor and his people jubilee singers of a nation they themselves created, celebrants of its beauty, chanters of its wealth and its freedom. In Du Bois the "more perfect" Union Lincoln called for awaits a melding of the black and the white that will be achieved by policy alone, but only gradually, holistically, through true spiritual growth.[13] *The Souls of Black Folk* is a journey into the wilderness that persistent sectionalism had preserved.[14]

This final gathering Du Bois envisions – a harmonizing of black voices with white – puts him in the oldest New England tradition. Like a circuit rider or itinerant minister, journeying south from the Housatonic River in Massachusetts to Atlanta, venturing north from Fisk University in Tennessee to Harvard, crisscrossing the Black Belt on foot and via Jim Crow car, Du Bois lets his writing map the itinerary of returnees. Americans in pursuit of soul, weary travelers, seek a far-off home. The spiritual discovery he lets his book perform is his people's, America's own, "on their way."[15] Their region is neither North nor South but a more remote country, defined by its distance from the much-desired destination.

Not rooted or grounded but diasporic – and belonging to no sections at all – Du Bois's American folk, white *and* black, are souls whose home is the road. Their strength is persistence, despite an ever-receding goal. Thus he cites the spiritual: "*Let us cheer the weary traveler, Cheer the weary traveler, Let us cheer the weary traveler / Along the Heavenly way*" (*Oxford* 239). Sectionalism, which split the nation along bloodied regional seams, parceling identities geographically, had segmented the way of both black and white Americans. Du Bois now bids all Americans of the early twentieth century to hear, heed, and cheer those who, singing in processional, stitched and may stitch the ragged and disparate sections of America together. He lets progress depend upon this errand, this itinerary broader than any region or section. One cannot claim a country as one's own who has not walked its roads – from Philadelphia's streets to Atlanta's: who has not wandered from the Housatonic to the Cotton Kingdom. He who has not trodden the dusty steps, ridden the Jim Crow car into and through countries of the black folk, does not know America.

Du Bois's chapters thus grant his native New England, and the North in general, none of the separate chosenness its abolitionist agitators claimed. For Du Bois in *Souls*, New England's own redemption still depends on its reunion with the larger nation to which it belongs. Its pilgrims too are "weary." The book's narrator often has a companion, a Northern and a white one, whom he brings with him to their own shared land behind the veil: "Out of the North the train thundered, and we woke to see the crimson soil of Georgia stretching away bare and monotonous right and left" (*Oxford* 157). There is much for this witness to absorb as the train penetrates historic ground; much to be related to this traveler looking out from the window of the train. "But we must hasten on our journey," reminds the narrator: "If you wish to ride with me you must come into the 'Jim Crow car' . . . Usually the races are mixed in there; but the white coach is all white" (*Oxford* 158). Thus, moving in fan-like forays, tracing through his chapters the tenuous vectors of the rail lines, strumming the expansive mystic chords, Du Bois fills the role of census-taker. House to house, county to county, depot to depot (and, later, nation to nation), Du Bois the soul seeker goes, and he takes with him a companion seeking his own completion and redemption.

What genre, what medium, what method will prove most hospitable to such delicate soul-work? A professionally trained sociologist, his academic education empirical, by the time he writes *Souls of Black Folk*, Du Bois the sociologist has become a poet. And yet the poetics of *The Souls of Black Folk* exhibits, too, the impress of sociology with its empirical exactitude, and the vision of this later book still carries the observant rigor of his earlier. In both groundbreaking works, Du Bois's challenge is to describe a people who are pervasive yet invisible, physically present and yet uncounted in America. To look back, even briefly, at *The Philadelphia Negro* is to see Du Bois developing a means, as Jewett did, to count those not yet counted. What evolves from one book to the next is the meaning of the census; or, we might say, the census as bearer of meaning.

"The final design of the work," writes Du Bois in "Chapter One" of *The Philadelphia Negro: A Social Study*, "is to lay before the public such a body of information as may be a safe guide for all efforts toward the solution of the many Negro problems of a great American city" (1). Technically, the *Philadelphia Negro* confines its attentions to the "long narrow ward, extending from South Seventh street to the Schuylkill River and from Spruce street to South street" (1). Like Jewett, the writer of this text would instill in the public the confidence to draw from narrow glimpses insights much more broadly applicable. Certainly a goal Du Bois, the sociologist, pursues is the improvement of wards like the Seventh. And by recommending the study's findings to "all efforts" made to remedy the "many Negro problems" existing across a range of "great American cities," Du Bois links Philadelphia to other sites, its potential improvement to rehabilitative efforts in other cities. But another – which will prove even more important to Du Bois – is sociology's use as a school for higher forms of sympathy and discernment.

Indeed, Du Bois's Introduction to *The Philadelphia Negro* already makes plain his intention to render his account of conditions in the Seventh Ward in terms capable of stirring broad hope and idealism – terms that address not only one city's ills but the notion of the city itself as an ingathering of striving souls. Thus *The Philadelphia Negro*, a scientific treatise, addresses itself not only to urban planners but to all those whose "heart-quality" will submit facts to the test of "moral conviction" as well as method (3). Du Bois's decision in *The Philadelphia Negro* to perform all census taking himself, rather than relying on the "varying judgments of a score of census-takers," is motivated by the decision that a "personal" sensibility of "unvarying quantity" may restore through "heart-quality" what it sacrifices in cold objectivity (3). Du Bois goes out on a limb to protect this "heart-quality." That is, even before *The Souls of Black Folk*, we see Du Bois taxing himself to discover the proper methods of not only collecting data, but also of harvesting its depth of meaning; its bearing, as it were, on soul. To know a place, whether Spruce Street or Dunnet Landing, requires sensitivity to a place's spirit, that spirit not fully accounted for by local truism or cold scientific objectivity. To discern such spirit will require an investigator capable of going the full emotional distance, of opening the doors to emotional identification and extension. In *The Philadelphia Negro*, not only the questions on the survey but genuine human interest lead the sociologist from door to door.

Thus, in a later itinerant journey, a weary door-to-door, the speaker of *The Souls of Black Folk* relates a drastic sectionalism that impedes understanding, obscures and frustrates the tally of souls. It is impossible not to read irony in such chapter titles as "Of the Meaning of Progress" and "Of the Faith of the Fathers." Progress is a hollow word in those zones, in the zone Du Bois calls the "Black Belt." Planted by Southern slavery (and sectionalism, and secession) but exploited by Northern capitalism, the waste of resources and sapping of human initiative in the Black Belt are, Du

Bois dramatizes, a bitter harvest reaped by both sections. It is not only the ruin of the peculiar institution of slavery that strands the black man in his lazy life. The depredations of Northern capitalists who "rushed down . . . to woo this coy dark soil" continue to sow a fertile regression. Depopulation and waste; persons arrested in invisibility; households but husks of boarding and brick – it is a census-taker's nightmare:

> On we wind, through sand and pines and glimpses of old plantation, till there creeps into sight a cluster of buildings, – wood and brick, mills and houses, and scattered cabins. It seemed quite a village. As it came nearer and nearer, however, the aspect changed: the buildings were rotten, the bricks were falling out, the mills were silent, and the store was closed. Only in the cabins appeared now and then a bit of lazy life. (*Oxford* 163)

The South's "plantation" and the North's "mill" advance each other's ruin, and this process is the same post-bellum as ante-bellum. Such scenes show Reconstruction bringing no genuine freedom but only a devolution into idle misery, an extreme efflorescence of social anomie.

Behind the veil, in fact, the "Union" imposed on South by North acts as a corrosive, atomizing force, breaking down connective social tissue and loosening bonds:

> So we ride on, past phantom gates and falling homes, – past the once flourishing farms of the Smiths, the Gandys and Lagores, – and find all dilapidated and half ruined, even there where a solitary white woman, a relic of other days, sits alone in state among miles of Negroes and rides to town in her ancient coach each day. (*Oxford* 165)

Here the discourse of sociological reportage rendered with full spiritual gravity, demographics as it might be rendered in expressionist art. The most telling phrase, of an almost Scriptural starkness, is "miles of Negroes." Reducing persons to an undifferentiated swarm, making place uncanny with shifting, shadowy movement, the glimpse of the Black Belt given in this phrase is only in part economic. For these miles have lost more, and need more, than commerce; they also have more, and are more, than their poverty. Their obscurity, their darkness, is also in the eye of he who sees them thus.

The sociologist of *The Philadelphia Negro*, the demographer, commences now to find in this belt a robust coherency, to discover how these miles might nevertheless comprise a "complete world." Recognition of persons by persons makes the most unpromising burg into a capital. Thus, the unprepossessing Albany, Georgia is not just a nondescript village but "the centre of the life of ten thousand souls; their point of contact with the outer world, their centre of news and gossip, their market for buying and selling, borrowing and lending, their fountain of justice and law" (*Oxford* 160). To such places, and to places even smaller, even more nondescript, he now goes who would bring progress. "Miles of Negroes" must be disaggregated, and a count of living souls must be undertaken.

As in Jewett, knowledge in Du Bois – full sympathetic knowledge – requires a "return." Prior acquaintance gives history, familiarity, and texture to phenomena obscure and indistinct. The narrator of "The Black Belt," a weary traveler, an itinerant, had gained this understanding in the chapter called "The Meaning of Progress." There, disaggregated from the swarm, suddenly amid the miles, he had found Josie years before:

> There at last I found a little school. Josie told me of it; she was a thin, homely girl of twenty, with a dark-brown face and thick, hard hair. I had crossed the stream at Watertown, and rested under the great willows; then I had gone to the little cabin in the lot where Josie was resting on her way to town. The gaunt farmer bade me welcome, and Josie, hearing my errand, told me anxiously that they wanted a school over the hill; that but once since the war had a teacher been there; that she herself longed to learn, – and thus she ran on, talking fast and loud, with much earnestness and energy. (*Oxford* 132)

The scene is full of what Du Bois in *The Philadelphia Negro* called "heart-quality." The ardency of this Josie with her great vivacity centers the composition, and a richly knit tableau coheres around her. Further, the "progress" initiated by the encounter with Josie leads not out of, but *into* the Black Belt, into the lived reality of Josie's existence behind the veil. For notwithstanding her circumstances, Josie's world has a dynamic internal composition – a there-ness of willowed hill, cabin, and school – from which she draws energy and to which she gives human face. The scene's unities have a compelling power one had not expected. If we imagined the meaning of progress to be a leading *out* of darkness, out of the "Egypt of the Confederacy," out of the Black Belt, we did not entirely comprehend. The lyricism and the personalization making intimate the encounter between the narrator and Josie allow for a far more fundamental kind of progress: understanding. One who has not rested under the willow and then heard Josie's need confessed in the detail that "but once since the war had a teacher been there" has not made the journey in discernment and empathy that is, for Du Bois, precondition to all genuine progress.

Extension of sympathy, along with development of data into images, reportage into history, ungainly vernacular into fullest musical idiom are additional responsibilities borne by a new kind of itinerant "minister": a sociologist seeking soul. Or, might we say: a poet? Du Bois marks the passage into sympathy and thus necessarily beyond what, in *The Philadelphia Negro*, he calls "cold objectivity" by allowing his prose a lyrical and homiletic timbre. Many scholars have been interested in why Du Bois prefaces each of his chapters with bars of music.[16] Here, an additional thought: to imbue observation with vibrancy, part of the necessary work the book's flexible speaker sets himself is to find, as it were, the music of the Black Belt. It is as though the demographer's standard form, the questions to be asked (number of persons, number of rooms, father's occupation, mother's occupation, age of children living at home) secured answers too fast and too thin, crowding out sensibility and absorption. Du Bois's paragraphs give the impression of a sensibility filling the hollow chambers of the statistical. The visitor's experience of the Black Belt is not only of a population but of that population's own lived experience – of its culture – and to render this exacts experiential knowledge. Each confiding or arrogant, yellow or nut brown, wizened or smooth-browed child is set within his clean or dirty, proud or shamefaced genealogy; each child's missed days of school are set within the constraints of the growing season, of the gendered pecking order; each man's ambition or sloth is set against the economic and racial constraints he faces.

The narrator's own trajectory of understanding, his growth, is crucial. As he teaches his charges, his own education progresses: it is the Burkes (with their "great fat white beds" in a room of "bad chromos" who "discreetly [go] away to the kitchen while I went to bed") and the Dowells (with their "four rooms and plenty of good country fare") who in fact give life to these "miles of Negroes" (*Oxford* 134–135). Fullness of experience, soul, throbs in the poorest house – even that of the Eddingtons on whose beds "herds of untamed insects wandered" (*Oxford* 135); and even in the little crude classroom, which, though lacking the "New England vision of neat little desks and chairs," is yet a school: "There they sat, nearly thirty of them, on the rough benches, their faces shading from a pale cream to a deep brown, the little feet bare and swinging, the eyes full of expectation, with here and there a twinkle of mischief, and the hands grasping Webster's blue-black spelling book" (*Oxford* 134). The genre scene, primitive as it is, is imbued with a sympathy and vitality transcending the sociological. Art, the inspired art of the narrator of *The Souls of Black Folk* – a figure no longer simply a sociologist, no longer simply W.E.B. Du Bois – elevates the life of the Black Belt.

And yet that same art, too, has a different function; that same art alienates and distances. Life behind the Veil remains obscure.

For all the richly rendered detail, there yet hangs between this world (the world of Josie and the Black Belt) and the larger world – and between the narrator and his readers too – a barrier, a curtain, a medium of obscurity. Du Bois's highly stylized, highly literary prose stands in for this Veil. The scrim of style, tissued and vibrant but also opaque, falls over and around the brutal facts of African

American life. It separates the writer, his subjects, and his readers, all from the other. It would be wrong to call Du Bois's style artificial, and yet it is rarely simply expository or even frank. Mannered, formal, this style looms the veil.

In the chapter called "The Black Belt," the paragraphs read often more like operatic recitative than prose ("All is silence now, and ashes, and tangled weeds") (*Oxford* 161); the sentences press beyond the denotative into the figurative ("The hill became steep for the quiet old father") (*Oxford* 136); and pulsating rhythms, dreamlike images, accumulate and overtake the narration of events ("Back toward town we glided, past the straight and thread-like pines, past a dark tree-dotted pond where the air was heavy with a dead sweet perfume") (*Oxford* 163). To take in a sentence like this last as a piece of English style, style touched with Tennyson and the Song of Songs, by Whittier and Browning, is to be alerted to the pervasive poeticization of the whole work: to inversions of syntax ("ten miles we have ridden and seen no white face") (*Oxford* 161); to homely folk allusions allowed to ripen ("three hundred lonesome square miles") until they become something more (*Oxford* 160). The allusion to the old song is delicately filigreed with musical alliterations ("three hundred lonesome square miles of land, without train or trolley") and then made, through expressionistic repetition, to vibrate and thrum ("in the midst of cotton and corn") (*Oxford* 160). The tone of the writing is lent, through these stylistic refinements, a distance, an archaism so rich it can even accommodate allegory:

> Three hundred bales of cotton went through it last year. Two children he has sent away to school. Yes, he says sadly, he is getting on, but cotton is down to four cents; I know how Debt sits staring at him. (*Oxford* 161)

It is as if one stood at the perpendicular, staring down the axis of the Veil that separates those outside from understanding those inside, not only those inside but both prevented from achieving full personhood. The function of the errand on which Du Bois leads his readers, and the meaning of the progress he deems possible, converge. Indeed, the further one goes, the more conscious of the veil one becomes: its obscurity thickens.

Du Bois's prose epitomizes the quality one notices in much regional American literature of the nineteenth century's final years: a tone of melancholy habituated to ruin. Dramatic but not psychological, registering grief as an undercurrent afflicting whole populations, the tone describes a general mood which, once acknowledged, has convening power and thus spiritual force. Within this tone's echo, readers and indeed all Americans may find the venerable, collective relations that make of mere persons, souls.

The souls Du Bois describes abide in a region that America's racial history makes ineluctably separate, but they share, too – and this is part of what informs Du Bois's tone with hope of reunion – the sadness that is the common inheritance of post-bellum America. Like Lincoln, Du Bois sees the salutary virtues of this sadness, its power to heal sectional wounds. And so too do the two poets to whom we can now turn, Edwin Arlington Robinson and Robert Frost. These poets, from the vantage point of their own ruined and abandoned regions, let their poetry mark an epochal turn in the national culture.

Yet who shall hear these poets? Who, assembling these scattered souls, living and dead, shall resurrect the voice of "the people"? As I have been arguing, the question haunts New England's literature of the post-bellum period. It also explains regionalism's backward-looking temper, and the civic attentiveness of its poets. The burden of commemoration, the poet's classic office, is to set heterogeneous and inchoate materials in forms capable of persistence. To engrave an image with the perseverant earliness one sees on shields or coins; to raise an echo like a bas relief, its archaism rounded and reverberant – this is the thrust of this post-bellum work of recovery. These New Englanders retrieve from heterogeneity and mutability the many forgotten dead, gathering the spirit of them in their manyness. Thus a nation recovers the *e pluribus unum*. What individual figures have been, who they were, may be unrecoverable. But the impress of these figures can be recovered; their spirit may, in fact, be more resonant once it is non-identical with personhood.

181

Statuary is the art form traditionally best adapted to this task, as William James (at the time) and Robert Lowell (later) expressed in their commemorative works on Saint-Gaudens's beautiful bas relief of the Massachusetts 54th. Indeed, Lowell, to whom we return in Chapter 8, turns over whole volumes to such artisanal service. Lowell lets his sonnets' formality, even their sometimes stiffened, armored, and weighted quality, signal history's historicity, its heaviness on its pedestal. Before Lowell, though, Robert Frost and, before Frost, Edwin Arlington Robinson took up the classic responsibility that falls to the national poet: convening power.

Edward Arlington Robinson is not appreciated enough for the great civic poet he was, and for the way his poetry gathers in, even as it pities, the social body. Diminishment, especially social diminishment, and reduction, in particular the insidious fall from pride to mere boast or grandiosity – these, in Robinson, are conveyed in language itself orotund with bad faith. Indeed, Robinson's most profound contribution to American poetry is the haunting collective voice of a populace not fully a "people." Along with a small-minded "us" and a grasping "our," Robinson's "we" is the voice of a self-promoting, yet degraded, social consensus. The loss of vital ancestry, of the dead, is compounded by the negligent vacuousness of lesser heirs.

"We go no more to Calverly's" is the first line of the poem called "Calverly's," in *The Town Down the River*. First published in 1910, the volume's voice is that of the unsaved remnant. A weak "we," a soulless, posthumous people breathes its small sureties and imposes its nervous concerns. Without vision or mastery, but only "fond self-shadowings," this "we" has its most honest moments when it admits itself remaindered:

> We go no more to Calverly's
> For there the lights are few and low;
> And who are there to see by them
> Or what they see, we do not know.
> (1920: 330)

Set in a Maine town decimated by war and hopelessness, "Calverly's" is a regional poem and a poem reflecting on region's false consciousness, on the constitution of a "there" by those who need it to be there. "Calverly's" is the generic name for a place where toasts are drunk and strained jollity raises the night's nobody to a hero; it is the symbolic name for hale fellowship rendered imperishable by recollection. Having once sung and been sung about, having lifted voices in company, the "we" preserves a kind of vitality not to be confused with life. "No fame delays oblivion / Yet Something else survives," writes Robinson in the similar "Scattered Lives." In Calverly's, the shoulder to shoulder of iambic singsong gives each barfly his dubious immortality:

> There'll be a page for Leffingwell,
> And one for Lingard, the Moon-calf;
> And who knows what for Clavering,
> Who died because he couldn't laugh?
> Who knows or cares? No sign is here,
> No face, no voice, no memory;
> No Lingard with his eerie joy,
> No Clavering, no Calverly.
>
> (330–331)

Formal finish, allusions to the poetic only intensify the hollowness, the sense that Leffinwell, Lingard, and Clavering will never achieve any better commemoration than in the fond stylizations of the drinking song. Such stylization deceives, for it blurs distinctions and obscures the foolishness of persons. "Calverly's," however, has soul, though bleak soul. It arranges its insignificant actions on a frieze where their insignificance, their lack of distinct individuality, may sound. In composition, "scattered lives" cohere.

A more extreme case, "The House on the Hill" is a poem without content: a song sung to be sung, a song guiding the singer by the hand. Its Beckett-like etiolations are summed up in the refrain, "There is nothing more to say." The plain effort to go on, to put one foot ahead of the other, becomes poetry:[17]

> They are all gone away,
>   The House is shut and still,
> There is nothing more to say.

> Through broken walls and gray
>> The winds blow bleak and shrill:
> They are all gone away.

> Nor is there one today
>> To speak them good or ill:
> There is nothing more to say.

(81)

"The House on the Hill" may describe, gesture toward, what seems a conventional romantic ruin. And yet, it is as though the house were mere prop, an occasion for a poem but not its subject. Rather, the poem's power derives from the somnambulistic transactions of a "we" and a "they." The chronic, apparently routinized recitation of "their" absence "today" is no different from their absence any other day. "Today" is as gratuitous and place-filling a detail as the automatic "more" in "nothing more to say." Overextended and truncated, the poem's triplets proliferate to no purpose. "Shut and still," "bleak and shrill," "good or ill" are shibboleths, sterile pairs mustered for rhyme's sake, each rung through its predictable variations. Robinson makes clear, though, how the urgency to say is not exhausted, but rather stimulated, by having nothing to say. The urge to expression births a final superfluity, a four-line refrain:

> There is ruin and decay
>> In the House on the Hill:
> They are all gone away,
>> There is nothing more to say.

(82)

Look, these verses say, "we" talk, and "we talk in rhyme."

Reading the Maine depressive Robinson, one thinks back with longing to Jewett, for whom "those few words that escape us in moments of deep feeling look but meager on the page." Meagerness is the keynote in Robinson, and individual psychology is a straitjacket, always preventing any genuine human contact. For Jewett deep feeling may, through forms of social intercourse (friendship,

184

reading), soften rigid forms. In Robinson, a less consoling writer, human bravado and the burdens of self-presentation turn persons and even societies toward static, repetitive enactments of roles. Robinson's gift is to show the vocal, and thus spiritual, range narrowed by the pinch of repressive discipline and by the exigencies of false cheer. Violent, stigmatizing explosions of internal pressure (the suicide of Richard Cory, the grief-maddened destructiveness of Reuben Bright) prompt Robinson's "we" to sterner constraints on the self. So plated are the lives Robinson's poetry treats, they sacrifice all meditative poise, all breathing space. What these lives have instead of feeling is frontage and gait. And yet, how much tragic feeling, how much the chafed will struggles to make its voice sound, to sing a song of – anything.

Robinson's attachment to traditional form and his social pessimism are, in other words, darkly complementary. The more finished the verse, the more tortuously rationalized and patted into graceful form, the more vacant the thing that lies beneath. Robinson's poetry enacts again and again the hardening of repression in reaction formation, the freezing of internal life in mere acting, in the scabbard of social performance. Can we credit the querulous, swaying music of learned compromise? Should we pity or reject the hacking rhythms, or ingratiating fluency, or urgent pounding stresses in which grief – inchoate, savage, wordless – finds form? How but with irony to see the transparent falsities of the drinking song, the dandy's tuneful humming, the ode's base flattery? Form's very stiffness, its unyieldingness in Robinson describes its too desperate purposes. Form facilitates repression, endurance, dissimulation. Form schools the hardening, the falsifying of the human voice.

And yet: would it be better for Eben Flood to stumble and fall splayed on the ground, or is it better that he adjust his gait to tetrameter and he himself to his drinking place? Would it be better for the wife in "Eros Turranos" to spit out the truth of her husband's mendacity; or (for her own sake, for his, for those who pity them both) to stay in rhythm and on course down the slope of evasions that the poem's stanzas provide? Ought we distrust on principle all

185

nimbleness, all brilliancy, just because Richard Cory puts a bullet to his head and because we knew, always knew, that he would?

Not so, Arlington Robinson's poetry suggests, unless we would mute the very human comedy, the pathetic pageant souls put on – their dances with many veils. Every form in Robinson is heavy with the history of its usage, ponderous or worn thin from the weight of human feeling it must carry. Human culture's self-per-petuating repetitions are, Robinson shows, also its signs of conscious life. Tradition's inwrought music – the filigree of stanzas, the delib-erateness of meter, blank verse's dogged stamina – describes civiliza-tion's persistence, soul's self-preservation. Lost souls find no more fitting medium to conduct movements out of time and into eternity than that most measured of disciplines, poetry. In the work of Edwin Arlington Robinson, poetry is where we live. In the formal frieze of social routine, in the mellifluous falsities of inherited utterance, souls in procession sing their hearts out.

By the time Robert Frost titled his second volume a "Book of People," he had in Edwin Arlington Robinson the example of the New England regionalist as sad national tribune. It is this role he develops most amply in his most under-read volume, the book called *New Hampshire*. There, Frost's speaker comes "as census-taker to the waste / To count the people in it" (174).

A curio cabinet of congealed folkways, artifacts, and meanings, *New Hampshire* is a work of collective cultural salvage. From its over-specified title through its various excursions down arcane lanes of forgotten folkways, through its evocation of defunct customs, norms, and myths, the book takes as given the "scattering" of lives, and it applies itself to recovering such old forms and advancing their rehabilitation. The necessary petrification of all unique things, along with the precious endowment of the given, raise the question (a cultural as well as a poetic one), "what to make of a diminished thing?" (120) To retrieve from dishonor, to protect from annihilation things brought low; but more: to reinstate within the longer proces-sion, to record in the tally what no longer lives as fact or person – such is the nature of the census Frost performs. Frost captures the stoical, weight-bearing quality of the poet's task when he writes in the volume's title poem "New Hampshire," "No state can build / A literature that shall at once be sound / And sad on a foundation of well-being" (168). History, and poetry itself, both weigh on the speaker of "The Census-Taker," as he admits, "The melancholy of having to count souls / Where they grow fewer and fewer every year / Is extreme where they shrink to none at all" (176). So, too, then, the melancholy of a writer inheriting from Robinson the evacuated and increasingly brittle structures of New England expressiveness: this tradition's reticences and discretions, its custom of obscurity, its provincial way of talking to itself. The opportunity to take the world as one finds it, to make do with the materials given, is an obligation Frost never evades. Nor does he evade its grief.

In particular, in *New Hampshire*, Frost explores both the comic and tragic aspects of regional ingrowth and involution, of sectional pride as it preserves eccentricity. He explores the desiccation of life itself, of soul, as New England's principles (retained, naturally, *on* principle) calcify. "New Hampshire," the title poem of the volume, is a sportive verse disquisition on local pride as planned inutility, while the second poem, "Star in a Stoneboat," makes mischief with the idea of indigeneity. It finds in the Granite State's very building blocks, its stones, only the most spurious foundation. But by the volume's third poem, "The Census-Taker," satire and mischief bottom out in darkness. "The Census-Taker" gives a fearsome account of a world abandoned to indigeneity: "I came," the poem begins,

> an errand one cloud-blowing evening
> To a slab-built, black-paper-covered house
> Of one room and one window and one door,
> The only dwelling in a waste cut over
> A hundred square miles around it in the mountains:
>
> (174)

Frost's "census-taker" arrives at a world in sectional extremis, a world cut off even from itself. Ad hoc combinations ("slab-built"; "black-paper-covered") belie claims of purpose and integrity. The region now flayed by weather and abandonment always cut and

187

built waste, always made not wholeness but the makeshift. The houses "slab-built, black-paper-covered," the gouged-out forest are what remains of a way of regional life always cutting itself down, cut off and sterile ("It never had been dwelt in, though, by women," the poet reminds us).

Thus, the poet tallies the spiritual consequences of such wastage: a country where "the people" are not to be found:

> I came as census-taker to the waste
> To count the people in it and found none,
> None in the hundred miles, none in the house,
> Where I came last with some hope, but not much,
> After hours' overlooking from the cliffs
> An emptiness flayed to the very stone.
>
> (174)

In this poem of the aftermath, the phrase "the people" is allowed to vibrate between its plural sense (multiple persons) and the more abstract one, where many-ness becomes spiritualized and the people become the People. Denuded not only of its trees, but of the very human life the logging of these trees was to have warmed, this landscape is stripped of everything that could supply human interest. Not a tree stands. That flutter of fall crimson Frost so often lets stand for human desire ("Without a single leaf to spend on autumn," "Or branch to whistle after what was spent") is long past: no flirtation, no consummation, no heartsick grief rouses this landscape. Rather life breeds non-life, like the tree "bringing out its rings in sugar of pitch," luxuriantly (175). "An emptiness flayed to the very stone" shows the region skeletonized, the human visage in every doorway melted off the landscape's very bones (174).

Is it a solace then? Or is it a mere symptom of his melancholy that the speaker, lacking even one soul to count, lets himself go in reverie, lets himself fancy that the wind "said something of the time / Of year or day"?

> the way it swung a door
> Forever off the latch, as if rude men
> Passed in and slammed it shut each one behind him
> For the next one to open for himself.

I counted nine I had no right to count
(But this was dreamy unofficial counting)
Before I made the tenth across the threshold.
(175)

Who is it the speaker counts here? Whom would he resurrect, or
kill, as he girds himself to fight the very skeletons, arming himself
with the "pitch-blackened stub of an ax-handle / I picked up off
the straw-dust-covered floor"? Again, one does well to note the
mortared hyphenates, for they convene not only the materials, but
the makers, of long departed axes; they conjure the men who kicked
up dust. These with their human industry, their ad hoc carelessness,
made a human racket and at least left someone housekeeping to do.
These departed souls, counted by the census-taker, comprised a
human company: life lived where they did. Their very negligence
and rudeness carved human print.

In their wake, what can human beings do but declare their own
peoplehood in counting what is gone? "Where was my supper?
Where was anyone's? / No lamp was lit. Nothing was on the table.
/ The stove was cold – the stove was off the chimney" (175). The
depression the census-taker records in this deserted logging cabin is
one felt for lost civilizations, and it is epic loss he acknowledges:
"the houses / Fallen to ruin in ten thousand years / Where Asia
wedges Africa from Europe" (176). And yet, in uttering, in singing
the loss, the poet assumes a civic and civil office: he joins that procession to which he himself, tenth through the door, belongs.
Whether it is pacing through wilderness as demographer or verse
maker, or as the public servant who combines both functions, the
reason for his errand is to sound the cry.

Art's census, Frost shows, no less than the demographer's, preserves the forms souls know to hearken to. Like the narrator of *The
Souls of Black Folk*, like Mrs Todd in her doorway, and like the "we"
who haunt Calverly's, Frost's census-taker finds in the New England
region a civilization souls make:

"The place is desert, and let whoso lurks
In silence, if in this he is aggrieved,

189

Break silence now or be forever silent.
Let him say why it should not be declared so."

(176)

Will he find one soul to answer in the waste of New England?
One thing is for sure: the land itself will not count him, will not
confer on him existence. Only answering echo, countervoice breaking the silence, will. The errand to count souls, as vital as any in
post-bellum America, is reconsecrated in Frost's "The Census-Taker."
Drawing force and conviction from earlier literary census takings,
the poem claims candidly, nakedly, its need for the human striving
company that gives the people life:

"It must be I want life to go on living."

Notes

1 No one writing on Lincoln's poetics can afford to miss Allen Grossman's great essay, "The Poetics of Union in Whitman and Lincoln"
(see Michaels and Pease, *The American Renaissance Reconsidered*). As I
have acknowledged before, the impact of Grossman's teaching and his
work on me extends beyond his treatment of Lincoln to his treatment
of human values and of the human as they are sustained in the forms
of poetry. As a teacher and poet, Grossman cherishes form, and he
maintains and renews the forms of the past, letting his lines sound
the meters, flow into the shaped stanzas, and return again and again
to those places where, apostrophic, his precursors broke silence with
speech. As a literary critic, Grossman never loses sight of language's
greatest office: to sound and to preserve the sounds of human speech.
Poetry, for Grossman, is essentially language lent to persistent value
and to the persistence itself. In this sense, Lincoln is a poet, an artist,
and a theorist of crafted language. What he marked out at Gettysburg
was a rhetorical and poetic as well as physical field. For further analysis of Grossman and his poetics see my entry, "Allen Grossman," in
Haralson, *The Encyclopedia of American Poetry*. On Civil War death
counts and death ways, see also *Lincoln at Gettysburg* by Gary Wills;
The Language of War: Literature and Culture in the US from the Civil War

190

to the Second World War by James Dawes; *America's God: From Jonathan Edwards to Abraham Lincoln* by Mark Noll; and *This Republic of Suffering: Death and the American Civil War* by Drew Faust. See also the classic studies, *Patriotic Gore* by Edmund Wilson and *Trumpets of Jubilee* by Constance Rourke.

2   In highlighting "soul" and in emphasizing souls as opposed to, say, citizens in post-bellum American culture I am not seeking re-exceptionalize or sacralize Americans, or to re-mystify the rights and duties of responsible and accountable citizenship. The constitution of a representative, enfranchised, protected citizenry was, as such critics as Priscilla Wald, Saidiya Hartman, Brook Thomas, and Nan Goodman have all shown, a major cultural work of the period. Indeed, just what uphill work it was to constitute a citizenry fully representative is reflected in the titles of their books. See Wald, *Constituting Americans: Cultural Anxiety and Narrative Form*; Hartman, *Scenes of Subjection: Terror, Slavery and Self Making in Nineteenth-Century America*; Thomas, *American Literary Realism and the Failed Promise of Contract*; Goodman, *Literature, Law, and the Theory of Accidents in Nineteenth-Century America*.

My work in this chapter is meant to pursue something different from citizenship. In emphasizing soul, I attend not to the rights and recognition of individuals – to the way in which each person must count – but to the necessity of a *count*, of spiritual census-taking as it is achieved in literary language. Taking my language from Jewett and Du Bois, I probe the meanings of "soul" and "souls" for writers of the period, and I try to describe the way in which the activity of counting souls enters the repertoire, becomes a test, of the American writer. I do so, first, in hopes of excavating, of bringing into view a dispositive, pivotal epoch in what we might call the history of American hope – the epoch, not incidentally, that saw the emergence of Jamesean pragmatism. With Richard Rorty, who described the function of Jamesean hope in his book, *Achieving our Country*, I argue here, as I did in *The Line's Eye*), for literature as it realizes belief.

3   The post-bellum period saw sectional hardenings and the calcification of regional stereotypes so chauvinistic as now to seem very crude, even grotesque. Moral triumphalists of every region assumed that virtue was their special province, while regional and ethnic humor was so dominant in the culture as to comprise nearly all of what was called humorous. The classic treatments of American humor are nearly all catalogues of different regional or ethnic types. See Constance Rourke, *American*

Humor; Walter Blair and Hamlin Hill, *America's Humor*; Robert Hendrickson, *American Talk*; Daniel Hoffman, *Form and Fable in American Fiction*; and, for a roundup of Civil War regional truisms, see Daniel Aaron's "Writers and Politics" in *The Unwritten War*. But the stage for post-bellum typing was already set, as Lawrence Buell has written, in the ante-bellum period. As Buell explains, both Connecticut Federalist Timothy Dwight and, several generations on, civil dissident Henry David Thoreau "contemplated with grim relish the possibility that the American union might dissolve, and they were emboldened to do so because they believed that New England's moral fiber and institutions were sounder than those of the other regions. Thoreau on the necessity of keeping Massachusetts free of the slaveholding influence is a reincarnation of Dwight on keeping Connecticut free of Jeffersonianism" (Buell, *New England Literary Culture*, 323–324).

The nineteenth-century depth of investment in sectionalism explains why Frederick Jackson Turner, best known for his "frontier" thesis, worked even harder and assumed he'd make his mark as a scholar of "sectionalism." It was against this older, more established, idea in American culture that Turner's famous "frontier thesis" was counterpoised. For Turner, the experience and the narrative of frontier endowed Americans with a shared history of trial and error, an ever-beginning and renewable sense of life's plasticity. Sectionalism, Turner was convinced, had always been the greatest threat to this ethos of the frontier. In his landmark essay, "The Significance of the Section in American History," Turner quotes the Whig Platform of 1858, letting Lincoln himself make the case against sectionalism. As Lincoln warns, "formed by the conjunction in political unity of widespread geographical sections, materially differing not only in climate and products, but in social and domestic institutions . . . any cause that shall permanently array the different sections of the Union in political hostility and organized parties, founded only on geographical distinctions, must inevitably prove fatal to a continuance of the national Union" (Turner, *The Significance of the Section*, 199).

See Philip Fisher's *Still the New World* for a brilliant argument that updates Frederick Jackson Turner's thesis by insisting that post-bellum American literature holds the frontier open. For Fisher, an ethos of "creative destruction" has always prevailed and still does to this day. He argues that the market and the transportation systems that link isolated communities cut through other forms, especially ethnic forms, of membership. However, this is not only because of America's essentially deracinating tendencies but also because the value of variety, of fundamentally religious and Calvinist derivation, sees identity as inconsistent with soul.

4   See, for instance, Gillman and Zagarell's chapters in *New Essays on Country of the Pointed Firs*, edited by June Howard. Both offer readings that seek to lay bare the "nativist" or "nationalist" tenor of Jewett's book, readings that assume Jewett's "inclusive and restrictive" use of regionalism. Zagarell, interpreting Jewett's sentence, "We possessed the instincts of a far, forgotten childhood; I found myself thinking that we ought to be carrying green branches and singing when we went," writes: "These references are instances of Hellenism, the celebration of the cultural superiority of Greece that flourished in Europe and the United States in the nineteenth century and that, as Martin Bernal has shown, had strong racial overtones" (53). I wonder though if Michael Bell is not right in wondering whether readings of so strong a "polemical or even political intention . . . may tend less to overcome this marginalization than to perpetuate it" (*The Problem of American Realism* 70–71). Against the suspicious reading of Zagarell, Tom Lutz makes an interesting case for the "cosmopolitanism" of recent literary historical trends, showing how critics treating the work of "local colorists" assume cosmopolitan positions when the "exclusivity" of writers under discussion would seem to require a larger, more generous critical view. See Lutz's excellent wide-ranging work on the history of regionalism, *Cosmopolitan Vistas, American Regionalism and Literary Value*, which chronicles a history of narrow cosmopolitanisms, including our own. See also, *No more Separate Spheres: a Next Wave American Studies Reader* edited by Cathy Davidson and Jessamyn Hatcher, which endeavors to overcome rather than perpetuate the marginalization Bell warns of. The correctives offered in its excellent introduction, and the spirited debate conducted in its pages, are worth attention. The volume tracks, as Lutz's book does also, the critical notions passing through their own stages of creative destruction.

5   The classic statement of this case comes in Werner Berthoff's still magisterial *The Ferment of Realism*. There Berthoff writes, "The prime source of imaginative energy in American local-color writing was in the tension put upon the older agrarian–mercantile order of life by its triumphant industrial successor" (90) and calls typical of local color

"the huddled courage of resistance to a fundamentally ruthless and destructive pattern of outward history" (97). But Berthoff himself is unwilling to call the work, at least the best of it, nostalgic, rather arguing, as I do, that the images it yields compose the fragments of a book of the people, "an essential history of their lives' common conditioning" (100). Again, see also Lawrence Buell's pithy work on local color in *New England Literary Culture*, especially the wonderful section, "New England as a Country of the Imagination: The Spirit of Place."

6 New understanding of the importance of ethnography and of cultural, racial, and ethnic differences as objects of study distinguishes some of the most interesting work of the last decade. Some excellent works on the culture as object include Nancy Bentley's *The Ethnography of Manners*; Steven Conn's *Museums and American Intellectual Life*; Sarah Blair's *Henry James and the Writing of Race and Nation*; and Bill Brown's *The Material Unconscious: American Amusement, Steven Crane and the Economics of Play*.

7 These were writers dedicated, as Werner Berthoff once put it, to composing the "fragments of a book of the people, an essential history of their lives' common conditioning" (*Ferment* 100).

8 See Ammons's "Jewett's Witches" in *Critical Essays on Sarah Orne Jewett* (ed. Gwen L. Nagel) for a thorough and fascinating treatment of Mrs Todd as herbalist.

9 See, for example, Elizabeth Ammons and Valerie Rohy's *American Local Color Writing 1880–1920*, an anthology organized to show the "relationship of local color writing to structures of dominant power" (viii), with gender and race treated focally, and Fetterly and Pryse's *American Women Regionalists, 1850–1910*, which admires how regionalism creates a "climate within which writers can avoid reliance on sexist, racist, or classist stereotypes in the depiction of character" (xviii). Study of such literature can, its editors promise, provide a foundation for "a feminist literary that has evolved from literary practice" (xx). The best critic treating imperialist ideology as it penetrates and permeates local and "feminine" spaces is Amy Kaplan. See Kaplan's *The Anarchy of Empire in the Making of US Culture* as well as her earlier *The Social Construction of American Realism*. June Howard's recommendation, to which I subscribe myself, is that Jewett ought to be read, not alongside regionalists and not alongside women, but "with other authors of the late nineteenth and early twentieth cen-

turies who are striving to tell a 'story of civilization'" ("Unraveling" 379).

10   "Reading," as Fetterly and Pryse note eloquently in their anthology of *American Women Regionalists*, is a synonym for listening, and regional texts thus are a place of "empathic connection" (xvii).

11   The role of the market in replacing this older form of "exchange" is the subject of much excellent critical work which treats the Civil War as a chronological dividing line separating the agrarian, localized culture of the ante-bellum period from the urban, interstate, and interregional markets of post-bellum America. Richard Brodhead's excellent *Cultures of Letters* is exemplary. Brodhead's excellent treatment of Louisa May Alcott as prototypical writer, "Starting Out in the 1860's," focuses on Alcott's discovery of a new market niche in *Little Women*, in which "letters" is a culture supplanting that of any place. Brodhead's reading of local color writers, including Jewett, argues that regionalism provided various kinds of access: to impecunious locals who gained access to circulating media as promulgators of regional authenticity, and to well-heeled tourists eager to consume, as tourists, lost portions of America. Amy Kaplan has also argued persuasively for how post-bellum commercialization of regions offered new opportunity to writers steering the novel between other social practices, including journalism and popular fiction. Another strong general essay concerned with local color realism in the marketplace is Louis Budd's essay, "The American Background" in the *Cambridge Companion to Realism and Naturalism*.

12   The role of Jamesean belief, and not just subversion or double consciousness, has been underestimated in studies of Du Bois, but it is a crucial factor in such essentially pragmatist and optimistic works as *The Souls of Black Folk*. *Souls* is a text that, as Arnold Rampersad argued, would "convert and . . . seduce the American people, white and black, into sharing Du Bois's optimistic view of black culture" (68). Suspicion of the optimistic and prophetic aspects of Du Bois's work is currently running high. A new collection, *W.E.B. Du Bois on Race and Culture*, erring on what James called the "toughminded" side, collects skeptical and materialist essays and excludes those focused on "soul." Rampersad's closing essay in that collection gently queries this approach, reminding how much *The Souls of Black Folk* gave Du Bois "latitude for an exploration of racial meanings not only in the areas of history and sociology but also in art, religion, and psychology"

(301). Rampersad's superb interpretive biography of Du Bois, from which I have learned much, rather argues that the "greatness of *The Souls of Black Folk* . . . lies in its creation of profound and enduring myths about the lives of the people" (Rampersad 88).

13   Eric Sundquist, in his 1982 essay "The Country of the Blue," pointed to what he called, eloquently, the "agony of retrospect" (*Realism* 9), arguing for the influence of the Civil War on Mark Twain – who showed in *Pudd'nhead Wilson* and other works that the Civil War was not a "clean break." But he points out too that Melville and Hawthorne's works "preced[ing] the Civil War" seem "in retrospect . . . to have comprehended in advance its effects and aftermath." Sundquist's later treatment of post-bellum literature in *To Wake the Nations* is the best account of this "agony of retrospect" that I here apply to Jewett, Du Bois, and Robinson.

14   I mean for this discussion to build on the work of others in developing understanding of Du Bois as an essentially pragmatic, optimistic, and faith-based thinker. Cornel West pioneered this line of inquiry in *The American Evasion of Philosophy*. Important contributions to the field include Ross Posnock's *Color and Culture*; Mike Magee's *Emancipating Pragmatism*; Len Gougeon's *Virtue's Hero*.

15   Julia Bader's treatment of "ghost-towns" argues that the "scenes of dissolving vision" behind the realist narrative "intimate the existence of a world beneath or beyond this one, which is *in*comprehensible and *dis*ordered" (Sundquist, *American Realism* 198). Or, as she puts it elsewhere, these scenes mark a place of "emotional devastation." As with other criticism assuming realism and verisimilitude to control threats of "emotional devastation" particular to women, Bader's observations, I think, limit themselves. She is hardly wrong, but perhaps she stops too soon. As I try to show in this chapter, in the literature of the period, the devastation of dissolving vision and the countervailing emphasis on forms of consensus pertain not just to women but to the whole disunified people.

16   Though Robinson's *oeuvre* is too large, and can seem dated and mannered in its tones, his omission from such accounts of American poetry as Jay Parini's *Columbia History of American Poetry*, or, more precisely, the reduction of his *oeuvre* to a vestibule for Frost to pass through, tipping his hat at his mentor, seems unfortunate. Parini is wrong, as Pearce was, to reduce Robinson's accomplishment to transforming the "egocentric nineteenth-century poem into a vehicle to

196

express the exhaustion and failure of its primary impulse" (260). It is not the exhaustion of the ego that Robinson so much chronicles as that of the social ethos, of the "people."

17 I propose here, in other words, something different than has been said of Robinson ever since Frost called Robinson "a poet with an old-fashioned way to be new," so prompting critics to follow in probing the extent of Robinson's application of old forms to new materials. Still the best of these is J.G. Levenson's "Robinson's Modernity," which points out that, forms aside, in Robinson "[d]oubt is certain, disbelief plausible, despair sympathetic, and hope obscure," and, moreover, that Robinson "derived these principles not only from temperament and the circumstances of his private experience, but also from the cultural situation of his time" (Barnard 158). Levenson's tour of Jamesean despair and the will to believe seems to me altogether apt. Yet against, or in an overlay, I would hold for the rapid aging of Robinson's world, an aging of America that rediscovers the sheltering utility of the old.

References

Aaron, Daniel. *The Unwritten War: American Writers and the Civil War.* New York: Alfred Knopf, 1973.

Ammons, Elizabeth, and Valerie Rohy, eds and intro and notes by. *American Local Color Writing: 1880–1920.* New York: Penguin, 1998.

Barnard, Ellsworth, ed. *Edward Arlington Robinson: Centenary Essays.* Athens: University of Georgia Press, 1969.

Bell, Bernard W., Emily Grosholz, and James B. Stewart. *W.E.B. Du Bois on Race and Culture: Philosophy, Politics and Poetics.* New York: Routledge, 1996.

Bell, Michael Davitt. *The Problem of American Realism: Studies in the Cultural History of a Literary Idea.* Chicago: University of Chicago Press, 1993.

Bentley, Nancy. *The Ethnography of Manners.* Cambridge: Cambridge University Press, 1995.

Berthoff, Warner. *The Ferment of Realism: American Literature, 1884–1919.* New York: The Free Press, 1965.

Blair, Sarah. *Henry James and the Writing of Race and Nation.* Cambridge: Cambridge University Press, 1996.

Blair, Walter, and Hamlin Hill. *America's Humor: From Poor Richard to Doonesbury*. New York: Oxford University Press, 1978.

Brodhead, Richard, ed. *Cultures of Letters. Scenes of Reading and Writing in Nineteenth-Century America*. Chicago: University of Chicago Press, 1993.

Brown, Bill, *The Material Unconscious: American Amusement, Stephen Crane and the Economies of Play*. Cambridge, MA: Harvard University Press, 1996.

Budd, Louis. "The American Background." *The Cambridge Companion to American Realism and Naturalism: From Howells to London*. Ed. Donald Pizer. Cambridge: Cambridge University Press, 1995.

Buell, Lawrence. *New England Literary Culture: From Revolution through Renaissance*. Cambridge: Cambridge University Press, 1986.

Conn, Steven. *Museums and American Intellectual Life*. Chicago: University of Chicago Press, 1998.

Davidson, Cathy, and Jessamyn Hatcher, eds. *No More Separate Spheres: A Next Wave American Studies Reader*. Durham: Duke University Press, 2003.

Dawes, James. *The Language of War: Literature and Culture in the U.S. from the Civil War to the Second World War*. Cambridge, MA: Harvard University Press, 2002.

Du Bois, W.E.B. *The Oxford W.E.B. Du Bois Reader*. Ed. Eric Sundquist. New York: Oxford University Press, 1996.

Du Bois, W.E.B. *The Philadelphia Negro: A Social Study*. Intro. by Elijah Anderson. Philadelphia: University of Pennsylvania Press, 1995.

Du Bois, W.E.B. *The Souls of Black Folk*. Intro. by Nathan Hare and Alvin Poissant. New York: New American Library, 1969.

Faust, Drew. *This Republic of Suffering: Death and the American Civil War*. New York: Alfred A. Knopf, 2008.

Fetterly, Judith, and Marjorie Pryse, eds. *American Women Regionalists, 1850–1910*. New York: W.W. Norton, 1992.

Fisher, Philip. *Still the New World*. Cambridge, MA: Harvard University Press, 1999.

Frost, Robert. *The Poetry of Robert Frost: The Collected Poems, Complete and Unabridged*. Ed. Edward Connery Lathem. New York: Henry Holt and Company, 1969.

Gougeon, Len. *Virtue's Hero: Emerson, Antislavery and Reform*. Athens: University of Georgia Press, 1990.

Goodman, Nan. *Literature, Law, and the Theory of Accidents in Nineteenth-Century America*. Princeton, NJ: Princeton University Press, 1998.

Haralson, Eric L., ed. *Encyclopedia of American Poetry: The Twentieth Century.* Chicago: Fitzroy Dearborn, 2001.

Hartman, Saidiya V. *Scenes of Subjection: Terror, Slavery and Self-Making in Nineteenth-Century America.* New York: Oxford University Press, 1997.

Hendrickson, Robert. *American Talk: The Words and Ways of American Dialects.* New York: Viking, 1986.

Hoffman, Daniel. *Form and Fable in American Fiction.* New York: Oxford University Press, 1961.

Howard, Jane, ed. *New Essays on The Country of the Pointed Firs.* New York: Cambridge University Press, 1994.

Jewett, Sarah Orne. *The Country of the Pointed Firs, and Other Stories.* Preface by Willa Cather. Garden City: Doubleday, 1956.

Kaplan, Amy. *The Anarchy of Empire in the Making of U.S. Culture.* Cambridge, MA: Harvard University Press, 2002.

Kaplan, Amy. *The Social Construction of American Realism.* Chicago: University of Chicago Press, 1988.

Levenson, J.C. "Robinson's Modernity." *Virginia Quarterly Review* 44 (Autumn 1968): 590–610.

Lutz, Tom. *Cosmopolitan Vistas: American Regionalism and Literary Value.* Ithaca, NY: Cornell University Press, 2004.

Magee, Mike. *Emancipating Pragmatism: Emerson, Jazz, and Experimental Writing.* Tuscaloosa: University of Alabama Press, 2004.

Michaels, Walter Benn, and Donald Pease, eds. *The American Renaissance Reconsidered.* Baltimore: The Johns Hopkins University Press, 1998.

Nagel, Gwen L., ed. *Critical Essays on Sarah Orne Jewett.* Boston: G.K. Hall, 1984.

New, Elisa. *The Line's Eye: Poetic Experience, American Sight.* Cambridge, MA: Harvard University Press, 1998.

Noll, Mark. *America's God: From Jonathan Edwards to Abraham Lincoln.* New York: Oxford University Press, 2002.

Parini, Jay, ed. *The Columbia History of American Poetry.* New York: Columbia University Press, 1993.

Posnock, Ross. *Color and Culture: Black Writers and the Making of the Modern Intellectual.* Cambridge, MA: Harvard University Press, 2000.

Rampersad, Arnold. *The Art and Imagination of W.E.B. Du Bois.* Cambridge, MA: Harvard University Press, 1976.

Robinson, Edwin Arlington. *Collected Poems.* New York: The Macmillan Company, 1922.

Robinson, Edwin Arlington. *The Town Down the River*. New York: Charles Scribner's Sons, 1920.

Rorty, Richard. *Achieving Our Country: Leftist Thought in Twentieth Century America*. Cambridge, MA: Harvard University Press, 1998.

Rourke, Constance. *American Humor: A Study of the National Character*. New York: Harcourt, Brace and Company, 1931.

Rourke, Constance. *Trumpets of Jubilee*. New York: Harcourt, Brace, and Company, 1927.

Sundquist, Eric, ed. *American Realism: New Essays*. Baltimore: Johns Hopkins University Press, 1982.

Sundquist, Eric, ed. *To Wake the Nations: Race in the Making of American Culture*. Cambridge, MA: Harvard University Press, 1993.

Thomas, Brook. *American Literary Realism and the Failed Promise of Contract*. Berkeley: University of California Press, 1997.

Turner, Frederick Jackson. *The Significance of Sections in American History*. University of Virginia: P. Smith, 1959.

Wald, Priscilla. *Constituting Americans: Cultural Anxiety and Narrative Form*. Durham: Duke University Press, 1995.

West, Cornel. *The American Evasion of Philosophy: A Genealogy of Pragmatism*. Madison: University of Wisconsin Press, 1989.

Wills, Gary. *Lincoln at Gettysburg: The Words that Remade America*. New York: Simon & Schuster, 1992.

Wilson, Edmund. *Patriotic Gore: Studies in the Literature of the American Civil War*. New York: Oxford University Press, 1962.

8

Disinheriting New England
Robert Lowell's Reformations

> Calvinism is a too-conceived abstract-expressionist Church of
> Rome.
>
> (Robert Lowell (*Collected Prose* 276))

At the end of his career, in the poem "Phillips House Revisited,"
Robert Lowell reflects on the figure of his dead grandfather, the
Yankee entrepreneur he had remembered in the early poem "In
Memory of Arthur Winslow." Now, checked in to Phillips House
with a chest complaint, his room in the same elite wing inhabited
forty years before by the dying Arthur Winslow, Lowell meditates
on the martial efficiency of his closest Protestant forebears, the
Winslows. Represented in this poem, as throughout Lowell's work,
by the team of mother Charlotte (still the "*femme militaire*") and her
redoubtable father, Arthur, the Winslows can be relied upon always
to get the last word, even on the matter of their own extinction
(*Day by Day* 78):

> But these forty years grandfather would insist
> have turned the world on its head –

New England Beyond Criticism: In Defense of America's First Literature, First Edition. Elisa New.
© 2014 Elisa New. Published 2014 by John Wiley & Sons, Ltd.

their point was
to extinguish him like a stranded crab.
He needed more to live than I,
his foot could catch hold anywhere
and dynamite his way to the gold again –
for the world is generous to the opportune,
its constantly self-renewing team of favorites.

(*Day by Day* 87–88)

A few poems earlier, in a lyric addressed "To Mother," Lowell probed his mother's ability to make the elegance of her parlor itself a reproach; or, more exactly, to furnish the stiff-backed milieu that Boston deems elegant (*Day by Day* 73). In "Phillips House Revisited" Lowell discovers what undergirds this perverse aesthetic of discomfiture: a classic Protestant knack for turning disadvantage to advantage. Embracing discomfort as a badge of honor and birthright, Lowell's family solicits and bestows the "gracious affliction" Sacvan Bercovitch called the badge of the American self.[1]

No surprise, then, that Robert Lowell's recollection of his mother's rebuke – "Why do we keep expecting life to be easy, / when we know it never can be?" (78–79) – resonates in his memory of Arthur Winslow, as Arthur Winslow's ferocity tints all his representations of her. Arthur Winslow, like his daughter, does not need good fortune to feel his chosenness. Quite the contrary, Winslow assumes that the world's generosity to "the opportune" flows chiefly to those who "improve the time" without expecting improvement to bring pleasure – or progress to mean change. The elect are those opportunely situated in the same straits their forebears endured: down the generations, God beaches these elect on the same lonely strand their forefathers found. Arthur Winslow's pilgrim's progress is thus the fulfillment of a destiny not despoiled by vulgar luck. God's "self-renewing teams of favorites" become so precisely by never courting His favor.

Charlotte's joyless exploitativeness, like Arthur's grim instrumentalism, makes her a charter member of this team. Her courting of adversity is not a personal or even a family trait; it is a broad cultural pattern. And this is why, of course, Lowell's indictment of his family's vices has never been mistaken for simple indiscretion, but has instead always been taken as a profound, or at least thorough, re-evaluation of the American soul. Indeed, Lowell's deployment of confession and of the personal to myth-making ends is what best sustains his reputation. Lowell is the poet whose auto-da-fé of representative Americanness unwrites the exemplary Protestant self. As the title of one critic, Philip Cooper's, study tellingly suggests, Lowell's claim to posterity's notice is through "autobiographical myth."

Lowell's self-scourgings, however, are addressed to the self as construct, and thus as much to the "American individual" as to his own tortured person. There is an affective deficit which, in Lowell's diagnosis, afflicts his New England culture. What Lowell finds wanting in Protestantism is its very repudiation of want; and, in his immediates, a Yankee disaffection as corrosive as Yankee instrumentalism. Lowell indicts Charlotte and Arthur not only for making conveniences of those they do not in any personal way want; but, more than that, for wreaking a kind of vengeance on the idea of want itself. Kin to New England's most corrupt native son, the self-sufficing Gilbert Osmond of Henry James's *The Portrait of a Lady*, Arthur and Charlotte see need itself as lack of mettle.

Reacting, then, to this heritage of affective parsimony, Lowell develops a poetics and a career more hospitable to human need. Specifically, he cultivates a model of selfhood not in fact mythic but quotidian, not representative but historical, and, most importantly of all, not sufficed by affliction but beseeching succor from day to day. If for Charlotte and Arthur there is nothing so base as Lowell's own "fear of not being wanted" (*Day by Day* 124), the poet's rejection of their legacy necessitates an embrace of need and an openness to ministration that profoundly marks his subsequent work. As he crafts and refines a poetics of quotidian mediacy, Lowell consecrates himself to possibilities of lesser immediacy, and greater satisfaction, than Protestants countenance. As the heir to Protestant immediacy becomes the poet of mediacy, the artist finds in the "blessèd structures, plot and rhyme" forms capable of appeasing soul and talent both (*Day by Day* 127).

This is to say that Lowell's lines above shed light on a less Reformed, more catholic – and of course more Catholic – Lowell than the autobiographical myth sustains. "There is no way of telling," Albert Gelpi commented, "how Lowell's poetry would have developed had he remained a Catholic; or whether the style of *Life Studies* which we associate with his lapse of faith would have occurred anyway and been accommodated into the expression of a developing religious sensibility" (Gelpi 58).[2] Let us entertain the possibility that Lowell's poetic development is cognate with the development of this genuinely "religious sensibility," a sensibility which, while no longer expressing itself in any kind of orthodox observance, finds full and complex expression in the poems themselves. In *Day by Day* (1977) Lowell will have separated himself from the exhausted, Weberian Protestantism of Arthur and Charlotte Winslow by casting off the sufficiencies of Protestant selfhood and the externalities of Protestant time. He will have learned rather to make his poems hold the spiritual charge of a relation to time more tenuous and "day to day," a relation to the material world more sacramental than efficient and, most crucially, a relation to *relation* itself more open.

The Protestant culture Lowell inherited had come to believe in, to embrace, the liberation of the self from any agency but that installed in the self by God; Lowell will avail his later work of forms external to the self. Openly supplicant, candidly in quest of confessors, Lowell's poetic persona – whether he addresses the Virgin Mary or his last wife, Caroline; whether his subject is Easter or his own recurrent lapsing into mental illness – is that of a man soliciting intercession, charity, and understanding, and of a poet making his poetry the vestibule of such plaints. Lowell's voice takes on the plangency of one who knows the absolution he seeks cannot come from within. As a young convert to Catholicism, Lowell had spent hours in the confessional; as a lapsed Catholic, he makes his poetry hold the imprint of that experience as he seeks structures of regularization, avenues of displacement: as he seeks custodians who can receive his want. What come to be Lowell's most characteristic poetic gestures – the solicitation of a hearing ear, the discovery of a conveyancing image or voice – are transactions between the solitary imagination and the interlocutor or substance that holds this absolution. The poet whom Robert Lowell becomes and the brief, revelatory event his mature poems strive to record are both born in a counter-Reformational rediscovery of confession.

This is to say that the "confessional" school that Lowell earns credit for inventing may trace a greater share of its origins than we have supposed to the confessional: a place where articulation given into the hands of another secures absolution. The poems of Lowell's maturity read, one after another, like missives to a mediating power from the mouth of one who knows he cannot cure himself, who knows, as Lowell famously puts it in "Skunk Hour," that "I myself am hell." Lowell's work demonstrates how the Protestant liberation of self to its own recognizance, soul to its own rigor, is an enterprise doomed to fail, since the self is not cleansing but polluting. As the poet of "Unwanted" knows when he compares himself to a "sailor dying of thirst on the Atlantic" (*Day by Day* 121), the native element of the Protestant hypos is inimical to genuine self-knowledge. Protestant self-cleansing is easily degraded into sanctimonious narcissism or the notebook ramblings of the confirmed "case." Thus Charlotte Winslow "go[es] on cleaning house / for eternity" and making it unlivable (124); the poet's own self-examination risks the same sterility and stasis:

> Alas, I can only tell my own story –
> talking to myself, or reading, or writing,
> or fearlessly holding nothing back from a friend,
> who believes me for a moment
> to keep up conversation.
>
> (*Day by Day* 121)

To make of determined work more than another kind of inversion; to produce art whose power to heal extends beyond quelling the symptoms of one sufferer; to shape a space of interlocution not narrowed by monomania or compromised by patronage – these are goals of Lowell's mature creative life and the achievements of his "confessionalism" at its best.

Understanding of just how thoroughly Lowell's voice is altered, tempered over time by the mediating influence of the confessional mode, takes us back to *Land of Unlikeness* (1944). There we listen in on an earlier Lowell: on the Catholic apologist girded, paradoxically, in full Protestant armor. Lowell's elegy for Arthur Winslow, the most memorable poem in that volume, sets Protestant cupidity in stark contrast to Catholic mercies, but it does so in the manner of the classic Protestant jeremiad. Setting off from the convert's smug "This Easter," Lowell makes his elegy express all his disappointment at the failure of forefathers to know failure for failure, affliction for affliction.

The poem has great power. Winslow is a sharply etched depiction of self-aggrandizing self-effacement.

> This Easter, Arthur Winslow, less than dead,
> Your people set you up in Phillips' House
> To settle off your wrestling with the crab –
> The claws drop flesh upon your yachting blouse
> Until longshoreman Charon come and stab
> Through your adjusted bed
> And crush the crab. On Boston Basin, shells
> Hit water by the Union Boat Club wharf:
> You ponder why the coxes' squeakings dwarf
> The *resurrexit dominus* of all the bells.
>
> Grandfather Winslow, look, the swanboats coast
> That island in the Public Gardens, where
> The bread-stuffed ducks are brooding, where with tub
> And strainer the mid-Sunday Irish scare
> The sun-struck shallows for the dusky chub
> This Easter, and the ghost
> Of risen Jesus walks the waves to run
> Arthur upon a trumpeting black swan
> Beyond Charles River to the Acheron
> Where the wide waters and their voyager are one.

Winslow's career epitomizes a family knack for turning any setback into an advantage. Though eventually consumed by the "crab," cancer, Winslow is a man whose hardshelled tenacity had allowed him to prosper anywhere. As a young man on the make, Winslow's skill at bottom-feeding permitted him to turn a spell of Western exile into a literal goldmine, and thus to make alienation pay. Lowell presses the crab imagery as far as it will go, developing the ironic interplay between Arthur Winslow's consumption by the cancer and the casual consumption of luxury seafood by his still hale coevals to suggest the inevitable isolation of a man "set up" in an elite hospital and left to fend for himself by "people" just like himself. Left to die alone, Winslow is, in fact, paid the highest compliment "Your people" can pay: he is left in peace to enjoy the affliction God visits only on favorites (*Selected Poems* 11).

As the above explication should indicate, Lowell's chief poetic device at this stage is the image. Just as images of the crab – mythological and culinary – are set against one another, Lowell makes similar symbolic use of the heralding trumpets of the judgment day. The faulty hearing of Lowell's doddering Massachusetts kin evokes the invalidism and invalidation over time of the Congregational faith. While this faith's vitality once inhered in its preaching, now the trumpets of the End devolve into ear-trumpets for the insensible. These, deafened rather than roused by preaching, are pathetic shadows of their sermon-drunk kin. Fittingly, Arthur Winslow is conveyed to the afterlife on a "trumpeting black swan," the image cousin by pun to the "trumpeter swan." Lowell's revision, which imbues the descriptive "trumpeter swan" (the stylized bird of genteel parlor prints) with sound and present action, only sharpens the irony flowing against the Winslows, whose triumphalist individualism is, as it were, trumped, both from the social and the religious standpoint. From the commoners' "Boat Club," Boston Garden, the swan boats cast off; they "coast" while Arthur founders. At the same time, the man once contemptuous of all aid but his own is transported from his "adjusted" bed by a Jesus who "runs" him "Beyond Charles River to the Acheron" (*Selected Poems* 11). He who despised charity is now the object of it. He whose feet could catch hold anywhere, who was, above all, "opportune," is demoted from martial pilgrim to patient sinner, or sin-consumed patient. Either way, patience, a Catholic virtue, is Protestant indignity.

The indignity, though, is apparently no more than Winslow deserves. Poetic justice requires that the man who has hogged the American road lose driving privileges in the afterworld. By the end of the poem's first stanza, the value of hearty Protestant individualism – along with its sacralization in American culture – is indicted for its partiality to "favorites." Lowell exposes in Winslow the specious rationalization of self-interest that may occur when the expanse of a continent is made to incarnate individual designings: when expansionism is ratified as destiny on the belief, in Bercovitch's terms, that "America was consecrated from eternity for the New England Way" (*American Jeremiad* 7).³ Rejecting any seamless or "natural" identifications of "individual," "continent," and "nation," Lowell dismisses the romance of divine design as mere "craft." Winslow's journey across America, his archetypal push west, is not Manifest Destiny, but adventurism, pure and simple. A fisher after booty ("the craft that netted you a million dollars, / Hosing out gold in Colorado's waste"), Arthur Winslow sustains a family instinct for the main chance, reprising the equivocal ethics of Revolutionary era ancestors who either "whipped" or backed the king, depending on how the wind blew. In the instance of the Winslows, the difference between good timing and craven opportunism is effectively null.

Lowell's elegy for his grandfather, Arthur Winslow, is a tour de force: it maintains its energy and texture through the complex imbrication of image chains. Yet the poem's particular effectiveness flows from other sources as well: namely, from Lowell's experimentation with temporal elements, his striving to create a certain range of moods, and his marked (though not markedly successful) attempt to transfer authority outside and away from the thunderous voice of its prophetic and autochthonous speaker. Temporally speaking, Lowell arranges the details around Arthur Winslow in a manner peculiarly arrested, without dynamic thrust, while the poet writes from the vantage point of a time more vital, signaled by the vibrantly present sacred date: "This Easter." Indeed, as Lowell proceeds in itemizing what there was to remember about Winslow, the affective dynamism of the elegiac form seems oddly to spend or exhaust itself; and where elegy was, now there is only epitaph. This formal hardening is, Lowell's poem seems to demonstrate, not inevitable, but rather a result of the process of Protestant hagiography that arrests and inscribes individual persons into eternal types. As Protestant saint, Arthur Winslow lies in the bed his forebears made. The poem that traces his life's progress is, finally, a portmanteau of inert epithets, or epitaphic tags, which signify the satisfaction of Protestant progress in stasis. A headstone easily preempts the Protestant elegy.

This attention to lyric time is, then, one way that Lowell uses his early poems to distinguish the sterility of Protestant certainties from the more contingent ethos he will go on to explore. Another way will involve sustained use of the second-person addressee, and, in particular, his development of a newly tentative, or what we might call subjunctive, quality of tone. Gabriel Pearson long ago argued that Lowell's objects are always being "reapprehended, and, as it were, redeemed for attention by being locked and cemented into larger structures" and that Lowell's end is to achieve a "controlled remoteness" (Bloom 31).[4] Pearson's evocative observation permits elaboration. Lowell's aim is not so much the achievement of remoteness from the subject and objects of his existence, but rather a literally mediated relation to them. The poet presents – admits into evidence, as it were – objects, perspectives, and reminiscences, whose ultimate meaning will only be revealed by a trusted interlocutor, by a mediator in whose hands burdens may be deposited. This shift in authority – from the poet to his addressee, from an immediate to a displaced source of wisdom – shows up in the elegy for Arthur Winslow only in the last stanza, where, unrelated to any species of Protestant address, the shift jars. The maladroitness, even near ludicrousness of the stanza entitled "A Prayer for My Grandfather to Our Lady" serves to suggest how momentous for Lowell is this renunciation of authority:

> Mother, for these three hundred years or more
> Neither our clippers nor our slavers reached
> The haven of your peace in this Bay State:

> Neither my father nor his father. Beached
> On these dry flats of fishy real estate,
> O Mother, I implore
> Your scorched blue thunderbreasts of love to pour
> Buckets of blessings on my burning head.
>
> *(Lord Weary's Castle* 28)

Renouncing the jeremiad of the foregoing stanzas as well as the prophetic authority of his own current practice, Lowell commends his soul and those of his "people" to the mercy of a Mother bountiful in forgiveness. The awkwardness of these lines – with their reachings after a sublimity that seems, in "blue thunderbreasts," merely cartoonish – marks a crisis. The grandeur, and sometime grandiosity, of Lowell's early mode is in a register too hyperbolic, too stiffly rhetorical for any genuine "imploring": what the needy speaker beseeches cannot really be "Buckets of blessings" poured from "blue thunderbreasts": he needs a softer, simpler affective register. We see how much he needs that register here, and so are prepared to greet it in the justly hailed volume *Life Studies*, a breakthrough book in so many ways – but among them: the first to show Lowell finding the poetic, but also cultural and even spiritual usefulness of a more mediated poetic practice. There, and in subsequent books, Lowell will move away from Protestant hardness, and individualism itself, as he seeks to define a poetics and assemble a body of work capable of thriving in provisional, rather than providential, time.

Lowell will not have to discover this poetics entirely on his own. As is well documented, Lowell was a poet who took influence from a variety of sources. Axelrod showed just how influential William Carlos Williams was, in this regard as in others.[5] The poet, dissatisfied with his earlier method, learns from Williams the affective as well as formal advantages of a different kind of poetics. After hearing Williams read "Asphodel, That Greeny Flower" at Wellesley College in 1956, Lowell marvels at the impact of Williams's "simple confession, something that was both poetry and beyond poetry" (Mariani 244).[6] If Lowell's description of Williams's poem as "confession" is notable, he was in fact probably predisposed to such description.

210

For "simple confession" was a characteristic Lowell had already discovered in the work of a host of religio-literary changelings like himself: Augustine, More, Herbert, Newman, Hopkins. But closer to home, he had given considerable study to another middle-aged poet thinker and Protestant heir who, as he like him, put by prophecy for more candid genres.

Jonathan Edwards, whose biography he planned to write at the precise time of his conversion to Catholicism, is a crucial figure for Lowell. In Edwards, the archetypal Protestant, Lowell discovers the germ of another kind of faithful poetics. This poetics is neither precisely Catholic nor Protestant, but rather grounded in an Augustinian confessionalism, which, at the source of both, renders the Protestant/Catholic distinction factitious. In Edwards, Lowell rediscovers, in effect, the lost soul of his heritage in a New England Way redeemed of sectarian sharpness, patriarchal self-possession, and Weberian zeal. Lowell's Edwards is not the pitiless and martial Christian soldier of the Winslow way, but rather a genius of feeling, a theorist of affective life. True legatee to the school of Cambridge Protestants made visible in Janice Knight's *Orthodoxies in Massachusetts*, Edwards has more in common with the recondite John Cotton than the outgoing Benjamin Franklin, more in common with Nathaniel Hawthorne than his more "representative" neighbor, Ralph Waldo Emerson. By the end of his career, this Edwards has become for Lowell the quintessential model of the Christian-poet without portfolio, his temple the page. Exiled, but actually liberated, from the burden of representative Protestantism as Lowell is himself, Edwards serves as Lowell's most important instructor in the poetics of the "day by day."

While Lowell never writes his biography of Edwards' career, Edwards, in a very real sense, writes Lowell's. In his poetic treatments of Edwards, Lowell maps two related, but ultimately opposed Puritan traditions: one defined by typological repetitions that subsume process, change, and variety; the other adopting a stance expectant and penitent before the contingencies of history. Not accidentally, these are the two primary movements of Lowell's own career as well.

211

The pivotal moment in Lowell's characterization of Edwards surely comes in *For the Union Dead* (1964). The volume is most often remembered for its scouring critique of war-mongering, colonialism, and racism at home, and perhaps also for the voice of its speaker, Lyndon Johnson's scourge and the counter-culture's spokesman. But *For the Union Dead* is, through and through, a New England book, a book whose focus is Manifest Destiny and its victims – here including, especially, its victors. Hardshelled New Englanders win, but wincingly. They bear the costs of Protestant duty as an internalization of predation that rots or breaks down the soul while carapacing it in a rigid representativeness.

If the younger Edwards, the anointed head of renascent orthodoxy at his Northampton lectern, had already shown signs of this syndrome in *Lord Weary's Castle* (1946), here he is joined by others. In his company, on his graciously afflicted "team," Lowell also finds Arthur Corning Clark, schoolmate and poor rich boy whose "triumphant diffidence" and "refusal of exertion" make him a paragon of the Protestant sufficiency. The tense inversion of Clark's life is poignantly transcribed in the palindrome of his birth and death dates, which Lowell carefully transcribes: 1916–1961. There is Robert Gould Shaw himself, the greatest of the "Union Dead," who, while honored as martyr to the cause of racial justice, is perforce rendered, in life as in death, a man too hard to give vent to mortal weaknesses. Whether trapped in death or its near cousin, duty, Shaw's breathing is within bronze: he "seems to wince at pleasure, / and suffocate for privacy" (*Selected Poems* 110). Even Moses appears in *For the Union Dead* as a misguided evangelist or a calloused casualty of a primeval Great Awakening – or a mere lobbyist, eaten up inside. Lowell's Moses is not unlike those pols from "July in Washington" who arrive in the Capital "bright as dimes / and die disheveled and soft" (127). If, as Lowell laments in that poem, the rigid artillery of the New England Way rolls over the green earth without gentleness ("The stiff spokes of this wheel / touch the sore spots of the earth"), the Protestant soldiers of this movement do not escape undamaged by its progress, even though it is they, in fact, who roll it along (136).

212

Indeed, these men like needles or daguerreotypes – each trapped in the static imperturbability his culture demands, each carrying his "house" on his back – are, unlike their prefiguring types in *Land of Unlikeness* and *Lord Weary's Castle*, more sympathetic than earlier prototypes. They are "poor," rather than graciously afflicted, sinners; and, as such, deserving of a new charity. Lowell's Christian soldier must be rescued from Winslow's lonely deathbed, and who better for the mission than one of his own? While the nation may render his faculties of will and eternal vigilance all the honor rendered earlier saints (Shaw's high-strung eliteness earns him comparison to a greyhound, while the monuments to his "wasp-waisted" comrades grow "slimmer and younger each year"), the poet has a more tender and pitying image to bestow, that of the encumbered turtle: outside, all armored plates; inside, all rot (*Selected Poems* 136).

This image – of fresh growth trapped in the casket of the past – makes *For the Union Dead* one of Lowell's most unified and effective volumes, for it dislodges and frees Lowell's poetics from the recursive and finally sterile endeavor of writing jeremiads against the jeremiad. The critique of historical succession that commandeered the matter and form of earlier work, exhausting lyricism in hortatoriness, and entangling the censor of Protestant selfhood in baroque reenactments of the very selfhood he censored, has found new ground, as the Protestant avatar now earns the poet's solicitous pity. Poignantly unoriginal in his singularity, this paradigmatic Protestant cannot escape himself. His adamantine individuality is reproduced again and again in shields and commemorative busts, in urns spilling slime, and in statues uncannily breathing: a pathetic Boston drinker "snores in his iron lung," while in Maine towns, "fresh paint / on the captains' houses hides softer wood" (*Selected Poems* 116, 130). Indeed, it is with what can only be called a new strain of charity that Lowell now regards those

> all in outline, uniformly gray
> unregenerate arrowheads sloughed up by the path here,
> or in the corners of the eye, they play
> their thankless fill-in roles . . .
>
> (*For the Union Dead* 16)

Pity the Protestants! What better way, then, to show this care, to model such solicitude, but by redeeming Protestantism's hero, Jonathan Edwards. Lowell's conceit of the petrified integument constraining mere mortal flesh gets most brilliant, and pivotal, deployment in "Jonathan Edwards in Western Massachusetts," where the poet's pity expands, and his former suspicion of Edwards as the Protestant Ironsides is replaced by close identification: "I love you faded, / old, exiled and afraid." On pilgrimage to Northampton, site of Edwards' professional glory days, the poet recounts to have found nothing but "the round slice of an oak / you are said to have planted." Now so brittle, it is "only fit for burning." This stump is all that remains of the renowned Edwards who "stood on stilts in the air" (*For the Union Dead* 42–43). The quintessential New Englander, elevated by training, temperament, and family heritage to high office, Edwards turns out, in the end, as just another turtle, one of the poet's own kind. As Lowell had written in "The Neo-Classical Urn":

> . . . I rub my skull,
> that turtle shell,
> and breathe their dying smell,
> still watch their crippled last survivors pass
> and hobble humpbacked through the grizzled grass.
>
> (*Selected Poems* 126)

Like the rotting Arthur Winslow, like the poet himself subject to "night sweats," Edwards confesses to be nothing but "flaccid solids / vapid, sizzy, scarse fluids." It may seem an ignoble kind of fall for Lowell's most august forebear to suffer, but the descent from Jeremiah to turtle is actually a moral rise. In Lowell's earlier exploration of the unripe Edwards, he had made Edwards complicit in a revival with fearsome consequences. Edwards himself had seen his career advanced, and his conscience troubled, by a talent for the vatic resembling Lowell's own (9).

Thus Lowell indicts the callow younger Edwards of Northampton whose "White wig and black coat, / all cut from one cloth," blur together the man and his orthodoxy (*Selected Poems* 122). Silhouette of his sect, anointed outline, Edwards had commanded a rhetoric febrile and affecting; his gift, not unlike Lowell's, was for turning visceral horror to collective, homiletic ends.

In "Mr. Edwards and the Spider" this was the Edwards he? had memorably deployed his own uncle in a thought-experiment on hell ("Josiah Hawley, picture yourself cast / Into a brick-kiln where the blast / Fans your quick vitals to a coal") that probably brought on Hawley's suicide (*Selected Poems* 128). Indeed, in Lowell's clearly self-reflexive treatment of the episode, the mistake Edwards makes with Hawley follows from a broader confusion of general and particular, Adam's sin and one's own, that characterizes the Great Awakening. In Lowell's interpretation of his own history, national and familial, a culture collapsing individual sins into typical ones creates fertile conditions for Josiah Hawley's reversion to congenital madness, renamed intense spiritual "experience." And if one man's psychotic episode could be mistaken for a genuine religious experience, how then to prevent a more violent and widespread transmission of madness among a populace ready to call all kinds of irregularity "religious affection"?

> The multitude, once unconcerned with doubt,
> Once neither callous, curious nor devout,
> Jumped at broad noon, as though some peddler groaned
> At it in its familiar twang: "My friend,
> Cut your own throat. Cut your own throat. Now! Now!
> September twenty-second, Sir, the bough
> Cracks with the unpicked apples, and at dawn
> The small-mouth bass breaks water, gorged with spawn.
>
> (*Selected Poems* 30)

Here the vitality and changefulness of time that the seasons mark fall into neglect. Harvests are left unpicked, daytime sanity is broken by competing nightmares hawked by vying clerics, and the new is literally eaten by the old. But Lowell shows Edwards apprehending in Hawley's embrace of family pathology the literal consequences of a belief system that visits the patriarch Adam's sin down the generations from father to child. The New England way over which Edwards presides "awakens" men into their parents' rather than their own days. The Puritan imperative "to live ancient lives," as Theodore Bozeman has it, hostages the day. Awakening is, in this perspective, a reanimation of the past that gives no quarter to the present. The poet who will later regret walking in the "dinosaur / death steps" (*Selected Poems* 103) of the father hints early on at the revolt to come in his striking portrait of Jonathan Edwards waking out of the Awakening.

What saves Edwards from the entombed stink of the archaic turtle, from being Arthur Winslow, is simply his fall off the "stilts" of his high Protestant sinecure. It is, in Lowell's rendering, this fall that permits his rediscovery of a simpler, more "original" version of Christian confessionalism, the early Church confessionalism of Augustine who, as ancestor of both Aquinas and Calvin, Roman Church and Reformed congregations, bequeaths the forms of a piety genuinely catholic. The strain of orthodoxy that Lowell will observe Edwards to pursue post-Awakening is an orthodoxy reinfused with the soul that predestinarian applications (and particularly a covenant theology collectivizing individual into eternal communities) perforce occlude. Infused with this new, yet also quite normative, strain of piety, Jonathan Edwards in Western Massachusetts sheds the thickened sensibility of sectarian fathers to cultivate other faculties, and more responsive ones: attention to beauty; susceptibility to love; readiness to imagine the Mind that imagined its own mind and so to train imagination as a pious faculty.

One of the most moving and remarkable achievements of Robert Lowell's poetic career must be this counter-intuitive yet acute reinterpretation and rehabilitation of Jonathan Edwards from mainline evangelical paragon to devotionalist and mystic. In "Jonathan Edwards in Western Massachusetts," Lowell addresses the spirit of Edwards, musing, "You too must have been green once," and then finds it is so (*Selected Poems* 122). Edwards evicted from his station of wooden eminence is precisely master of the present and of the spiritual fertility of the common day. No longer standard-bearer of individual Will, apocalyptic appetite, and ostentatious self-denial, this other Edwards is a poet of highly developed perceptual sense, an empiricist of what Marianne Moore later calls "observatory nerves," and a lover paying nearly Marian homage to a beloved wife. This Edwards makes "affection" and affectedness the constitutive principles of redemption.

Whereas Lowell cannot help but find the millenialist Edwards complicit in partitioning God's country into sectarian principalities ("I could almost feel the frontier crack and disappear. / Edwards thought the world would end here"), Edwards in Western Massachusetts is released from the invidious elitism and interests of his former "circles" to a genuine catholicity of interests and pursuits (*Selected Poems* 120). On a further frontier, Edwards finds a world exfoliating itself from minute to minute. He delights in what Hopkins called Creation's "pied beauty," reading the variety and complexity of nature as Being's gracious, and ongoing, consent to Itself. This same delight in mimetic reciprocities – in the call and response of growth and creation – is now expressed in Edwards's touching submission to his wife's ministry. If Nature is the sacramental book where God records his consent to Himself, earthly marriage schools His creations in the harmonics of the Divine benevolence. Nature's symmetries and a woman's voice inspire Lowell's ecstatic Edwards to a kind of creative action modeled on God's making:

> . . . The soul
> of Sarah Pierrepont!
>
> So filled with delight in the Great Being,
> she hardly cared for anything –
> walking the fields, sweetly singing,
> conversing with some one invisible.
>
> Then God's love shone in sun, moon and stars,
> on earth, in the waters,
> in the air, in the loose winds,
> which used to greatly fix your mind.
>
> Often she saw you come home from a ride
> or a walk, your coat dotted with thoughts

you had pinned there
on slips of paper.

(*Selected Poems* 121)

In these verses Jonathan Edwards – in the spirit of Augustine and More, Newman, Hopkins, and Lowell himself – forgoes narrow dogmatisms. He trades in the sectarian's coat to put on God's surplice. The change is expressed in the difference between, "White wig and black coat, / all cut from one cloth" and, on the other hand: "from a ride / or a walk, your coat dotted with thoughts." Uncanny metrical cousins, the former line describes a man of self-sufficient rigor and unvarying consistency, a representative Puritan; the latter, a man who wears his longing for God on his literal sleeve and who seeks fresh terms for his devotion day by day. Lowell's depiction of Edwards "writing, writing, writing," shows Edwards converted to a kind of creative activity eschewing predestinarian certainty for a more plangent and instantaneous mode (*Selected Poems* 123). The very singing echo of the phrase, "writing, writing, writing," evocative of Sarah Pierrepont's own song, suggests Edwards's assent to the reality of human incompleteness and his embrace of constant mimetic effort as a making in God's image.

At what he saw as a parallel stage in his own life, Robert Lowell adopts a style of writing informed by a similar imperative to make creative action the wellspring of constant devotion. "Jonathan Edwards in Western Massachusetts" is, in effect, a displaced rehearsal of Lowell's spiritual process: it depicts an Edwards born to walk the "dinosaur / death steps" of his line instead of finding a more spontaneous and imaginative mode of spiritual exercise. By means of "Jonathan Edwards in Western Massachusetts" and other poems in *For the Union Dead*, Lowell readies himself for the shift into a more traditional "confessionalism" than he had yet practiced, indeed a confessionalism that is, perhaps, the one element of his Roman Catholicism to survive into his maturity.

There is a question whether my poems are religious, or if they just use Christian imagery. I haven't really any idea. My last poems don't use religious imagery, they don't use symbolism. In many ways they seem to me more religious than the earlier ones, which are full of symbols and references to Christ and God. I'm sure the symbols and the Catholic framework didn't make the poems religious experiences. Yet I don't feel that my experience has changed much. (*Collected Prose* 250)

The confessionalism of Lowell's late years is characterized by an immediate and literal reading of Augustinian time rather than the now culturally over-determined Protestantism Lowell inherited. This is to say that it shows a greater attention to, and investment in, what may be realized in a "day." Augustine's celebrated Book 11 of the *Confessions* describes the wonder of such a day in this way: "Of these two divisions in time, then, how can two, the past and the future, *be*, when the past no longer is and the future is not yet?" (264).[7] As Lowell had occasion to ponder while editing the *Confessions* at Sheed and Ward in the 1940s, and as his intense reading in such Catholic thinkers as Etienne Gilson and E.I. Watkin taught him, an Augustinian temporarily mandates responsive devotion to the advancing of Glory in our own time and in our own estate: Glory cannot be endowed or inherited. Such works as Watkin's *Catholic Art and Culture* and Gilson's *The Spirit of Medieval Philosophy*, the primer texts of Lowell's conversion, only reinforced this sense. The table of contents of Gilson's *The Spirit of Medieval Philosophy* (Chapter III. Beings and Their Contingence; Chapter IV. Analogy, Causality and Finality; Chapter V. Christian Optimism; Chapter VI. The Glory of God) is itself a suggestive digest of Lowell's developed poetics. Such a poetics requires an activist image-maker, the poet as upholder and actualizer of a revelation exacting constant renewal. Poetic achievement, in this view, proceeds from a discipline necessarily quotidian; and revelation, from a certain assiduity of vision never sufficient in itself, but responsive to, vibrating with, exigent phenomena. As Gilson puts it: "to realize this glorification not only being is required, but action" (145).[8] If the New England Way squandered this poetics, and Edwards fell, only to be lifted up by it, its modern hero for Lowell will be a poet like Hopkins, whose "sanctities" Lowell describes in an essay of the forties entitled "Hopkins' Sanctity": "to be thoroughly in act is human perfection; in other words it is to be thoroughly made. According to Catholic theology, perfection demands a substantial transformation." As he goes on: "for Hopkins' life was a continuous substantial progress toward perfection," while "the beliefs and practices of most modern poets more or less exclude perfection, . . . and . . . insofar as perfection is shut out the poetry suffers" (*Collected Prose* 168).

I am not contending that Lowell remains in any sense a regular Catholic. Three wives and many lovers; the disorientations of a career alternating spells in the hoosgow and seasons on the cover of *Time*; residence on two continents and years of manic depressive illness – these all took their toll on any kind of regularity in Lowell's life, religious or otherwise. His lapse from Roman orthodoxy aside, Lowell is too much the ironist in the end to continue fashioning verse paraphrases of such sentences as this: "The contemplation of our Lady, type and exemplar of the contemplative Church, sees horizontally the ends of becoming, the issues of history" (Watkin 218).[9]

Subtract the Church, however, and what remains is a discipline and a set of predilections that a poetry, like a Church, may harbor. And Lowell's mature poetics may be said to harbor these with a kind of vehemence. A receptiveness to ministration; a sense of history as determined by small daily transactions; a search for some more tender guide to personal redemption than the past had bestowed – these are the obsessional givens of Lowell's later work.

After Lowell no longer writes poems to the "Lady of Walsingham," a thematic constant remains the invocation of the wife given salvific power: an "old flame" of "flaming insight"; the "Tenth Muse . . . in [her] white and red dresses like a tablecloth"; the "nymph" with "her soaring armpits and her one bare breast," or the "Dolphin" who "guide[s] by surprise" (*Selected Prose* 101–102, 124, 125, 246). More fundamental, though, will be the structural integration, and architectonic integration, of mediate form expressed in Lowell's embrace of the blank verse sonnet.

220

The sonnet is Lowell's cathedral. With its historic openness to female intercession, its intense *durée*, and its opportunities for affective shift within the compact span of its fourteen lines, the sonnet proves one of Lowell's most durable and efficacious forms. In it, personal materials may be exposed to the pressure of historic time and so to the response of an interlocutor, screened but ever present. In the sonnet, Lowell can allow the "blessèd structures, plot and rhyme," to enable supplications of an older sort. Sometimes, the lyrics are overly private and sometimes, too, the form itself over-stylizes. But the cumulative effect of the sonnet sequences is to purchase release for a poet once encased in the iron casket of the jeremiad and arrested in a cartoon of his own representativeness. The evanescent temporality of the sonnet as Lowell practices it makes complacency fatal and insight, urgent. Nothing may be relied upon to exist but the moment. As Lowell writes in "Fall Weekend at *Milgate*":

> The day says nothing, and lacks for nothing . . . God:
> but it's moonshine trying to gold-cap my life,
> asking fees from the things I lived and loved
> > (*Selected Poems* 231)

Renouncing the Weberian sanctifications of use value in such lines, Lowell puts aside all those devices by which we redeem time past with a specious "improvement." The world instead vibrates with sights, actions, whose value may not outlive the instant. Snagged on time passing, admitting he is "counterclockwise," Lowell lets his lines stall with paradox, accumulating the tension of what's lost as it's found.

> I watch a feverish huddle of shivering cows;
> You sit making a fishspine from a chestnut leaf.
> We are at our crossroads, we are astigmatic
> and stop uncomfortable, we are humanly low.
> > (*Selected Poems* 231)

All the progress obtainable in the lines above is that availed in a view of cows hoarding warmth, or in the sight of one's wife making "a fishspine from a chestnut leaf" – revelatory sights that emerge from the crucible of Augustinian time. Making by unmaking, his lines "under pressure," Mark Rudman puts it, "of a moment that will not recur,"[10] Lowell assembles images of ambitious diminishment, fertile desiccation (158). Sonnets like the above render the human day a mystery replete with nothing but itself. And if Lowell's late work is wracked by the pain of this, it is also infused with a certain devotional awe and *agape*. It turns out that the very "astigmatic" view, drastically foreshortened and feeling the strain of its reach as an emptiness of grasp, opens a space for sudden, brimming instants of vision. It happens that the valves of confession open inward, too. Revelation rushes in: "It's amazing," Lowell observes in his last volume,

> the day is still here
> like lightning on an open field,
> terra firma and transient
> swimming in variation,
> fresh as when man first broke
> like the crocus all over the earth.
>
> (*Day by Day* 53)

By the end of his career, writing poems under the motto "let nothing be done twice," Lowell is no longer writing autobiographical myth or reprising the gracious afflictions of Arthur Winslow. Positioned within history rather than outside as its representative, the "confessional poet" of *Day by Day* is obliged to renew all vision, re-address all suits each day.

From his early intense exposure to Catholicism and from such guides as Edwards, Lowell has come to recognize the "one unpardonable sin" is not, as his mother had it, want, but rather want's denial. Thus the mature poet may find release from the stance of the self-possessed visionary. He may embrace the necessity of an artistic vision imbued with need and the humility of action that substantiates need. On this, his "Epilogue" does no less than insist. Lowell writes at the last: "*The painter's vision is not a lens, / it trembles to caress the light*" (*Day by Day* 127).

Notes

1 See Bercovitch *The Puritan Origins of the American Self.*
2 See Gelpi's essay "The Reign of the Kingfisher" in *Robert Lowell: Essays on the Poetry.*
3 See Bercovitch *The American Jeremiad.*
4 See Gabriel Pearson's article "The Middle Years" in Harold Bloom's *Robert Lowell.*
5 See Steven Gould Axelrod's *Robert Lowell: Life and Art.*
6 See Paul Mariani's *Lost Puritan: A Life of Robert Lowell.*
7 See F.J. Sheed's translation of *The Confessions of Saint Augustine.*
8 See Etienne Gilson *The Spirit of Medieval Philosophy.*
9 See E.I. Watkin's *Catholic Art and Culture.*
10 See Bercovitch's *The Puritan Origins of the American Self.*

References

Axelrod, Stephen Gould. *Robert Lowell: Life and Art.* Princeton, NJ: Princeton University Press, 1978.

Bercovitch, Sacvan, ed. *The American Jeremiad.* Madison: University of Wisconsin Press, 1978.

Bercovitch, Sacvan, ed. *The Puritan Origins of the American Self.* New Haven, CT: Yale University Press, 1975.

Bloom, Harold, ed. *Modern Critical Views: Robert Lowell.* New York: Chelsea House, 1987.

Cooper, Philip. *The Autobiographical Myth of Robert Lowell.* Chapel Hill: University of North Carolina Press, 1970.

Gelpi, Albert. "The Reign of the Kingfisher: Robert Lowell's Prophetic Poetry." *Robert Lowell: Essays on the Poetry.* New York: Cambridge University Press, 1986.

Gilson, Etienne. *The Spirit of Medieval Philosophy.* New York: Scribner's, 1936.

Lowell, Robert. *Day by Day.* New York: Farrar, Straus and Giroux, 1977.

Lowell, Robert. *Land of Unlikeness.* New York: Cummington Press, 1944.

Lowell, Robert. *Life Studies* and *For the Union Dead.* New York: Farrar, Straus and Giroux, 1964.

Lowell, Robert. *Robert Lowell: Collected Prose*, ed. and introduced by Robert Giroux. Farrar, Straus and Giroux. New York: 1987.
Lowell, Robert. *Selected Poems*. New York: Farrar, Straus and Giroux, 1977.
Mariani, Paul. *Lost Puritan: A Life of Robert Lowell*. New York, London: W. W. Norton, 1994.
Pearson, Gabriel. "The Middle Years." In Harold Bloom, ed. *Modern Critical Views: Robert Lowell*. New Haven, CT: Chelsea House, 1987.
Sheed, F.J (translator). *The Confessions of Saint Augustine*. London: Sheed and Ward, 1942.
Watkin, E.I. *Catholic Art and Culture*. New York: Sheed and Ward, 1944.

Further Reading

Axelrod, Stephen Gould, and Helen Deese, eds. *Robert Lowell: Essays on the Poetry*. New York: Cambridge University Press, 1986.
Bushman, Richard. *The Great Awakening: Documents on the Revival of Religion, 1740–1745*. Chapel Hill: University of North Carolina Press, 1989.
Heimert, Alan, and Perry Miller, eds. *The Great Awakening: Documents Illustrating the Crisis and Its Consequences*. Indianapolis: Bobbs-Merrill, 1967.
Lambert, Frank. *Inventing the "Great Awakening"*. Princeton, NJ: Princeton University Press, 1999.
Moore, Marianne. *The Complete Poems of Marianne Moore*. New York: Penguin, 1981.
Rudman, Mark. *Robert Lowell: An Introduction to the Poetry*. New York: Columbia University Press, 1983.
Williamson, Alan. *Pity the Monsters: The Political Vision of Robert Lowell*. New Haven, CT: Yale University Press, 1974.

Part III

Matriculations:
In Academic Terms

9

Winter at the Corner of Quincy and Harvard

The Brothers James

A few steps from where I work, at 12 Quincy Street in Cambridge, is the site where, between 1866 and 1881, the most illustrious New England family of all, the Jameses, lived.

The house itself is gone. The Harvard Faculty Club now occupies 20 Quincy, but it is, nevertheless, a source of constant pleasure to remind myself that 12 and 20 Quincy still stand together, within the same compact cluster of buildings, on the same rounded corner a half block from Massachusetts Avenue, just outside of Harvard Yard. Of course, the Yard had a more rural aspect in the days of the Jameses. Then, the area now taken up by the three great libraries – Widener, Houghton, and the undergraduate library, Lamont – was just bare common. But the view from my building is otherwise much as it was in the 1870s, with little paths leading then, as they do today, from outside the campus in, and the in-and-out flow of foot traffic weaving Cambridge into the rhythms of the University.

William and Henry James did not grow up in this house, but from the late 1860s through to the 1870s, it was here, just across

New England Beyond Criticism: In Defense of America's First Literature, First Edition. Elisa New.
© 2014 Elisa New. Published 2014 by John Wiley & Sons, Ltd.

the way from President Eliot's, where their parents and sister lived and they called home. Here they lived during the years when, as two insecure, mood-bedeviled young men of irregular upbringing, they nevertheless launched what would be two of the most brilliant and influential careers of any Americans. Both traveled frequently and extensively. Nevertheless, it was from 20 Quincy that the young Henry James – roughly the age of a Harvard senior – completed and sent off to his father's friend, J.R. Lowell, editor of the *Atlantic Monthly*, what would be his very first literary publication. Scribbling in an upstairs room at 20 Quincy, Henry posted – or may have walked with – his early reviews and stories across Harvard Square and out Brattle Street to Elmwood, where Lowell would have read them in his square and sunny rooms before the fire.

Even though Henry James did not remain in America, much less Boston; even though he chose to live in Europe and, finally, to become an English citizen; even though he made clear that, all devotion to his parents and especially his brother, William, aside, he found America culturally impoverished, and New England harsh, stiff, and crude (or *nude*, as he liked to say); James nonetheless bore an affection for the region and evinced an interest in it not compromised by his sense of its deficits. Indeed, the more distinct the unlovelinesses of the New England scene, the richer the fund of experience it presents a consciousness capable of apprehending them. Long passages of his work on Hawthorne, published in 1876, make just this point and so, too, do subsequent works. In, for instance, "A New England Winter," a novella of 1884 about a young expatriate man who visits Boston for a season (the death of James's parents in 1881 occasioned two winter stays at 20 Quincy), a Europeanized young American hero successfully resists the charms of New England, not extending his stay beyond winter, despite his mother's clever attempt at "sugaring for the young man's lips the pill of a long deferred visit to Boston" (*Complete Stories* 81). Boston, in fact, provides this condescending young man more entertainment, more complex forms of stimulation than he had expected – "The houses – a bristling, jagged line of talls and shorts"; "the air was traversed with the tangle of the telegraph" (112). There is even the frisson of erotic complexity in the suitably named Mrs "Mesh." One marks that there is less to hold the interest in the "academic suburb," Cambridge, to which one, or the young protagonist, walks from the Back Bay. The unprepossessing route to America's greatest institution of learning is over an "exaggerated" bridge (past what is now MIT) and then along a "wide blank avenue where the puddles lay large over the bounding rails," the whole way offering sights "denuded," "nude," "bare," "mean," and full of "gaps" (100–113). The destination, Harvard, is something of an anticlimax: "the collegiate precinct, low, flat and immense, with vague, featureless spaces and the air of a clean encampment" (113).

It is not a flattering picture. Nor, by the way, is it completely inapt, even today. Stretches of Massachusetts Avenue, on the Cambridge side anyway, are still puzzlingly raw and unkempt. And yet, for one on whom nothing is lost, even ugliness may have magic to bestow. And New England has certain secrets, or even certain "jokes" (as James hinted in Hawthorne), to share with those of imagination. The greatest of these: winter itself, New England's most splendid season.

The hero of "A New England Winter," burdened with such imagination, has no choice but to become a connoisseur of Boston's skies, of the lights and obscurities clarified by the winter cold. He cannot prevent himself from taking in the facades that "seem to have been scoured, with a kind of friction, by the hard, salutary light," from feasting his eyes on "brilliant browns and drabs, their rosy surfaces of brick" (90), from raising his eyes to the "arching blueness" or lowering them to the "ice" that "had a polish which gleamed through the dusk" (104).

So utterly bedazzled by the New England light is Henry James that if he didn't have quite so much to satirize in New England manners and mores (and he does have an immense amount), his novel of 1885, *The Bostonians*, might easily be mistaken for a paean to the New England winter. Whether one is simply waiting mundanely for a streetcar in the morning of a winter weekday (the "weather was brilliant enough to minister to any illusion"; "as if the touch of the air itself were gloved, and the street-colouring had the richness of a superficial thaw") (114; 119); or, observing the everyday winter dusk over the Charles ("the picture was tinted with a clear, cold rosiness. The air, in its windless chill, seemed to tinkle like crystal, the faintest gradations of tone were perceptible in the sky, the west became deep and delicate, everything grew doubly distinct before taking on the dimness of evening. There were pink flushes on snow, 'tender' reflections in patches of stiffened marsh, sounds of car bells, no longer vulgar, but almost silvery") (95); or, stepping from a warm room, crowded with partygoers, into the January sharpness ("a splendid sky, all blue-black and silver – a sparkling winter vault, where the stars were like myriad points of ice") (72). New England weather, and New England, gives life a "festive complexion" (114).

The pivotal chapter of *The Bostonians* occurs on a winter afternoon in Harvard Yard itself, conveying James's hero and heroine past the corner occupied by 12 and 20 Quincy Street. In this chapter, the raffish Verena Tarrant, budding celebrity feminist, brings a young Southern suitor to see the College. By the time they have left Verena's neighborhood of Cambridgeport (whose "little wooden houses, with still more wooden dooryards looked" – then as now – "as if they had been constructed by the nearest carpenter and his boy") and by the time they have made their way up the more groomed blocks of Massachusetts Avenue leading to Harvard Yard ("a long avenue which, fringed on either side with fresh villas, offering themselves trustfully to the public, had the distinction of a wide pavement of neat red brick") (130) and have found their way into the Yard ("the irregular group of heterogeneous buildings – chapels, dormitories, libraries, halls – which, scattered among slender streets, over a space reserved by means of a low rustic fence, rather than inclosed"), they are well on their way to falling in love (132).

Only in New England, James's satire gives us to understand, would a pretty young woman and a young man enjoying a sunny walk work quite so hard to wring moral improvement from their date. Only in New England (where, after all, the "Boston marriage" was invented, James's sister Alice one of its pioneers) would Verena trouble herself so much with keeping the secret of this walk, concealing it from her great friend and other suitor, the well-to-do Olive Chancellor, whose Bostonian techniques of siphoning off excess libido involve readings in German philosophy, edifying lectures, and, when these don't work, suffering jouncing horse-car rides, the better to chasten patrician instincts. Nor does Verena, herself Bostonian, skip even one improving stop on the Crimson tour. Debating history and the future of man and womankind with her date, she not only has him admire the Library, but also go in to see the Reference Desk, to meet a librarian, and, even, to riffle through the drawers of the card catalogue. Only then do the lovers make their way past dormitories and classroom buildings to their final destination, Memorial Hall, erected for the Civil War dead. A full tour naturally follows.

Not so sexy, one might say, and yet James knows otherwise – as Hawthorne did too. Both well understood that the New England Way, with its intolerance of tepidness and its tolerance of doubleness, with the wide latitudes it gives fervency and the low regard in which it holds compromise, is a fertile atmosphere or love, which, like the ravishments of winter, may sneak in when one is not looking.

Walking across Harvard Yard on so many winter days, the sound of conversations rising and falling about me, it is not hard to pretend sometimes that I hear the voice of that same William James just steps behind.

Handsome in tweeds, with his straight nose, his keen eyes and his manly beard, William James was such a fixture in Harvard Yard, and such a hero of the institution, his charisma still charges the air – particularly in winter.

In keeping with his faith in the in-between, in the prepositional moments of our experience, James delivered as much instruction between classes as during them, pausing on the brick paths or halfway down staircases to ponder and expostulate, laughing or chaffing or pausing with interlocutors. If his brother Henry was probably mistaken, carried away by the weather perhaps, when he wrote, again in *The Bostonians*, that "Harvard knows nothing either of the jealousy or the dignity of high walls," he might be forgiven the exaggeration, with William for a brother. William's informality was his own, but it is also true that he probably could not have become himself without so much in the way of New England stiffness and Cambridge parochialism to work against. Harvard's particular formality provided an excellent backdrop and stimulus for his more out-of bounds personality.

Not that James hasn't been – as the most distinguished figures at Harvard inevitably are – institutionalized and monumentalized. What must be the ugliest building on Harvard's campus is called William James, and James's lectures and letters, both published and jotted – complete with jokes – are preserved in Houghton, what must be the most fortified archive in the world. There, in the hush of the paneled reading room, an hour spent poring over James's most casual jottings has a sacral feel. And yet, even in an atmosphere of such pomp, it is wonderful how much salutary vagary – which is to say, how much heart, and poetry – aerates the work of James. The most local of Harvard locals, a lifer, James nevertheless evinced throughout his whole career a spirit as free of parochialism as it was true to many aspects of New England's oldest articles of faith. Certainty left him skeptical, but uncertainty inspired him with belief. He had a nature so ebullient and open, and an attitude to knowledge so experimental and contingent, that the various disciplines in which he worked had to expand to accommodate him, and had to discipline itself to make its case against relaxation, of reason against belief, and all certainties to be judged according to their usefulness. The fields we now call Philosophy, Psychology, Religious Studies – not to mention those branches of Sociology, Political Science concerned with the preservation of pluralism; not to mention those branches of Aesthetics concerned with the experience of making, and beholding, the work of art; not to mention those reaches of popular culture concerned with self-care and self-help, good habits – all these were just gaining disciplinary outline during the years James worked in these fields, and all these bear James's stamp. Yet his mark cannot be called a stamp at all since James was the last person to think knowledge would remain still within its outline.

Or to imagine that elite institutions, or classes, had any monopoly on what was true. Thus, James defended and befriended psychics and séance holders, aesthetes and anarchists, depressives and light-weights, arguing against systems but also working the system as necessary when more practical expedients were called for. In an age of Jim Crow and quotas, James was the mentor who mattered most to W.E.B. Du Bois, to Gertrude Stein, to Horace Kallen, and to Charles Sanders Peirce, four of twentieth-century America's most influential thinkers and artists, recognizing genius even when it broke the rules. One cannot imagine it was administratively simple, but James gave Gertrude Stein an "A" even when, instead of her blue book, she turned in a note to Professor James regretting that she did not feel very much like completing an examination paper that day. Neither did James.

It is as a teacher, and as a teacher of teachers, that William James bestowed the greatest lessons. James saw the teacher not as dignitary but as exemplar of strenuous experience, a kind of intellectual animal living in the eventful element of thought. While James's Harvard was, and remains, a place enamored of the formal lecture, James's test of a good lecturer was, as his colleague George Herbert Palmer recalled, whether that lecturer: "'wallowed,' that is, moved unobstructedly, through his matter as the whale does through the sea, twisting and turning at his pleasure, tossing up foam for mere sport, and plunging or rising as the fancy strikes." Palmer confirmed: "James always wallowed" (33). A similar anecdote is related of a small seminar James liked to hold in his house, one in which he brought out a little blackboard and, after trying to balance the board first on a chair and then on a table, he finally gave up on inferior solutions and threw himself full length on the floor, holding the board with one hand and lecturing from the carpet. Students privi-leged to witness such performances were, of course, already accus-tomed to James's unorthodoxies.

"Life is in the transitions," James famously wrote. It is a hospitable maxim, one to which any reader of New England's literature profit-ably returns.

James's vacillations charm. Late for lunch over on Irving Street, James would often draw shy, hungry undergraduates along with him, and he drove his wife, and himself, crazy with the many invitations he bestowed. It is related that on one such occasion, irritated at the bell heralding yet another awkward collegiate visitor, James instructed Mrs James to inform visitors that her husband was, regrettably, unavailable. Before the visitors had turned away, however, Professor James had himself rushed to the door, waving them in with his "Come in, Come in!"

References

James, Henry. "A New England Winter." In *Complete Stories 1844–1891*. New York: Library of America, 1999: 65–122.

James, Henry. *The Bostonians*. New York: Penguin Classics, 2000.

Palmer, George Herbert. "William James." *William James Remembered*. Ed. Linda Simon. Lincoln: University of Nebraska Press, 1996: 27–35.

10

Upon a Peak in Beinecke

The Beauty of the Book in the Poetry of Susan Howe

A scrap of Emily Dickinson's "cream laid" notepaper traced with graphite, the face of the manuscript buffed and eroded by time and the friction of the oblong envelope (acid free) in which it is stored.

A strip of denuded gray homespun or of the muslin once used for bed-curtains, the fabric threshed by time to a mere crosshatch of warp and woof: porous, skeletal.

The ambered tissue of a nineteenth-century frontispiece overleaf.

A crushed, torn origami, one friable finger's length, shaped like a weathervane, ripped from a Webster's dictionary, 1840 edition, tiny crumbles sifting from the edges.

The black-and-white photograph of a young blonde girl with a shoulder length pageboy hairdo, wearing a toga. The photo is not actually black and white, but rather a study in grays brightened by a black backing or a white detail. Here it is a warm, – nearly brown – gray pebbled with darker graphite and there: pale-steel clouded with ivory. In folds and yokes of the girl's clothing, and the clothing of the others shown with her, various matte mid-grays cue us to

New England Beyond Criticism: In Defense of America's First Literature, First Edition. Elisa New.
© 2014 Elisa New. Published 2014 by John Wiley & Sons, Ltd.

see red, blue, or green. Only at the composition's center, where a gleam from below lights up the girl's hair and bodice, is there a true pearly white.

What else? A Xerox-shaped rectangle, a photo offset or photocopy of a microfiche strip, the rectangle bordered black and centered on one thick ivory page of a book of published verse. Within the gray rectangle separate words (*"praise,"– "thunders," "kills"*) are repeated according to some pattern, with discrete words enclosed in thick lozenges of border.

A fraying square of white silk from the wedding dress of a Connecticut minister's wife. The image of a man, walking abstractedly, random pieces of paper pinned to his coat. He wrote on every inch of paper he could find, and then came home to his wife, after days of hard riding, with his coat covered in scraps.

Can words composed in holy awe betroth him to Christ, marry his sin to redeeming graceful love? He prays it might be so, for his tradition tells him the Word is a wedding garment. Along with his wife's wedding garment, some of his scraps may still repose in drawers in Yale's Sterling and Beinecke libraries.

Such delicate and perishable objects, their structures resolving to non-structure, or non-structures to structure, are central in Susan Howe's poetics.[1]

Typically, these objects to which Howe gives a nearly ritual power are ones she has personally salvaged and then subjected to a unique process of composition. Trained originally in the visual arts, Howe makes poetry (rather than merely writing it) as painters make art. From the personal libraries and scrapbooks of her own parents and forebears, from local libraries in small Massachusetts, Connecticut, Berkshire, and Adirondack towns, and from the great institutional archives where books deemed worthy of keeping reside – Harvard's Houghton and Yale's Beinecke – Howe retrieves the articulate textual remnants of her New England past. Later, at home at her table, sitting near a window that brings in light broken by tree shadows, she coaxes these objects into second growth. She exposes their surfaces to the changing light on her desktop, and then the technological light of the photocopier. After she has copies in hand, she begins the delicate grafting and quilting operations that give her pages loft and texture, and even a sort of grade, and she also composes the meditative or lyrical stanzas closest, in traditional terms, to what we call poetry.

Legibility, transparency, and even navigability are aspects, but hardly the most salient, of her poetry's features. How could they be, in this poetry so many featured, this poetry ambitious of exceeding, while including and honoring lyric form?

By and large, English readers expect that poems shall express the personality of an individual self, a self for whom the lyric "I" is spokesperson and whose subjectivity is represented by the supposed transparency of print. Poetic success, in the traditional model, is achieved best when the set of highly dense and quite material conventions, the poetic apparatus, can be made to seem sheer. For the extent to which print can be a communicative medium depends upon the individual voice that confers beauty by washing the world with vision, leaving it glistening. Traditional books of poetry will, in fact, contain any amount of obscure printed matter, but all such matter will be suspended within a life-giving fluidity of the lyric voice that contains and masters them. "Readings" are generally expected to enhance this experience of absorption, translating poetry on the page into sounds whose referential rather than acoustic or musical qualities will pierce the intervening crowded space of the room full of chairs, persons, microphones, and hearing aids.[2] One hears a poem at a "reading," or reads a poem in one's own mind, but the poem, we presume, is not altered. Only the delivery system is different.

Moreover, in America, poetry is often justified, if at all, only for its capacity to elevate us morally, to offer edification or improvement. It is expected that, as the poet aims his work at producing insight, his reader travels via printed lines on a journey whose end will be his own deeper understanding. As the popularity of explicit hortatory themes withered in America, it nevertheless remained a given that poetry and philosophy were hortatory forms. For instance, readers accepting that an arrangement of lines need not mimic a "psalm," that lines need not scan or count off in numbered stanzas to earn the right to be called poems, still wanted their poems to end with a redemptive bang. Readers assumed that the lines of a poem would conduce toward growing clarity, its progress initiated from the left and going to the right-hand margin of a single page. Development on the page, in other words, would mimic growth or revelations within the psyche or soul of the reader, with destiny of poet and soul joined. The traditional poem ministers to this destiny.

What makes the poetry of Susan Howe so different is that the poem is not a minister or medium of transparency. The poet does not stand outside. She is, often at much risk, vulnerability, and exposure to herself, inside the poem, her voice one tactile, historical object among other objects in the poem. Her quest for the beautiful poem is not for what frames or contains. If the lyric speaker is usually outside her book, her "voice" containing the poem's contents, here the lyric voice sounds from within, and lyric consciousness has no special privileges.

> If the book is to be opened
> I must open it to open it
> I must go get it if I am to
> Go get it I must walk if I
> Walk I must stand if I am
> To stand I must rise if I am
> To rise I had better put my
> Foot down here is where
> Consciousness grows dim
> (*Pierce-Arrow*, 57)

Howe shows in such lines that poems have a weight and volume, palpabilities and opacities running counter to trained expectations. Though her poems can be called experimental and seem, on first glance, radical, this Connecticut poet is a secret sharer dwelling in the neighborhood of Wallace Stevens, who wrote that "The greatest poverty is not to live / In a physical world (325)." As in Stevens, so in Howe. Not only is it axiomatic, in Howe, that the greatest poverty is not to live in a physical world, but also that the physical world is historical. Such convictions have implications. To journey into the literary past is not, and will never be, for Howe, a matter of mere exercise of mind. The intellectual life of the poet will need more than clarity of vision, will be held accountable to disciplines more palpable than the cerebral ones – to farming, quarrying, harvesting; to the work of pioneer wives packing and unpacking, storing and arranging; even to uncomplaining attendance in a Hartford office. Even when the tools she uses are electronic – and she does use them – the most dematerialized of processes will retain its tactile feel or else lose purchase on the beauty of the objects it seeks. Even a Google search does, for Howe, retain the palpable labor intensiveness of mining or agriculture, or an arduous handicraft.

It is no surprise, then, that Howe lets us see the process of making poems as painstaking, even excruciating. The poet's greedy raid on the archive will always uncover more of the disintegrating paper mobiles, each lovely in its way, than can ever be represented adequately. There is a certain pathos attached to work of this kind, for there will always be a fatter pile of photocopies, a taller haystack of the lovely mobiles, than any publisher will ever include in a book, always the prospect of diminishing returns for labor expended. Sometimes one feels how charily Howe has set down words, feels a Frostian thrift implicit in Howe's craft of honoring diminished things. And sometimes one senses, conversely, a certain luxuriousness in the enterprise, so lavishly deliberate, even prodigal,

Which fossil-like sprays of print, some black and distinct, some blurred and eroded, will find a place within the area of Howe's page? How to "frame" these? Shall the simple window-sized rectangle of a single page best frame the scrap or image, or ought the scrap instead form, say, part of a diptych, conversant with its facing page? If part of a diptych, shall the shard or flake be shadow or herald, announcing its coeval, and if so, shall it appear in line with, or raised above or below? Should the font or typeface be as distinct, more distinct, or less distinct than that on its facing page?

What of the rhymes or patternings, the principles of coagulation and scattering, that unify or loosen the pages? Shall there be threads

239

of theme carrying through an actual narrative story line, or shall images pool in coagulant interknit structures – verb-less, objectless, and yet visually or sonically dense? To what extent shall individual words comment on, reflect each other through sonic imitations or visual punning, and to what extent shall the individual line, or even the grammatical sentence, frame a given stretch or movement of the poem? When, and with how much information, shall the poet offer teacherly exposition; when should she narrate in a twenty-first-century plain style what she experienced when she wrote the poem? How much weight should she give to such passages?

What about the physical book as it organizes and is itself altered by an interval of reading? Books are read, Howe lets us see, by sunlight or lamplight, on divans or in bed or at library tables, for work or diversion. What about the weight or importance of any one page within the mobile architecture of the book itself? Pages may be flat but books are made of 180 degrees; every page traces the arc from 0 degrees to 180 every minute or so. As the page turns, the reader's fingertip active, the geometries of relation between eye and print alter. Light dawns or spreads its bloom out from the spine of the book to the edge, and then light is sucked back into the thin crevice. We block it out, but each page we press to 180 degrees flat narrows back to nothing before it reopens. Reading constantly hazards triangles as well as rectangles. Only when we fail to open a book fully enough on the photocopier are we reminded of the way print slides on the diagonal down into a closed book, the inner margin an angled slope into the dark spine.

The mobile sculpture of the book is, what's more, a technology encased by, and dwelling in, the more complex architecture of the library. Houghton Library at Harvard, no less than Mt Vision in the Berkshires, is a complex site, creviced and craggy and promontoried. Nature and culture are interleafed and mingled to a far greater degree than we admit. Howe shows how certain "natural" spots on the North American crust – tracts of Adirondack acres where Protestants met Indians in war, for instance, or the Cape Cod coast, or certain becalmed Pennsylvania foothills where religious pilgrims preserved extreme cultural quietus – are textually fecund, full of articulate sounds and sedimented with printed matter the poet can detect and carry into the future. Conversely, she disallows merely mental or intellectual spaces. Libraries, and especially the great ones like Houghton and Beinecke, are features of an environment composed out of material indigenous and transplanted, made by persons native or migrant, of stone and wood, their door frames and elevator shafts constructed once and forever changing, though less perceptibly. In banks of oak shelving on slate floors, in their cooling systems and Dewey decimal systems and maps, these buildings have declivities and broad plateaus, accessible pathways and unnavigable outcroppings which, like a mountain or body of water, facilitate or impede, filter or speed engagement with their contents.[3] Like Keats who, in reading Chapman's Homer ("On First Looking into Chapman's Homer" (43)) compared it to the enlarged vistas "stout Cortez" beheld as he stood "Upon a Peak in Darien" (46), Howe stands upon her peak in Beinecke Library and surveys the American canon.

Susan Howe has written far more than can be comprehended here, and so in these pages I confine myself to looking at the last four, two from the 1990s and two from the early twenty-first century. These books will serve to represent Howe's mature work. *Singularities* (1990) and *Pierce-Arrow* (1997); the small, privately published *Kidnapped* (2002); and finally, *Souls of the Labadie Tract* (2007) allow us to watch Howe's mature techniques in motion and development. I shall concentrate on describing the poet's relationship to precursors and history in the volumes *Singularities* and *Pierce-Arrow*, and, more concisely, in *Kidnapped*, before going on to analysis of Howe's most recent, work, *Souls of the Labadie Tract*. There the poet becomes the courier between two Connecticut forebears, Wallace Stevens and Jonathan Edwards, making her own verse conversant with theirs.

Along with her colleagues of the L=A=N=G=U=A=G=E school, and in the tradition of William Carlos Williams, Howe's work has not only questioned the associated ideas of lyric subjectivity and self-possessive, self-assertive individualism, but has also traced both to certain aggressive syndromes of the Puritan mind. This given, Howe has also cherished Protestant thought and, especially in the traditions of Protestant literacy, has created an aesthetic field with semaphores up, attuned to beauty and prolific in producing it.

Illustrating this point is the cover of Howe's *Singularities* (1990), a cover that does not just illustrate but initiates and inaugurates the reading process. Tinted an antique powder-puff pink, the book's cover typifies books as decorative elements that furnished refinement as they "civilized" and domesticated the wilderness. Meanwhile, the cover's woodcut illustration tells a more violent story. The woodcut depicts a phalanx of black-hatted marksmen taking aim across what seems either a rolling sea or a planted field – in either case, someone is dying or drowning in the billows. Ambiguity also surrounds what lies between the shooters and their targets: sheaves, women, swaddled babies, or merely compacted leaves. Are the shooters in the woodcut perhaps uniformed British soldiers aiming at colonials in woodland settlements or, perhaps, colonials taking aim at Indians in longhouses? Battlefield and planted field share the same outlines, suggesting agriculture's slow-growth aggression, while the stylized foreshortened compression of the battles between whites and Indians, particularly those taking place around Deerfield at the commencement of King Philip's war, suggests a telescoping of many battles and of history itself as battlefield. The woodcut seems (in the manner of Williams's prologue to *In the American Grain*) to expose the fear of contact, to represent the cold blossom of pride that allowed Americans to treat the earth as – in W.C. Williams's words – "excrement of some sky (218)."

European trashing of the American wilderness, a despoiling as old as the first Europeans' arrival but renewed in every century, is a theme Howe pursues, especially in the second long poem of the volume, "Thorow." There Henry David Thoreau's alienation from the despoiling of America by commerce prefigures her own alienation before the cheap motels and gimcrackery of modern-day Lake George. Again one hears echoes of Williams, as Howe finds that the "pure products of America go crazy (217)." The very entering of the wilderness and settling it is a form of madness that wreaks vengeance on the land itself, turning it to ugliness for the sake of private possession and discreteness of soul. This does not mean, however, that the poet marooned by Lake George, living out a winter in cold winds next to glittering ice, denies sympathy with the volume's central perpetrator-victim, the seventeenth-century minister Hope Atherton who, lost in the woods during King Philip's war, was finally set aflame and ran to his death. Howe lets Atherton's purity of belief, his naked fear, his Protestant aloneness abide within and ignite her own lyricism. Through Atherton's stiff but lovely archaisms, Atherton's genuine if myopic convictions, his chilled and threatened accents, Howe finds a certain redemptive womanliness in Puritan clerical speech. Also, Atherton's womanish name, Hope, softens the barriers of time and alienation so that the poet, in effect, takes him in. Howe, the lonely poet holed up in the frozen woods, is no stranger herself to defensiveness, to wondering who is her enemy and who her friend.[4] It is a milder version of wilderness panic she experiences during her Sabbatical in the Mohawk wilderness, but she too fears marauders and girds herself defensively. She too suffers the syndromes of individualism, spasms of singularity.[5]

This "singularity" is at least part of the problem. Hence the plural title of the volume, *Singularities*, a title that de-exceptionalizes while it also takes names and apportions accountability. *Singularities* gives the lie to the Puritan settler's assertions of chosenness, it exposes the modern advertiser's exploitation of the niche, and it endeavors to find a place of kinship between the two aggressive proponents of chosenness, the Reverend Hope Atherton and his later-day nemesis, the woodland sojourner, Henry David Thoreau. To both of these, and channeling the communicative Whitman as well (for Whitman, as Christopher Looby notes, is interleafed with Howe's verse, as all poets, and persons, are tucked into his *Leaves*), the poet declares:

> You are of me & I of you, I cannot tell
> Where you leave off and I begin
>
> (58)

This relationality is crucial to the volume, and to historical understanding as Howe seeks it. Historical consciousness is a remedy for excesses of singularity, and a means of entering and sympathizing across lines of estrangement or aggression. It teaches us that we are interleafed, softens the distinctions of persons according to and along coordinates of proper identity, historical epoch, language, and compass points: Hope Atherton, a seventeenth-century English speaker living in western Massachusetts, is usually held distinct from Henry David Thoreau, a nineteenth-century English speaker living in eastern Massachusetts, who is ordinarily held distinct from Susan Howe, a twentieth-century English speaker living in southern New England. But these distinctions are nullified by language, which connects us all.

Only the most meager, most non-historical, uses of language, Howe shows, will confine themselves to expressions of a placed and mortal subjectivity — a person of one time and place. Poetry's richer capacities, its more elastic talents, may be used to achieve the resonant scattering, to help us hear sound forms that persist across spaces unbound by occasion. Indeed, the only kind of verse one hardly ever finds in Susan Howe is the "occasional." Rather, the single, double, and multiple panes of paper surface offered by a printed book are like springboards and landing spaces. The pages of a book entertain the commerce of syllables and nomenclatures. A page is where idioms and linguistic changes still in process leave their prints.

Howe's refusal of lyric singularity in favor of the space of the book may eschew the privileges of the individual, but it is anything but impersonal. As she carries Hope Atherton's pitiable, poignant singularity, she carries, too, that of her lyric forebears whose conventions of authorial power and forward thrust are her historical inheritance: "Work penetrated by the edge of author, traverses multiplicities, light letters exploding apprehension suppose when individual hearing" (41). But beyond this, Howe's emotional, even plangent tonal register reminds us that writing does not slake but extends need; writing consists in a disarmed exposure of the writer's mind, psyche, and heart to the unknown. The seigniorial distance and cutting frontage of authorship are always, happily, subject to ambush by reading, which turns the self into a thruway, a way of admitting the dead to take up habitation within one. Reading opens the book of the self to other

244

leaves, which then dwell somewhere therein, their force liable to discharge at any moment.

Thus the fascination with "Thorow," Howe's scout and guide, in *Singularities*. During her visiting professorship at an upstate university in winter, the poet finds not Thoreau but "Thorow." Thorow clears trails, we might say, within the imagination of Susan Howe, who becomes disidentified with her "self" just as "Thorow," spelled with an English rather than French set of ending vowels, is disidentified from his. Not identical with his name, Thor-row is now, as one correspondent puns, a god-like "Thor" who "rows" (down the Concord and Merrimack). Not only does Thoreau row, but he rows on "eau." Indian place names end with the suffix "et" and his ends with "eau" – both are words for water. Whatever the biographical personality Thoreau had, "Thorow" has riverine fluency and ready translatability; his name, like "Hope" Atherton, becomes not a singular label but a place of passage, a sort of pump. With "Thorow" at her back, the poet barricaded in her cabin ventures out, moves into "the weather's fluctuation"; she gets the Indian names "'straightened'" by which she means "more crooked." Now she may read American history differently, allowing the language of one epoch to wash over that of another, admitting the past to the present.

A sequence of examples will demonstrate how this all plays out within the volume. The setting is northern New York, mid-twentieth century, the Adirondacks, where a poet, sometimes lonely, lives in a primitive cabin through a cold winter. Indian wars were fought in this place, as they were along the wide belt of the Mohawk lands extending east to Concord. And so the poet, through the winter, keeps the Reverend Hope Atherton, who fled from Indians through the woods, and the naturalist Henry David Thoreau, in mind. The battles between whites and Indians, part of the archaic American experience, are yet more archaic, these conflicts now including the whole American continent and the epic history of war and terror. Howe endeavors to represent – all at once – the regular cycles of snow on earth, centuries of English and Indian habitation, fluctuations of fear, anger, and reverence. The ancient clash of bloodied arms achieves lucidity when, in Hope Atherton's "voice" it records:

loving Friends and Kindred
When I look back
So short in Charity and Good Works
We are a small remnant
Of signal escapes wonderful in themselves
(*Singularities* 16)

Yet Atherton's lucidity is achieved at the cost of much ambient depth of echo and many other sounds – of Indians, of woods, of seasons flowing through. It is as though the poet restricted language to the narrowest chamber to leave it in the care of the subjective voice. Thus, Howe lets the sound scatter, retrains it not only through the singular consciousness of a man's particular event, Hope Atherton's, into a larger surround, bouncing and rebounding off his cherished books and his dreams of Atlantic passage, his still-and-never-to-be-unlearned Continental and filial humility, the slow occlusion of European memories by New World flora and fauna, and these off each other, since sounds compose their own relations.

Otherworld light into fable
Best plays are secret plays

————————

Mylord have maize meadow
Have Capes Mylord to dim
Barley Sion beaver Totem
W'ld bivouac by vineyard
Eagle aureole elses thend
(*Singularities* 11)

Atherton's humility before old forms of authority, his instinctual awe before the dazzle of New World heights and expanses, his natural reaching for Biblical vocabulary to express exaltation, all these are compressed in these lines, the echo between worlds giving rise to a music no more crowded than history is. Obscurities in Howe are rarely opaque, although they may be refractory. What is "thend"? Perhaps it is " the end" subjected to the rules that allow "would" to be represented as "w'ld." Or something else – the thrumming sound, perhaps, of that eagle's wing, the concentric

246

inexactitude of the eagle aureole sharpened, sleeked by the "d" to a feathered edge. That "d" cinches rhymes that wavered in one line; read down the strophe's edge and you will find that, as *"dim"* is to *"vineyard," "totem"* is to *"thend."*

A few more pages and more radical crosscuttings and interleafings break the integrity and decorum of the page. The poem itself becomes a tool of crosscutting, a chisel releasing the plural singularities that populate false singularities. A vertical oblong of couplets, with white ribbons of double space between each and a theme of "marching," give page 12 a forward-leaning, epic-feeling surge across the gutter and between the leaves, impossible to ignore. Instead of ribboned lines, words not yet given semantic purpose, words not yet phalanxed or devoted to a cause, are arrayed in their native spirits – "Nature without check with original energy" (*Leaves of Grass*, 1891), as Whitman had it in "Song of Myself" (8). "Epithets young in a box" (*Complete Poetry and Selected Prose*, 13) the poet calls these syllables, these hard sounds unused to use, electric and many edged. Brilliant tessellated puzzle pieces milling in a square without the protocols of right to left to define their order, these words regain the density of epithets. Pictographic diagonals have just as much charge, or more than, laterals. Hence:

> architect
>> euclidean curtail
>>> (13)

Or

>> a
>>> severity whey crayon
>>>> (13)

Or

>>>> Shad sac stone
>>> recess
>>>> (13)

These little chimnied or cellared sheds of sound do not refuse all denotative gestures. They conjure, for instance, the actual phenomena

247

in a primitive world (human settlement staked out through geometry; the oblong whey-squiggles of loose bowels; a lovely sunlit pond incubating aquatic life), but their visual and aural shapes, stacked or leaning pyramids of c's and s's, Latinate clusters starting back in the palate, have an interknitness of their own.

In *Singularities*, the poet who was a visual artist has much to teach us about how forms confer beauty on other forms simply through patterns of resemblance and variation. For once, as she shows, thor ow (or eau) bursts the bounds of the singular person, once poetry leaps the fences of the lateral and the boundaries of the page, then, with the up-and-down joists of the book loosened, new species of poetic gravity, accountability, and kinship may descend. Once it is no longer human consciousness, with the lyric speaker in loge (lofted above, driving thought left to right in obedience to intention, past to future from nascency to destiny), words and thought may be seen in their more natural state. They splay and spread like lichen growth or tree fall, half living, half dead, turned face up, face down, some above and some below ground. From inside language's thicket, voices – even the poet's own voice – may be heard.

Choral, transtemporal, chthonic, language is beautifully crooked, branching and unlinear, turned and turned by tropings, cognitions, and recognitions.

That persons can never be transparent; that poetic "speakers," like philosophical "thinkers," are only by the most extreme suspension of disbelief reckoned to master, guide, or control materials; that there are other offices for the poet than Cartesian reflection or – even in America! – rhetorical (national) or homiletic (religious) persuasion – such convictions of poetry's coextensive relation with matter and complex ethical action inform *Pierce-Arrow* and *Kidnapped*, both of which highlight the poet's role as actor reactor, and accountable ethical subject rather than pure supervisory will. Indeed, as Stephanie Sandler has noted,[6] the accountability of Americans, including intellectuals and the institutions organizing intellectuals, to the exertions and dispositions of American power is a topic vital to Howe. We have seen this in her treatment of scenes of war in *Singularities*.

The idealized transparency or transcendent quality of the intellectual life are, as Howe shows in *Pierce-Arrow*, belied by how intellectual careers actually play out, with the levers and gears, the individual career trajectories, and high stakes power struggles of university life mimicking those less idealized. A career within the "ivory tower" is, as Howe reminds us, a trade like any other, where ideas may be pressed into service as tools, and the growth or stasis of disciplines liberated or impeded by demands of ego. And of course, competition between disciplines, like the age-old contest between poetry and philosophy, deprives both of claims to any transcendent poise and restores them to history.

Poetry itself is, these books remind us, a production, a profession, an institution. Thus *Pierce-Arrow*, largely set in the academy (art's patron and paymaster), finds Howe reflecting, as she had in other volumes, on the boundaries, constraints, and strictures governing creative life in New England's capitals of intellect.[7] Howe is not shy about allowing the tension between and among members of the intelligentsia to enter her poetics. Not for nothing does she, riffing on Thorstein Veblen, title the second part of *Pierce-Arrow* "The Leisure of the Theory Classes," as not for nothing had she given over pages of her work *The Birth-Mark* to exhuming and working through her own memories of Cambridge, Massachusetts in the 1950s. There, as daughter of a law school professor and an Irish actress, she came of age amid the posturing, genius, and tipsy grab-ass of the Cold War academy.[8] Not unambivalent, but also not dismissive of her own opportunities, Howe makes her poems reflect the experience of one born into not only her own life but into a way of life. Like Mather and Eliot children, Holmes and Lowell and James children – privileged for being what is called in academic parlance, "legacies" – Howe, daughter of a Harvard law professor, is informed by the name she bears and forever marked by the grid of Cambridge Streets. To have come of age at Harvard, a daughter of American law and the Irish stage, to be the sister of a poet and also an actor, are not incidental attributes but conditioning facts that Howe makes use of in her poetry. The tense, if often fruitful, tensions between creative temperaments and the bureaucracies that pay their livelihoods; the national, ideological, and religious imperatives or fashions that may elevate one strain of thought over another; the inverse or torqued relation of genius to success; the sharp byplay between intellectual centers and hinterlands; the ups and downs and variances within and between intellectual careers; and, finally – of a salience nearly impossible to exaggerate – the kinship customs and rituals of bequest, the protocols of transmission, inheritance, and memory that enable or interrupt the flow of ideas across time – to all these Howe opens her verse. A true New England native and student of its intellectual and poetic history, Howe appears in her verse as just that, representing the interimplicated history of intellectual life, poetry, and the professoriate.

Throughout her career, Howe has mapped with great precision the consequential descent of American poetry, like American philosophy, from American theology. Indeed, Howe has reckoned more precisely than any other contemporary poet the exquisite trade-offs and paradoxes of such an inheritance. "God's Altar needs not our polishing." Thus Cotton Mather had once inveighed against Anglo-Catholic aestheticizations, while Jonathan Edwards, of the same Calvinist tradition and a key figure for Howe, saw in "the beauty of the world" the Divine maker's Hand. Either way, the Calvinist–Cartesian regime required poetry's justification to be found outside the realm of art, its office outside the purely aesthetic. Ideally, poetry was countenanced as a device for producing inspiration, whether national or religious or both. Or, elevated language was to be a medium of praise and glorification, a means and mechanism of revelation, or a help toward godly conduct.

"From 1860 on in nineteenth/century American colleges/philosophy was an apology/for Protestant Christianity," writes Howe in *Pierce-Arrow* (71). A little later she quotes Charles Sanders Peirce admitting "One of my earliest recollections was hearing Emerson deliver his address on 'Nature' and I think on that same day Longfellow's "Psalm of Life'" (116). In these quotations we see that, not only are poetry's and philosophy's hereditary American duties fulfilled, their manifold accountabilities to standards ethical and improving summed up – but also their tutelary function is carried out, one institutionally insured. The great institutions of culture that provide Howe her key *mises-en-scène* do not leave disciplines to their own devices. At Harvard and Yale the homiletic imperative is never far off.

> Half of the company
> would try to portray
> some abstract quality
> Fear Courage Ambition
> Love Conceit Hypocrisy
> (*Pierce-Arrow*, 72)

In *Pierce-Arrow*, a poem with Charles Sanders Peirce at its center, Howe finds numerous ways to give density to the persons and forms of academic instruction, using the transgressive, brilliant anti-hero Peirce as avatar of this density. Peirce's most lasting contribution as philosopher may have been to prove the irrelevance, to question the existence, of such abstract qualities when estranged from practice. The mere idea of instruction – the transmission of mental matter via and through the institution of the professoriate (an idea parallel, in Howe's understanding, to poetry as a transparent medium for the conveyance of feeling or beauty) – was one Peirce doubted and dismissed, that vocal dismissal doubtless compromising and eventually dooming his claim to an office of "instruction" at a university. As Howe mordantly informs, Peirce regarded the notion of the university as "institution for instruction . . . grievously mistaken." (7) She lets Peirce's companion, Juliet, define his more intimate relation to ideas: "He loved logic (1)." Of course Peirce's own life-style, in particular his relationship with Juliet, a woman not his wife, made him notorious and lost him several academic posts, but Howe focuses more on the scandal of Howe's pragmatism. To "love logic" in this sense is a classic, pre-Socratic activity in which things are as they appear. For Peirce, the activity of pursuing the logical across a page of paper is an enterprise of the "passion-self" as edged and decisive as any march of epic warriors.

> Each assertion must maintain its icon
> (3)

251

As she develops her complex meditation on Peirce, a poem doubling as her own elegy to the departed husband, David, Howe gathers in a larger community of departed singers and thinker-lovers, communicants of Peirce and David. Howe herself writes that such poems as "The Triumph of Life" and the "Leave-Taking," by Swinburne, comforted her during years of loneliness in Buffalo, the lover-like fluency and plangent ripplings of Swinburne recalling her husband's skill at the tiller. George Meredith, and Swinburne, Peirce's late-nineteenth-century contemporaries, function in the book as his adjutants and secret sharers, all three blessed with a lover-like fluency that does not efface itself. Meredith is revealed through various personal effects – pens, pencils, and a period silhouette fashioned by Sir John Butcher; Swinburne through his desk and the discarded, much edited unfinished manuscripts he left. All three men are examples of unmetaphysical, untranscendant forms of immortality, as her husband's art – sculpture – exemplifies the idea persistent in material form. The poetic work does not transcend, does not "pierce" (Howe plays on Peirce's name here) or find some metaphysical persistence outside its physical form. But in some essential way, as Peirce's philosophy remains immanent, secreted or "pursed" within the vascular tissue of the manuscripts, within the expectant point of the pen, within the storehouse of the archive, so does Howe's poem. If conventional notions of poetic immortality make it depend upon transcendence of print, paper, and ink, these are turned on their head. In *Pierce-Arrow*, the arrow that would pierce is revealed as a purse, love still moist within. For it is, in the end, the great ardor of Peirce (for language, for his aptly named Juliet) that is expressed and reciprocated. Poetry itself, Howe shows, is inevitably an act of love.

The holder of such a view as Howe's will necessarily submit to wearing her own heart on her sleeve. The book, dedicated to the poet's late husband, the sculptor David von Schlegell, has Howe wearing herself on the cover and the back flap. Specifically, on the front we see a photograph of the young Howe in 1947 in a Cambridge, Massachusetts performance of *The Trojan Woman*, while the back flap shows her, in sunglasses, in front of the remains of the Pierce-Arrow automobile factory in Buffalo, New York, the struggling rust-belt city where Howe taught until her retirement in 2008.

This book of poetry, written between childhood and adulthood, Cambridge and Buffalo, is her vehicle too. The poet does not deny that as a writer of poems she plays a dramatic, a performative role, one among others in a lifetime of roles. This book, *Pierce-Arrow*, traces a poignant trajectory, that of the poet's own growth. The tender curve of the maturational arc – the arc of a girl's growth in and through forms of art, in and through stages of love – the nakedness and guardedness of the artist, the nakedness and guardedness of the woman – these themes lend a terrible tenderness to *Pierce-Arrow*. Liaisons with books and encounters with lovers share vectors. Both human and intellectual love aim dead at the heart.

As a younger poet, as one associating with the poets of the School of Poetry and Criticism at SUNY, Buffalo, Robert Creeley and Charles Bernstein, and as a member of the loose confederation known as L=A=N=G=U=A=G=E, Howe has, throughout her career, engaged in a certain amount of quiet polemicizing against the expectation that poetry should be weightless. Given the separation of the critical and the creative that has evolved in universities, the way Howe sends criticism to the school of poetic craft has put her, along with others, in a position of opposition. She found a kinswoman in Emily Dickinson (*My Emily Dickinson*), plus an alter ego in the Indian captive, Mary Rowlandson, and she has found foils and also valued interlocutors in such scions of the academy as Perry Miller and Helen Vendler.

Miller, author of *The New England Mind: The Seventeenth Century*, treated Americans as Augustinian agonists, lonely churches of one (in Niebuhr's phrase), and he dematerialized the Puritan inheritance by turning New England history into a history of ideas.

Helen Vendler, the twentieth century's most celebrated defender of the subjective lyric, has argued for forty years in favor of the individual agency and necessary boundedness of a poem. Poems are, Vendler eloquently argues, what "soul says," the particular textural and thematic signature of a poet's style confirming and affirming the unique texture of the individual (6–7).

Not so, Howe's stylistic cross-weave demonstrates. Universities, intellectual communities, the professoriate, are not merely the settings in which minds operate, providing rooms for minds to train limpid vision on *objets d'art*. Universities with their libraries and offices, their copiers and faxes, their sprawling neighborhoods of rental housing and substantial real estate, and not least their demographic instability and their transatlantic traffic, are part of the texture, entering the pure realm of ideas. Was America ever really America, its soul ever its own, Howe asks, when Boston rips off London? Nor is Harvard Harvard, nor Yale Yale, when Yale makes itself not-Harvard, Harvard makes itself not-Cambridge, Henry makes himself not-William or precisely William. National identities, like personal ones, are all so much annexation and occupation, so much ransoming, you kidnapping me, me you, every poet made out of her sisters and her uncles, volume after volume of imitation and theft down the years.[9]

Kidnapped demonstrates. In her first book of the twenty-first century, published in a limited edition of three hundred, Howe rewrites the American story of migration with materials from her own mother's family archive. In Howe's hands, the Manning family's journey to that most quintessentially American place, Massachusetts, is no Milleresque errand into the wilderness, no pilgrimage of individuals yearning for solitary redemption on the North American strand. The Manning immigration is best seen as a set of performances, of plays by a family of traveling actors. What is a family but a set of players? We feed each other lines. What are poets but estranged kin, kidnappers of the word?

Such scatterings and reunions of kin are themes that continue into Howe's most recent book, the *Souls of the Labadie Tract*. The volume is her simplest to navigate and, in many ways, her most beautiful; it may provide a good starting place for readers who are wary of postmodern experimentalism but lovers, as Howe is, of Wallace Stevens and Jonathan Edwards. As *Kidnapped* traced back along the branches of Howe's own family tree to Irish poets and playwrights, the title poem of this book traces Wallace Stevens to the Pennsylvania lands of his sectarian forebears, thus allowing

Howe to press into new tracts of Anglo-Protestant America. The central poem in the book, "118 Westerly Terrace," ties Stevens to Jonathan Edwards, and both to Howe herself. Imagine the book as a group portrait of three Connecticut poets sharing one ecstatic linguistic raiment and you have its central conceit.

I mean the image literally, for in this book Stevens and Edwards and Howe herself are literally dressed in verse and, too, in the formalized apostrophes of poetry. The language of address, the elevated discourse – whether of poetry or theology or America's characteristic fusion of the two – adorns the history of Connecticut as a bridal gown adorns a bride.

Both Edwards and Stevens had the kind of intimate physical relationship with the poetic word that Howe cherishes, and which she credits in part to her having learned from them. As Lowell too had been, Howe is struck (and who is not!) by the image of Edwards riding into the Connecticut hills with scraps of paper pinned to his coat, coming back from rides in the hills white-garbed, papered with godly sayings. Where is the text, where are the meanings, in this fluttering textual raiment; in this man who lets his faith ribbon his clothes? Edwards's notebooks and miscellanies, which Howe has visited at Yale, pose this question as well, represent a similar form of textuality, their meanings too copious for the conventions of print.

To follow Howe to the Edwards corpus at Yale's Beinecke Library today is to be struck immediately by the brimming, limpid quality of the life's work completed in Stockbridge – and by the explosion of intellect and faith that produced it. It is, for a start, prodigious in bulk. There are more than one thousand sermons, as well as autobiographical narratives of faith, copious scientific notes and essays, and ambitious philosophical pieces on mind, on Being, and on beauty. There are the deceptively titled "Miscellanies," which add up to hundreds of entries, long and short, ranging from mystical meditations on Christ's loveliness to comparisons of classical and Christian history to translations from the Hebrew. This is before we even arrive at the major treatises: *Original Sin, The Freedom of the Will, Treatise on Religious Affections.*

Yet it is not actually the bulk of Edwards's work that astonishes so much as its fractal density, the way the pages seem to grow ever more finely branching and reticulated, as though his writing could catch in its light the thinnest filaments of connection between the smallest particles of Being. Often Edwards's handwriting is so small, the letters like pinheads or filings, that one is hard put to imagine the quill delicate enough to sweep these tiny crests across the page. Somehow, though, these motes take direction, and a taut linear vibration is achieved, a page of even ripples. Other pages are cordoned off at the edges into squares and rectangles packed with pointillist citations of chapter and verse. Around the print of tracts from Scotland and into homemade notebooks made out of the front page of the *Boston Gazette,* Edwards crams odd polygons of text (news from the French and Indian wars; the sale of buckrams, dimity, broadcloth, ticking, wine), many of these harp-shaped and fretted and looking like spiderwebs in the eaves. Sometimes he uses sheets as long as scrolls, curled at the edges, and sometimes snuffbox-sized slips. Of the sermons, the most famous, "Sinners in the Hands of an Angry God," is scratched onto a petite pile of squares no larger than a CD jewel case, while the treatise *Original Sin* is 372 manuscript sheets of roughly legal size, each page crowded with a thousand or so words, the whole tucked modestly into a folder one inch thick.

Stevens too, for Howe, is a writer whose habits of composition become part of his corpus, the most material aspects of his textual life imbued with poetic liveliness. Edwards makes Glory a literal raiment, as he lets the page dress his thoughts: Stevens too has a peripatetic and distributed habit of composition. The daily walk to his job as insurance executive, the lines he scribbles on notepads to the office, the drafts typed by office secretaries, the transcription from notepads to standard eight by ten sheets, the recompression of stanzas back onto notepads, then, via the secretaries' typewriter back to the eight by ten format – these are not preparatory but intrinsic to Stevens's poetry, as are the two poles of office and home, workweek and weekend. Poetry is motion between media. Thus in "118 Wesley Terrace" Howe evocatively calls Stevens's walk to work an "Errand" (73), a Protestant allusion, the point being that the journey, as it were, is the errand. This account of Stevens's poetry gives the most literal account possible of his maxim, "It must change," where the "two by four inch scraps" (73), on which Stevens records thoughts as he walks, become as essential as the published volumes, and where bouts of nighttime and weekend bouts of composition during which he "transformed the confusion of these for these typed up 'miscellanies' into poems" (73) are where the poet really lives.

Although Stevens's poems have a monumental solidity that belies a liveness and quickness Howe rediscovers in their history, she uses the poem to follow this emergence of the poem "qua" from its many scattered incidents of cohering existence. Where and when does the poem acquire its "is," its thereness or address? At 118 Westerly Terrace? What then of the walks, where the ideas first emerged, or the office where they became print through the ministrations of stenographers? Or, at Howe's desk where, reading them, she also writes them? What is the poem's spatial and temporal address — the manuscript, the printed book? What of the house where the poem was written, or the countryside around and about that touched the poet's mind? Are these some of its genuine addresses? Do these addresses still speak, some speaking to us in tones soliciting response? Might not, for instance, the feeling that we "love" a poem or a poet, or can see the scene it depicts, or, even more obscurely, feel "moved" by its language, confirm the existence of still active addresses from these other sites?

Such questions established, the book's sections seem to guide the reader toward the wedding of poet and landscape, matter and mind, present and past, theology and poetry that Howe has always endeavored to represent. The pages of *Souls of the Labadie Tract* amount to a lovely fusion or wedding of adhesive media, percept, thought, printed word yearning and straining toward each other. And the book's final poem, "Fragment of the Wedding Dress of Sarah Pierpoint Edwards" appears in various guises. We see it literally, in the title of the book's final poem, and in a ghostly gray photocopy, a postage-stamp-sized square showing a thready edge of Sarah Pierpoint's actual dress.

257

And then appears a set of lace-like, pressed, delicate catalogue entries on the Edwards family. In the compost of book pressed on book, ripened by time, this detritus quickens into new delicate life. As Williams might have said, they grip down and awaken. These are not merely found objects or bibliographic refuse but a new wild growth, like wild ferns or thistles, sprouting from the page.

Though elliptical, full of gaps, the texture of a Howe poem is not less for being akimbo or tilted on the up–down axis, but more alluring. An appreciative reader of Howe now knows and comes to crave the tension of letting the eye catch in one of her tactile, bristling installations. There is, in the end, great aesthetic satisfaction in looking through the openwork, the pierced slubby lace of historical knowledge embodied in historical texts. One looks through the fabric as through a veil, the beauty not beneath but abiding in the crush and weave of the historical fabric itself. Nor is this activity simply retinal or visual or aloof. Humane, and good humored toward the lyric speaker, Howe does not exempt herself from the somnambulistic focus, the clenched drive of the rational self, the "workaholic state of revery / Destitute of Benevolence" (85). Burning her candle down, tracing the up-and-down aspirational phallic linear motions, as if ardor of quest could guarantee success proportional to noise of effort. The poet has a subject self but also suffers; she is relieved to meet her night-gowned forebears.

> For a long time I worked this
> Tallest rackety poem
> By light of a single candle
> Just for fun while it lasted
> Now I talk at you to end
> Of days in tiny affirmative
> Nods sitting in night attire
> (*Souls of the Labadie Tract*, 94)

It is a happy thing when the predecessors appear, Edwards or Stevens. To live in a world singly, unidimensionally, is to remain single and lonely when one might lie "happy down the grain." Everyone in his or her present time – Edwards, Stevens, Howe herself – had to live in a "house-island" (92), inside the shells of the one body, one gender, one historical moment, one house and family. And yet, Howe discovers, literate civilization creates openings for us – thresholds, doors – within the conversant architecture of the stanza. "Stanza" means room, of course. The poetic stanza, unenclosed, is naturally hospitable to poetic converse across time, as in Wallace Stevens's "rooms." Walking through them, the poet lets her voice loosen and receive. She utters, but is also blessed by apostrophes – "Back to the doorway flow / of life's energy" (82); "Afternoon at its most glossy / The foyer seems to smile" (92). Every poem, Howe's own included, is in receipt of inheritances that pass from ancestors, and every poem will become, in time, what Whitman called "nourishment." Stevens also wrote, in "Postcards from the Volcano," of children who would never know we were once "quick as foxes on the hill" (*Collected Poems of Wallace Stevens*, 158). Poetry brings living and dead to dwell on one plane: "In the house the house is all / house and each of its authors / passing from room to room" (*Souls of the Labadie Tract*, 77). But it also begins to show the present the way into archive and earth, into sedimented rather than singular existence.

> Two ages overlap you and
> Your predecessors – where
> They go to where far back
> Becomes silent and all lie
> Happy down the grain and
> Barrier self-surrender for
> Then all doors are closed
> (*Souls of the Labadie Tract*, 95)

To see, and to gain help from other poets, to see "what is secret, wild, double and various in the near-at-hand" (74), is what Howe honors Wallace Stevens for giving her in the central poem of the volume, "118 Westerly Terrace." Time, which laps us together, allows more still to be accomplished of the apparently finished than we think.

What makes us still consider Susan Howe an "experimental" or "avant-garde" poet is our preference for the beauty of authors over the beauty of books. Physical aspects of the poetic volume are still meant, in contemporary habits of reading, to evanesce. We expect that if the poem extends beyond the page, surely other recognizable closing devices will signal its beginnings and ends, edges and centers. We assume that the paper, leather, glue on which thoughts are stored are not part of the poem – that a poem is not a work on paper so much as a work despite paper. Notwithstanding that poems are made of black, clustered, twiggy, looped budwork of print of such impact they swim on our eyelids when we close our eyes; notwithstanding the sound individual pages make as they slip against each other, or the decisive thump they make clapping themselves closed after a session of silent reading; notwithstanding how the hands and the fingers experience, second by second, tactile contrasts between the stiffened leather or cloth or glazed paper cover that catch and brace the fingers, and the matte or silken page, smoothed to propel them – notwithstanding all this, poems are expected to transcend this embodiment, to present as little distraction as possible to the work of reflection. But the physical density and sensate clamor raised by the objects we use to read poetry can never be set to the side in the poetry of Susan Howe. The beauty of the book is in the book, in its itness and in the itness of the author who, in looking through, is also seen in the pane, the lens, on which she leaves her own print.

> Face to the window
> I had to know what ought to be
> Accomplished by predecessors
> In the same field of labor
> Because beauty is what *is*
> What is said and what this
> *It* – it in itself insistent *is*
> (*Souls of the Labadie Tract*, 97)

Within the true world of what "is," Howe denies living in a world in which nothing has ever died out. What "is" is never achievable by the singular self sitting by its rackety candle. This particular book is made of particular materials and relationships, by books that precede every poet's own book, the dictionaries full of words that precede her words, the libraries in which these books are held. Also of the cloverleaves on the highways spooling toward the libraries, the winter or spring or summer stand of trees growing around the libraries, and the leaves pressed and composted under the trees. And those buried under the trees with the dead.

Notes

1 For other treatments of the material aspects of Susan Howe's work, see Perloff, Schultz, Collis, and Quartermain. See also Howe's own Web site at the Electronic Poetry Center (EPC) and the site at Penn Sound. Walter Benn Michaels has argued that the emphasis on the materiality of texts is misguided. See his provocative *The Shape of the Signifier.*

2 "Transparency" gets a powerful and sustained critique in Charles Bernstein's "A Poetics." See also Marjorie Perloff's sustained analysis of the value, and limitations of transparency, in *Radical Artifice.*

3 Libraries are crucial spaces for Howe, and the experience of navigating a library as important as any similar experience of navigating through "natural" space. A good place to begin investigations into the material aspects of the American is Augst and Wiegand's *Libraries as Agencies of Culture.*

4 Howe's "autobiographical impulse," to use Hawthorne's phrase, complicates her eschewal of lyric subjectivity in interesting ways. Plainspoken scene-setting and contextualization of a given poem within Howe's life and career are as common and persistent as more difficult features of her work. She is a cooperative and quite enlightening interviewee (see those by Keller and Schultz for instance), and, along with Hejinian, often of interest to critics of women's autobiography (see Blau DuPlessis (123–139)). Tan goes so far as to devote a book-length study to the "Poetics of Autobiography."

5 See Nicholls ("Unsettling the Wilderness"), Tan and Collis, Ma and, again, Perloff, for treatments of Howe's materialist approach to history.

6 I am grateful to Stephanie Sandler for illuminating conversations on Howe's work, including several with Howe herself, and for many suggestions that much improved this essay. I am immensely grateful to

Susan Howe for an unforgettable afternoon in New Guilford – including to opportunity to see her workspaces, her personal library and beautiful environs – and for her visit to Harvard and reading in the spring of 2009.

7 See Nicholls ("Unsettling the Wilderness") and Schultz.

8 Howe's great attachment to, and ambivalence about, Harvard and the Cambridge of the 1950s is most on display in *The Birth-Mark*.

9 On the other hand, Howe is as generous at acknowledging her own intellectual debts as she is as incisive about the ransomings and thefts of academic/poetic practice. Acknowledgments of a kind other writers might put in citations – including mention of the printers, copyists, research assistants, editors, secretaries, and other amanuenses who turn a poet's fugitive thoughts into cogent, complete readable print – frequently become primary in Howe's work. It is an irony, then, that my own thanks to Charlotte Maurer, Madeleine Bennett, and Christopher Looby – through whose intelligent good offices this essay appears – should be filed in notes.

References

Augst, Thomas, and Wayne Wiegand. *Libraries as Agencies of Culture*. Madison: University of Wisconsin Press, 2001.

Bernstein, Charles. *A Poetics*. Cambridge, MA: Harvard University Press, 1992.

Collis, Stephen. *Through Words of Others: Susan Howe and Anarcho-Scholasticism*. Victoria, BC: English Literary Studies Editions, 2006.

Blau DuPlessis, Rachel. *The Pink Guitar: Writing as a Feminist Practice*, 2nd ed. Tuscaloosa: University of Alabama Press, 2006.

Howe, Susan. *My Emily Dickinson*. Berkeley: North Atlantic Books, 1985.

Howe, Susan. *The Birth-Mark: Unsettling the Wilderness in American Literary History*. Middletown: Wesleyan, 1993.

http://epc.buffalo.edu/authors/howe/

Howe, Susan. *Kidnapped*. Dublin, Ireland: Coracle, 2002.

Howe, Susan. *Pierce-Arrow*. New York: New Directions, 1999.

Howe, Susan. *Singularities*. Middletown: Wesleyan University Press, 1990.

Howe, Susan. *Souls of the Labadie Tract*. New York: New Directions, 2007.

Keats, John. "On first looking into Chapman's Homer." In *Complete Poems and Selected Letters of John Keats*. Intro. by Edward Hirsch. New York: New Directions, 1986.

Keller, Susan. "An Interview with Susan Howe." *Contemporary Literature* 36, No. 1 (1995): 1–34.

Ma, Ming-Qian. "Poetry as History Revised: Susan Howe's 'Scattering as Behavior Toward Risk.'" *American Literary History* 6 (1994): 716–737.

Michaels, Walter Benn. *The Shape of the Signifier*. Princeton, NJ: Princeton University Press, 2004.

Miller, Perry. *The New England Mind: The Seventeenth Century*. Cambridge, MA: Harvard University Press, 1954.

Nicholls, Peter. "Unsettling the Wilderness: Susan Howe and American History." *Contemporary Literature*, 37, No. 4 (1996): 586–601. Madison: The University of Wisconsin Press.

Penn Sound. http://writing.upenn.edu/pennsound/x/Howe.php.

"Unsettling the Wilderness: Susan Howe and American History." *Contemporary Literature*, 37, No. 4 (1996): 586–601. Madison: The University of Wisconsin Press.

Perloff, Marjorie. "Against Transparency: From the Radiant Cluster to the Word as Such" & "How It Means: Making Poetic Sense in Media Society." In *Radical Artifice: Writing Poetry in the Age of Media*. Chicago: University of Chicago Press, 1994.

Perloff, Marjorie. *21st-Century Modernism: The New Poetics*. Oxford: Blackwell, 2001.

Quartermain, Peter. *Disjunctive Poetics: From Gertrude Stein and Louis Zukofsky to Susan Howe*. Cambridge: Cambridge University Press, 2009.

Schultz, Susan M. "Exaggerated History." *Postmodern Culture*, 4, No. 2 (1994, January).

Stevens, Wallace. *The Collected Poems of Wallace Stevens*. New York: Vintage Books, 1990. (Original work published 1923)

Tan, Kathy-Ann. *The Nonconformists Poem. Radical "Poetics of Autobiography" in the Works of Lyn Hejinian, Susan Howe, and Leslie Scalapino*. Trier, Germany: Wissenschaftlicher Verlag Trier, 2008.

Vendler, Helen. *Soul Says: On Recent Poetry*. Cambridge, MA: Belknap Press of Harvard University Press, 1995.

Whitman, Walt. *Leaves of Grass*. Philadelphia: David McKay, 1891.

Whitman, Walt. *Complete Poetry and Selected Prose*. Ed. Justin Kaplan. New York: Library of America, 1982.

Williams, William Carlos. *In the American Grain*. New York: New Directions Publishing, 2009 (Original work published 1925).

Further Reading

Lennon, Brian. "Pierce-Arrow." *Boston Review*, October/November, 1999.

Nicholls, Peter. "The Pastness of Landscape": Susan Howe's "Pierce-Arrow." *Contemporary Literature* 43, No. 3 (1996): 441–460. Madison: University of Wisconsin Press.

11

Balm for the Prodigal
Marilynne Robinson's Gilead

> *Carrying a bucket along a slimy board,*
> *he felt the bats' uncertain staggering flight,*
> *his shuddering insights, beyond his control,*
> *touching him. But it took him a long time*
> *finally to make up his mind to go home*
> (Elizabeth Bishop, "The Prodigal")

If anything declares the existence of a unique New England sensibility it is the place reserved in its literature for surprise, for grace, and for the prodigal: for the inrush no action guarantees, for the exhilaration material fact can't contain or explain, and for the past's reappearance, not lost after all, but urgent and importuning. Addressed directly to consciousness, truth's fullness opens inner chambers which, like the Holy of Holies, are recessed from casual view.

As we have seen, this sensibility implied a social practice, too. John Winthrop saw imperfect civil society, including apparent inequalities between men, as God's way of teaching mankind charity. In his "Model of Christian Charity" Winthrop vouchsafed New

New England Beyond Criticism: In Defense of America's First Literature, First Edition. Elisa New.
© 2014 Elisa New. Published 2014 by John Wiley & Sons, Ltd.

England's sociality to a realm Invisible where love, a "ligament," obliged soul to soul in an interdependent corporate body. For Winthrop, this body inhered in "Christ," who was mysterious. For Winthrop's abolitionist heirs, this body was reconstructed in the Union. But in neither case (nor, indeed, in Wigglesworth's, in Edwards's, or even in Du Bois's) were worldly social bodies – whether towns, sections, or nations – to be sacralized. Received knowledge, accepted conventions, confirmed habits, old usages – all these human makeshifts could prove useful in making one's way through a wilderness, but they were not the Way. Whether in the realm of marriage or governance, the education of children, or the management of nature, the New England Way chronically withheld investment in worldly givens. These givens were, instead, revealed again and again to be temporal and contrived guises, performed or improvised maneuvers never fully cognate with the truer forms of Being they imitate. The stiff pageants, the crabbed *tableaux vivants* that recur in Cotton, Edwards, Hawthorne, and Lowell mime deeper movements that cannot be forced.

Coming to America in flight from the merely visible, the New England Puritan saw the human being, the ungraced soul, as over-developed, far-gone, a prodigal. To be Adam's descendant was to live, like Bishop's "prodigal," in the sty of the merely visible, in an atmosphere too close for perspective. To discover how one really felt required removal from the temporal round. Grace is precisely this removal, an experience whose signs and confirmations only increase unease, reassuring through the very lack of reassurance. Strange land, heavy weather, mixed rather than smooth metaphors, unlikeliness, uncanniness, reversal, disruption, trauma: to be jolted out of routine, to be whirled down into the black bubble of the vortex, to experience the uplift of conversion so as to recognize how stagnant and earthbound all the rituals of daily-ness – these are grace's presenting signs. This is why Mary Rowlandson, captive to the Indians, only finds her soul's home, her soul's rest, on a hard forced march in the snow far from the comforts of home. At the tenth or twentieth "remove" – then, and only then, does she feel the buoyancy of grace. Then does she drink the "wine of astonishment." Powerlessness releases the soul from the prison of the self. In the literature of New England, live, ductile consciousness, alert to the world, must be helped to recognize that Something it did not create has befallen it.

"Befallen" is not my word. It is Marilynne Robinson's, a resonant and rich term for how meaning drops onto and alters New England consciousness. It can be no accident, I think, that Robinson's *Gilead*, despite its Iowa setting, is the twenty-first century's first great New England work. Nor is it any accident that its title, *Gilead*, refers at least in part to the balm of writing itself, the insufficient but necessary resort of so many Protestant prodigals.

"I felt a palsy, here – the Verses just relieve," Dickinson wrote (*Selected Letters* 174). In Robinson's work, influenced by Dickinson's, writing is a comfort, a crumb bestowed on searchers graced by expression. For minds like Edward Taylor and John Cotton, who squeezed, or literally expressed, "Milk" for Christian babes out of the ABCs, and Robert Frost, who justified poetic expression by saying "strongly spent is good as kept," the letter is, if not sufficient, still necessary to faith. Literacy relieves cramped self of self, releasing it into the world's expanses. Writing does not solve or complete but it does ease the craving for meaning. Writing is thus, for the narrator of *Gilead* as it was for Robinson's literary ancestors, a practice of spiritual expenditure.

Perhaps it is for this reason that Robinson's narrator in *Gilead*, a minister named for theologian John Ames, says, "writing has always felt like praying" (19). John Ames exposes himself to an eclectic range of texts: Calvin, Leviticus, Feurbach, *The Nation*, the Gospels, James, children's riddles, Huxley, *Trail of the Lonesome Pine*, George Herbert, Isaac Watts, Karl Barth, Locke and, we presume, his ministerial namesake. He sips the honey of their surprise, the particular "delicacy" of each. The language of which books are made flows common, abundant, and unparochial through John Ames's faith; language's hydraulic movement keeps faith pure and sweet. Through reading, but also through watching, listening, and tasting words, Ames is able to observe the looming of the uttered and the made with pure Being. He is able to observe articulation, effortful and imperfect, catch perfection in its gossamer threads, one particular creation giving expression to Creation.

Language, in *Gilead*, is not restricted to the printed matter in books, to the "letter." No individual text, save the Scripture, keeps its power. Thus, while preaching matters, sermons themselves do not, since language's power is in its laving, its fluency and gush, its power to cleanse, to refresh, and most of all to move. John Cotton called Christ "The Fountain" for just this reason: his Word is fluency. Water has this same eloquence in *Gilead*. Labeled and unlabeled, muddy and clear, from the baptismal fount and from the tap, from the sprinkler, from tree limbs, in the depression a boot makes, from the cat's bath or the child's – all these broadcast Being's ampleness. Although it was his brother, John Edwards Ames, who had been named after Jonathan Edwards, John Ames is the one who sees waterfalls, sprinklers, who finds in every "iridescent little downpour" the end, as the original Edwards puts it, for which God created the world (*Gilead* 63).[1] Ames explains:

> There was a young couple strolling along a half a block ahead of me. The sun had come up brilliantly after a heavy rain, and the trees were glistening and very wet. On some impulse, plain exuberance, I suppose, the fellow jumped up and caught hold of a branch, and a storm of luminous water came pouring down on the two of them, and they laughed and took off running, the girl sweeping off her hair and her dress as if she were a bit disgusted, but she wasn't. It was a beautiful thing to see, like something from a myth. I don't know why I thought of that now, except perhaps because it is easy to believe that water was made primarily for blessing, and only secondarily for growing vegetables or doing the wash. I wish I had paid more attention to it. My list of regrets may seem unusual, but who can know that they are really. This is an interesting planet. It deserves all the attention you can give it. (*Gilead* 28)

To hold the door of perception ajar for meaning's gush, letting each moment re-create its fresher revelation, may lead, as this passage shows, to some preciousness. Just how much spiritual import, after all, can there be in a boy and girl on a date? How legitimate is it to put water's aesthetic and ritual functions ahead of its use in the growing of vegetables? There is, to be sure, some absurdity that

John Ames lets play around his scenes of revelation. Feeding his son in front of the TV reminds him of administering to him communion. TV broadcasts blessings, its "jugglers and monkeys and ventriloquists" comfortably share an afternoon for John Ames with meditations on Hagar and Ishmael (127). Karl Barth but also Jack Benny keeps the narrator company in his twilight years (128).

On the other hand, a lack of catholicity in taste, too much discernment or sectarian narrowness where the discovery of meaning is concerned, can lead to further absurdities. For example, John Ames relates the story of an old woman in his congregation who summons him for an emergency pastoral call. It turns out that the problem is the woman's sink. Ames has been called in to counsel the woman "considerably amazed that a reversal so drastic in a lawful universe could come, that cold water came from the hot faucet, and hot from the cold faucet" (132). Unconvinced, when urged by Ames that she might "decide to take C for hot and H for cold," she calls a plumber instead. Water, fluid as language and thought for Ames, obeys a much more mechanical set of laws for this woman whose insistence is, as it were, on a quick fix. She not only demands that the signifiers on her tap signify, but she also fears, superstitiously, that signifiers govern what *is*, that hot and cold do not exist but as we name them. This is sectarianism, religion of the letter (H or C in this case) at its most limiting. For it turns authority over to technicians, overvaluing correctness and giving up faith.

John Ames, on the other hand, confesses to have baptized a cat. He evinces equal joy in recalling formal and informal incidents of immersion – cat baths, bubble baths, sprinkler play – not because he pays baptism less honor than he ought but because, as he says above, we pay water (made for blessing) less than we ought. Honor, pedantry, and orthodoxy have no more monopoly on the Being than ignorance and faithfulness. In fact, the former depends – as hot does cold – upon the latter. John Ames argues that one divine substance flows through all names; between them, thus, are numberless relations:

> We participate in Being without remainder. No breath, no thought nor wart or whisker is not as stuck in being as it could be. And yet

no one can say what being is. If you describe what a thought and a whisker have in common, and a typhoon and a rise in the stock market, excluding "existence," which merely restates the fact that they have a place on our list of known and nameable things . . . you would have accomplished a wonderful thing, still too partial in an infinite degree to have any meaning, however. (178)

The problem, and this is the problem raised by the book's prodigal: what if faith does not easily flow, if water seems mere water? This ease and easiness of faith, this complacency, is not something everyone enjoys. Believers, churchgoers, may know with John Cotton and John Ames that Christ is a fountain. Those less orthodox may find a bit of succor simply in thinking about sprinklers. What, then, of those whom imagination, or even Providence, stints? What of those who cannot feel grace? What of the unelect? John Ames's obligation, his social duty to those less perceptually and spiritually blessed, occupies Robinson a great deal. This must be why she makes him not a mystic or a child, and not a poet either, but a minister who must translate his own vision, the individual ecstasies of Protestant belief, into an ethical social praxis. What obligation does this minister bear, and to whom? And to whom the greater obligation: the one better loved or the one in greater need? Is there balm in Gilead, Robinson asks in this novel, for the truly prodigal son?

Through the travails of one such – John Ames's namesake and godson, John Ames Boughton – Robinson subjects her narrator, and the tradition of the New England ministry, to exacting scrutiny. The Prodigal's redemption, his return to Gilead, tests the theology of grace as a social creed of relation, showing the gaps between communicative fluency, perception externalized, and genuine love or charity. "Does it seem right," asks this prodigal,

> that there should be no common language between us? That there should be no way to bring a drop of water to those who languish in the flames, or who will? Granting your terms? That between us and you there is a great gulf fixed. How can capital T truth not be communicable? (170)

Thus are the stakes raised – not only for Ames but for the New England Way he carries on, a Way whose social applications were always more vexed than their gifts to individual revenants. The minister-narrator's own family history shows the New England Way crossed now by compromise and now by absolutism; its history of taking now the easy way and now the hard; guilty now of exceptionalism and now of conformism. To all those who suffer the effects of the New England Way's vagrancy and volatility, its mistakes of identification compounded by mistakes of dis-identification, John Ames, as minister, is held accountable. And he cannot get himself off New England's Federal hook simply by calling hot water cold. As Jack Boughton comes to show, keeping faith with one's history is not only a matter of telling stories to one's children, or of openness of self or mind. It is also a matter of acknowledging and working to heal damage inflicted both in the name of chosenness and that of ecumenism. As much as blessings pile up, prodigal, so too does obligation, equally prolific. History, as the narrator admits, could "make a stone weep." It thus falls to him to find his highest calling, to stand for a true model of Christian charity.

Of the privative Augustinian power of sin to reverse progress John Ames is well aware, and he grieves, as we sense his author does, for "whatever hope becomes after it begins to weary a little, then weary a little more" (247). Not only incomplete but prone to deterioration (and degradation), vision and goodness weaken with age, and forgetfulness erases lessons learned. Robinson's second novel, like those of her many adopted ancestors, shows the New England Way beating its track west: no destiny fulfilled, no nationhood redeemed, and its journeyers still lonely.

Thus the test, the challenge, to a man so manifestly good as John Ames is to help precisely the sinner a minister ought to aid, but which the social mores and pressures of his town discourage. In Jack Boughton's past is the death of a young child he'd fathered, and the abandonment of that child along with the child's mother. That his bereftness reflects some sort of justice John Ames cannot ignore. Meanwhile, however, the impossibility of living legally with the black woman he loves – another minister's daughter, and teacher – makes

Jack Boughton important, too, for the moral development of the book's moral arbiter. His suffering tests the cosmic scheme of justice that awards one man a loving wife and another nothing but an empty bed, a bottle, and his own desperation. But more, it arraigns the Christian society that has ignored obligations to be just.

The fact that John Ames Boughton cannot marry his beloved indicts the town of Gilead itself, and the New England Way, for a hundred years of passivity. When first settled by Ames's Maine-born grandfather in the 1850s, Gilead was a Free Soil guerilla base, a sanctuary for southern runaways. However, by the time John Ames comes of age in the 1990s, his fierce old grandfather, who had joined with John Brown in Bloody Kansas, has become a pitied emblem of old-fashioned fanaticism, living on sufferance and politeness. Tolerated and honored, the Old Man's New England zeal is now a cause for embarrassment. The narrator Ames recalls a Fourth of July when, burning with his own shame, he heard his grandfather deliver a classic Election Day sermon. In the shame-faced and mocking response, Gilead's citizens show Iowa's radical fervor and especially passion for social justice grown tepid.

Nor do the dynamics of intergenerational friction, the rebellion of sons against fathers, help past and present to learn from each other: melioration cannot reverse violence, nor great conviction correct appeasement. Ames's father's flirtation with the non-violence of the Quakers, a mode of acting out against his own father's radical bloodiness, directs disinterested passion into filial rebellion, privatizing the social. It cannot be bad that a family loath to let itself rupture for religious and political reasons can mend its fences. But what, then, if the sons and fathers merely cancel each other out, each generation's innovations erasing those of the one before?

Compromise is, Robinson shows, compromising. Ames's father and grandfather had called each other Reverend, archly. The arch-ness is a compromise position which, like every other compromise position in this book, defines the middle ground where they, and their middle-of-the-road Christianity, have come to live. Like Iowa and Kansas, the Midwestern states where Maine's radical Abolition-ists took their last stands, John Ames's sense of rigor is often asleep in its chair. For him, the differences between Quaker quietism, moral senescence, and old men dozing in their chairs are important but hard to maintain in the modern world. His jocular descriptions of Methodists, Baptists, and Episcopalians, feebly distinguishing themselves from each other through styles of potato salad and church jokes, betray deeper unease. Once-vital theological distinctions have devolved into denominational tastes (like the flavors in Midwesterners' unending casseroles). John Ames's brother, named for Jonathan Edwards, is a German professor, while John is a minister, but they read the same books, pursue the same questions, and each enjoy certain honorifics of their station.

John Ames's relationship with his brother and the ministry's relationship to intellectual and literary vocations live also in uneasy compromise. John Ames dislikes his brother's intellectual pretensions but realizes that the ministry is, at least in part, cover for his own cerebral hobbies. The sermon genre, once a form of communal consequence, now mostly provides individual satisfaction to him: it is, fundamentally, academic. Meanwhile, his distaste for his brother's affected secularism, like his brother's for his more provincial piety, reenacts the schism that had opened a century before. In the middle of the nineteenth century, American Protestantism avoided rupture through physical separation. Going West led piety's revival on the prairie. Those remaining East accomplished its translation – into "Higher," more critical forms: history of religion, philosophy, poetry.

Heir to such a history, John Ames's appealing humility runs the risk of simple lukewarmness. What keeps his small-town, small-potatoes acquiescence to the limited platform, the limited scope of a Midwestern ministry in the Eisenhower era, from being simply mediocre, tame, tranquilized, and without courage? Perhaps what styles itself humble in this book is simply conflict-averse, not up to the civil disobedience for racial justice his grandfather stood for and Jack Boughton now needs. Gilead may be in its way Galilean, Christlike, and blessed for its very "little regarded" qualities. But its original mandate was to receive the stranger. This remains unfulfilled in the Gilead of the 1950s, a Gilead that's made its peace with keeping the Midwest white. Who is this minister of Gilead who, one hundred years after Gilead's founding as Abolitionist outpost, cannot protect his namesake from miscegenation laws? If a full century's passage has not liberated minds, what model of Christian charity does he serve? The privatization and domestication of Protestantism that have made his town comfortable for old white men keep it still closed to racial justice.

In the end, the limitations of the town of Gilead show New England's social ethos not to have worn as well as, and to have less to bestow than, its legacies of perception and consciousness. Brought West from Maine to Iowa (brought along with abolitionism, utopianism, and vigorous theological culture) are sanctimony, tribalism, sectarianism – and sufficient piety and filio-impiety to keep authority and the prodigality it fosters in a tense dialectic. Moreover, Gilead shows that where prairie Protestantism has forgotten its roots in protest, and where extreme behavior of any kind (whether radical virtue or radical sin, a father's shameful wanderings or a son's) is socially taboo, the withdrawal into private comforts (into favorite foods, baseball on TV) may keep the door barred to the needy.

Finally, Robinson does not give the tepid respectabilities of the New England Way a pass. Lack of charity and compromise of ministry cannot be redeemed by waterfalls, marital satisfaction, family peace, or even by language, however fertile a converting medium language is. To bring John Ames's "two thousand two hundred fifty" sermons, for a total of "sixty seven thousand five hundred pages," out from the attic will not answer the questions, nor provide succor, to the prodigal who needs answers and comfort (19). John Ames is not willing to tell his namesake that predestination has selected him for Hell, but the book makes it clear that he never brings the "drop of water" Jack Boughton asks for either (170). His relationship with Jack Boughton, full of miscommunication, remains, in Emerson's words, "oblique and casual." Motion is wasted, goodwill lost. The narrative Ames writes to his son is more than that son needs. The conversations with his namesake: far less.

What Robinson called in her book of essays the "Death of Adam" still accounts, as Emerson put it, for the "evanescence and lubricity of all objects" (*Essays* 46). The Fall as a name for erosion, slippage, and impermanence still, Marilynn Robinson avers, applies. Comforts may be found, but none that reverse mutability. Still, the very incompleteness of knowledge making her characters "lonely for they know not what" Dickinson also enlarges their sense of the possible. John Ames exults in a Divine understanding much less stingy than the human, a Divine forgiveness much more generous than moral rectitude, an effulgency far more fluent than language. As hot and cold are but letters on the water faucet – not water itself – thus the human will, in its surpluses and excesses, does not alter Being's flow, but only partakes of that flow.

> If I had had this experience earlier in life I might have been so much wiser, much more compassionate. I really don't understand what it was that made people who came to see me so indifferent to good judgment, to common sense, or why they would say "I know, I know" when I urged a little reasonableness and why it meant, "It doesn't matter, I just don't care." That's what the saints and martyrs say. And I know now that it is passion that moves them to their prodigal renunciations. I might seem to be comparing something great and holy with a minor and ordinary thing, that is, love of God with mortal love. But I just don't see them as separate things at all. If we can be divinely fed with a morsel and divinely blessed with a touch, then the terrible pleasure we find in a particular face can certainly instruct us in the nature of the very grandest love. I devoutly believe this to be true. (Robinson 204)

In this passage, and others, Robinson's narrator describes a fluency and adequacy of Being that breaks the skin of definition and engulfs diacritical meaning. "I suppose Calvin's God was a Frenchman, just as," John Ames jokes, "mine is a Midwesterner of New England extraction" (124). His quip is aimed at description's constraint within the local, not Being's. For this faithful speaker, as for Robinson herself, many of the particularities we imagine vital – arraigning them ugly or beautiful, functional or broken, too much or too little, saved or sinful, privative or prodigal – are, like the water tap, regulatory mechanisms on what Dickinson calls, simply, "Flood."

Robinson's Iowa, like her New England, is a place of reenactment and redaction, and her book retains a provisional quality, the quality of a "draught of a draught," as Melville put it to Hawthorne. Of the Midwest and the Northeast, of the twentieth and the nineteenth centuries, Robinson's Gilead is one of those places faith fashions, a zone of that expansive and yet straitened subsistence other chapters of this book have described. This zone, to which one arrives by reading, by writing, by the Word, is "not to be found," as Melville puts it, "on any map."

Notes

1   There is, to date, less literary critical interest in Robinson's Calvinism, even though the Puritan tradition, early and late, is of considerably more importance to this author than the feminist or post-modern theory. Some critics treating "spiritual" themes in *Housekeeping* include William Burke, whose "Border Crossings in Marilynne Robinson's *Housekeeping*" treats mysticism in Robinson, and Anne Marie Mallon's "Sojourning Women: Homelessness and Transcendence in *Housekeeping.*" One expects that the more explicitly Calvinist themes of *Gilead* will prompt critics working in Religion and Literature to greater attention. The first contribution to this field is Katy Ryan's essay "Horizons of Grace: Marilynne Robinson and Simone Weil" in *Philosophy and Literature*, and the interview conducted by Missy Daniels, which addresses Robinson's interest in pastors and Calvinism quite explicitly. Overall, the periodical press has evinced more interest in Robinson than academic writers have. The best critical study of Robinson's *Housekeeping* is to be found in Wendy Steiner's section in Bercovitch's *Cambridge History of American Literature* entitled "Post Modern Fictions: 1970–1990."

References

Bercovitch, Sacvan, ed. *The Cambridge History of American Literature. Volume 7: Prose Writing, 1940–1990.* New York: Cambridge University Press, 1994–2005.

Burke, William. "Border Crossings in Marilynne Robinson's *Housekeeping.*" *Modern Fiction Studies* 37.4 (Winter 1991): 716–724.

Daniels, Missy. "Interview: Marilynne Robinson." *Religion and Ethics Newsweekly*. PBS, March 18, 2005. http://www.pbs.org/wnet/religionandethics/week829/interview.html (accessed December 4, 2013).

Dickinson, Emily. *Selected Letters*. Ed. Thomas H. Johnson. Cambridge, MA: Belknap Press, 1971.

Emerson, Ralph Waldo. *Essays*. Boston: Houghton, Mifflin, and Company, 1882.

Mallon, Anne-Marie. "Sojourning Women: Homelessness and Transcendence in *Housekeeping*." *Critique* 30.2 (Winter 1989): 95–105.

Robinson, Marilynne. *The Death of Adam*. Boston: Houghton Mifflin, 1998.

Robinson, Marilynne. *Gilead*. New York: Farrar, Strauss and Giroux, 2004.

Ryan, Katy. "Horizons of Grace: Marilynne Robinson and Simone Weil." *Philosophy and Literature* 29.2 (October 2005): 349–364.

Steiner, Wendy. "Rethinking Postmodernism." *The Cambridge History of American Literature, Volume 7: Prose Writing 1940–1990*. Ed. Sacvan Bercovitch. Cambridge: Cambridge University Press, 1999–2005.

But now, on the poet's dis-privacied moods
With *do this* and *do that* the pert critic intrudes;
While he thinks he's been barely fulfilling his duty
To interpret 'twixt men and their own sense of beauty,
And has striven, while others sought honor or pelf,
To make his kind happy as he was himself,
He finds he's been guilty of horrid offenses
In all kinds of moods, numbers, genders, and tenses;
He's been *ob-* and *sub*jective, what Kettle calls Pot,
Precisely, at all events, what he ought not;
You have done this, says one judge; *done that*, says another;
You should have done this, grumbles one; *that*, says t'other;
Never mind what he touches, one shrieks out *Taboo!*
And while he is wondering what he shall do,
Since each suggests opposite topics for song,
They all shout together *you're right!* and *you're wrong!*
                    (James Russell Lowell, *A Fable for Critics*)

12

A Fable for Critics
Autobiographical Epilogue

Fair Harvard! We join in thy Jubilee throng,
And with blessings surrender thee o'er
By these festival rites, from the age that is past,
To the age that is waiting before.
                                    (Samuel Gilman, 1836)

I was not born a Yankee, a Brahmin or a Cantabridgean. The devotion to New England that inspired this book, though personal, owes nothing to indigenous belonging. Rather, like many other scholars of New England, I am a latecomer: a transplant rather than a native, a finder rather than founder. While the work of coming to know and write about New England has exacted of me considerable hard study, it has also furnished, expanded, and licensed my imagination. When I fear I may wander too far out of bounds, into that "extravagance" Thoreau described, I take some comfort in the company of other New England scholars, many of them converts to a passion for which nothing in their backgrounds prepared them.

New England Beyond Criticism: In Defense of America's First Literature, First Edition. Elisa New.
© 2014 Elisa New. Published 2014 by John Wiley & Sons, Ltd.

Joseph Conforti relates in his *Imagining New England* that it was growing up in gritty, industrial Fall River, Massachusetts, a Catholic child of immigrant mill workers, that turned his attention to a New England that was "at once geographically proximate and culturally remote." Conforti explains:

> My New England, then, was a gray ethnic city of mills, hills, and dinner pails. From their classroom windows teachers could easily point to half-abandoned factories. . . .The real New England seemed to reside somewhere beyond Fall River's hills, mills, and dense triple-decker ethnic neighborhoods. Fabled Plymouth was only forty-five minutes away. Thanksgiving acquired a special aura because of Fall River's proximity to the place where the 'Spirit of New England,' and of America, was born. (Preface, xi–xii)

Conforti makes clear New England's allure for him: some strangeness its charm, an oddly intimate sensation of unbelonging its passport.

Likewise John Demos's groundbreaking study of the Puritan family, *A Little Commonwealth*, that won him renown as a historian even without the PhD his Harvard advisers declined to award. He was the son of one Demetracopoulos, who, as Demos relates, had talked his way into Harvard's graduate program in philosophy more or less fresh off the boat, his only credential a diploma from a Greek missionary college. If the son did not fare as well in persuading his Harvard advisors to accept his anthropologically inflected book as a dissertation in history, it was perhaps because the field of American history had not yet seen the advantages of the personal perspective Demos, among others, was to bring. This was a perspective frankly experimental, susceptible to interdisciplinary influences, and one more imaginative, even literary, than was the norm. This was a perspective drawn to story and personality, to narrative – and to cultural, rather than analytic and intellectual – history. Not least, this was a perspective ready to treat Puritans not as stalwart Founders so much as persons fresh off boats.

In truth, Oscar Handlin, Demos's own advisor, was himself no New England fixture. He would have understood that the "Pilgrims" were what we call immigrants: what Emma Lazarus, beholding the influx of Jews like Handlin's parents, had called huddled masses. Of Lower East Side Jewish upbringing, Handlin had drawn on the capital of his impeccable dissertation, *Boston's Immigrants*, to write a book closer to home, his now classic study, *The Uprooted*. Still, that there was a legitimate way of connecting scholarly interest in New England with the personal experience of a New England transplant, or indeed between any subject and those who chose to study it, was still years away from being admitted. It was probably not until 1990, with Donald Weber's review essay in *American Literary History* of Andrew Delbanco's *The Puritan Ordeal*, that the odd cousinship of Puritan scholarship and immigrant critic was fully acknowledged; and, even then, with bemusement. "The historians will surely look with wary skittishness," Weber reflected, "at the linking of Cambridge, 1637, and Union Square 1908" (112).

They hadn't, in fact, seen anything yet. Sacvan Bercovitch's most mature, and also most personal, work on Protestant America, *The Rites of Assent*, just then in preparation, would give these historians a lot more to assimilate. In the frank and funny autobiographical essay with which he opens *The Rites of Assent*, Bercovitch, the Canadian-raised son of Yiddish-speaking communists, admits that it was not understanding or sympathy with the ministers of early New England that first sparked his interest in this particular time and place. It was rather an "epiphany of otherness as recorded in Kafka's 'Investigations of a Dog'" (3) that really led him to his subject. How, Bercovitch marveled, had an America so fantastic and counterfactual ever been dreamed up? So young a country, its piety mitigated by the Enlightenment, might have abolished the fables we'd spun of our origins. "The mists of antiquity cover the claims of Siegfried and King Arthur and the Trojan heroes who sired Virgil's Rome," writes Bercovitch, warming to his theme. "Scripture itself authorizes Joshua's claims to Canaan. But we *know* that the Puritans did not found the United States" (6). What made believable the idea of New England's centrality or America's destiny was, Bercovitch concluded, simply that we had believed it.

And believed it on the best academic authority. Intensifying Bercovitch's sense of unreality was the fact that the national fantasy had not been qualified, but rather coined and then disseminated out from the academy – from Harvard, no less. Who, then, Bercovitch wondered, was this Perry Miller who had pulled off an "intellectual construction of national origins from the esoteric writings of forty Protestant sectarians" (*Rites* 10)? The reader of Miller immediately grasps what Bercovitch was talking about, for did not Miller's masterpiece, *The New England Mind: The Seventeenth Century*, trace America's origins straight to St Augustine of Hippo on its very first page? Bercovitch lingered over how Miller's New England was made a place of epic, even, cosmic significance. Was it not in Miller just as it had been in Cotton Mather – as if the whole continent had "appeared out of nowhere – 'out of some place of darkness'" (*Rites* 10)? Such interpretative feats as Miller brought off would eventually suggest to Bercovitch that fascinating homologies, or parallel processes, could be obtained between America's national mythology and its emerging academic sociology. Both mythology and sociology were engaged, and both advanced, courtesy of ideological invention. In the beginning, though, Bercovitch was content to register "the anomaly as a cultural secret of academia" (*Rites* 10).

Consciousness of unfamiliarity – producing awe (if also bemusement) – has proven the greatest boon to the study of New England. From Bercovitch's disquieted fascination to Demos's search for ever-greater forms of expository immediacy; from Conforti's enchantment with Thanksgiving to Delbanco's sense of Puritan loneliness, ambivalence, and guilt, the best scholars of New England do not try too hard, in Frost's words, "to rub the strangeness" from their sight (Frost 68). Like Miller, who made St Augustine John Cotton's honorary uncle; or Bercovitch, who let Kafka tutor his inquiries into Calvin, I have learned not to try too hard to rub the strangeness from mine.

By the time I arrived to teach at Harvard in 1999, my second book, *The Line's Eye*, was in press and I had already begun to publish, or at least conceive, some of the preceding chapters.

I had left graduate school in the late 1980s with a dissertation arguing that, despite Emerson's attempt to "unwrite the Fall," American poetry had – fortunately (naturally!) – fallen. At my Columbia defense, my three Harvard-trained advisors, Ann Douglas, Andrew Delbanco, and Jonathan Arac, were kind in informing me that my argument, while plausible, showed a regrettably thin understanding of Adam's Fall – from which every New England child knew, as I did not, that "we sinned all." They reassured me, however, that mine was a deficiency not impossible to remedy over time, and so, at the University of Pennsylvania, in Philadelphia, while teaching my first courses, I reworked the argument of my dissertation and published it as *The Regenerate Lyric.* As I moved on to begin *The Line's Eye,* I had become sufficiently comfortable in other genres to move beyond poetry studies while also noticing how relatively little the findings of poets were reckoned in treatments of New England literature. In the classroom, I let curiosity carry me. The poetry of meditation naturally led me into a study of Puritan piety, and my fascination with verse jeremiads led me into sermonic literature. Points of doctrine in the poems of ministers, their arcane allusions, their inventive riffs on Scripture, took me from studying poetic conceits to clerical culture. Davenport led to Dimmesdale, Dimmesdale to Mapple, Mapple to Ahab, Ahab to Chillingworth, Chillingworth to Osmond, and so on. In the mid-1990s, I began teaching courses with the phrase "New England" in the title, and so I was led into new interests: It had taken only a few years of teaching and writing to put me reasonably in command of the New England canon that Harvard scholars had convinced generations is comprised of not the local but the national literature. And yet my academic command of the subject did not quite satisfy. The more my familiarity: the greater my wonderment. Like those I'd come to embrace as my guides and precursors, I was finding that intimacy with my subject only increased my sense of its strangeness. How had it happened that this provincial, clerically constrained tradition extending from Winthrop through Lowell (via the Mathers, Hawthorne, Melville, and Dickinson) had become the central and, for a long time, the defining tradition of American literature?

Harvard's campus is a stop on national bus tours. The very municipal signage asserts a sort of canonicity. Thus, with my arrival at Harvard in 1999, so began a more advanced, because more experiential, phase of my training. I had never contemplated the fact before coming, but most of the names in any standard American literature survey are names on the buildings in which Harvard students sleep and eat – and in which I now taught: Mather and Wigglesworth, Robinson and Emerson, James, Longfellow, Eliot, and Lowell. The nondescript bench on which I sipped coffee was, a helpful placard reminded me, the site of the first "New Town" location where poet Anne Bradstreet had settled with her husband Simon. A similar sign just inside the church across from Johnston Gate, where the shuttle bus picked up students and faculty, informed me that it was in this same church that Thomas Shepard (whose grilling of Anne Hutchinson was watched by Simon Bradstreet) had kept his congregation pining for Christ. On that same round corner, behind an iron fence, were some graves of original settlers, New Englanders who had lived and died too early for internment under the leafy knolls of Mount Auburn Cemetery. Even in winter, the hard ground of this churchyard was fringed with a matt of sturdy grass. And so, when I was teaching poetry in Holden Chapel (built when George Washington was a stripling, where undergraduates Waldo Emerson and Henry Thoreau rubbed sleep from their eyes, where William James first delivered "The Sentiment of Rationality"), I sometimes stopped for certain props – a piece of sod, say – from the graveyard. This I liked to pass around in frozen March to give my students the odor of mold, of earth – to remind them, as Wigglesworth and Shepard and Cotton had, of their own mortality.

So many Harvard interiors breathed the New England past – so many Harvard generations! The center upstairs from my office was called Du Bois, and the block on which my office sat, as another helpful placard informed, had been the site of William, Henry, and Alice James's teenaged years – if one could imagine that. Just outside the room in which we had our faculty meetings was an original Sargent portrait, this of the industrial lion, Higginson – founder of the Boston Symphony, friend of assorted Lowells and of Robert Gould Shaw, cousin of Emily Dickinson's preceptor, Thomas Wentworth Higginson. Dickinson did not have a building, of course, never having gone to Harvard, but she had a room with her own teacups in it, and the Houghton Library had her manuscripts. As a member of the faculty, I was permitted to visit and to peep into the very brown envelopes in which her manuscript slips were kept, to peek at the very string with which she had tied the packets of her poems, packets the cognoscenti called "fascicles."

To be sure, most of the names on my syllabus had at least some of their manuscripts in Houghton, the Fort Knox of archives, but one to which I had access. Even more valuable, I discovered, was the presence of all those other precious, if not technically rare, books in Widener Library, closed to the public but open to me and every other card-carrying Harvardian. Houghton Library was, I learned, for truly "rare" books; but there were hundreds, thousands in Widener's open stacks, leather-bound, satin-paged volumes of the 1840s, 50s, not antique enough to merit safeguarding in Houghton. These one might browse as one willed, turning perhaps the same pages as T.S. Eliot or Charles Norton Eliot, as Robert Lowell or Lawrence Lowell or James Russell Lowell had turned; or the same pages turned by their critical expositors. For I realized soon enough that my predecessors, the grandees of Harvard's long critical tradition, must have touched some of these volumes too, and I took to turning to the back of each book, to reading the purple date stamps from the age preceding our electronic one. Sometimes I even found a yellowing pasted slip on which a former borrower, one of my department's famous or infamous departed, had penned his name.

Of course the most beautiful books were often those more critically passé and discredited, but by this time, my confidence in analytic distance, in what some call the "genuinely critical," had more or less abandoned me. Belletrism? What was wrong with that? I mused, standing in the stacks and reading Horace Scudder's warm appreciation of Lowell, then Lowell's various epistolary tributes to Scudder. Fred Lewis Patee's tribute, in *Side Lights on American Literature* (1922), dedicated to his publisher, Ellsworth, came out just a season or so after that selfsame Ellsworth saluted him in *A Golden Age of Authors* (1919), and so it went with sundry other works of intellectual bonhomie. These were works whose ostensible purpose – and ultimate effect – was to establish the secure canon of New England writers, writers meriting wider recognition and appreciation. So much mutual appreciation lubricated the enterprise, so much delight and bouncing boosterism and zest for getting the word out: one really had to wonder what was so great about the "critical" after all.

For O, the titles that leapt off the shelf at me: no need for pedantic subtitles these! On New England Abolition: *Trumpets of Jubilee*; on the rise of my favorite New England dynasty: *The Lowells and Their Seven Worlds*; on Cambridge itself: *The Flowering of New England* – these titles preserved Henry James's "tone," a quality as precious as any mere idea. There was so much tone to find in Kenneth Murdock's edition of *Day of Doom*, illustrated with the woodcuts of Minnesotan Wanda Gag; in the older editions of Lowell's letters and their collected memorial editions; in *festschriften*, with their fond salutes, their creamy tissues and engravings of bearded worthies. Forget the Library of Congress system's PS classification, where I used to browse the library shelves for the newly published. How much better I preferred the old, the straightforward ALs – AL for American. Leather-bound, date-stamped in blue, these books I lugged home boasted bookplates establishing them as the estate donations of personal libraries. They'd not been published: they'd been *born* long ago and were now retired in Widener. Alternating my evening readings in the newer scholarship with older tomes, I spent long days holed up with the likes of Samuel Eliot Morrison and Vernon Parrington, and I began prowling antiquarian alleys and the Boston Athenaeum, too, where volumes consulted by my critical forebears, and by the authors themselves, quietly waited. I rediscovered the critics of the sixties: Anderson, who titled a book on Thoreau, *The Magic Circle of Walden*, and all students of Reuben Brower, especially Richard Poirier, indifferent to literary fashions and more limpid and lapidary a writer than anyone else I read – *A World Elsewhere* was a book that would never grow old. The most recent literary criticism of Elizabeth Bishop was well and good, but how much more satisfying to hold a copy of the geography text, circa 1879, from which Bishop must have copied the queries heading her last volume, *Geography III*! How much more interesting the account, dug out of the compressible shelving, of one Moorsom, a colonel from the Nova Scotia coast, whom Bishop described in so many of her poems! Why, for heaven's sake, had we gotten rid of illustrations, and what could be wrong with a frontispiece portrait of the author?

It was about this time, too, that I began to collect nineteenth-century ephemera. It was thrilling to find, in an old *Atlantic* or *Godey's*, one of my dead collegiate friends. Their credentials blazoned on the title page, these instructors had paved the way for later "public" intellectuals lending themselves to the task of general instruction. If their tones were a trifle plummy, their sense of their importance a bit too manifest, it was, I reasoned, not much worse than what one heard in the Faculty Room; there too one had colleagues who bore themselves with the grave seriousness of national treasures. Just who would be a fixture in the Harvard firmament and who an also-tenured; whose ideas would last and whose become mere subjects, *bête noirs* or whipping boys, of historical interest – these were not indifferent questions to my colleagues, or, I found, to me. For the Harvard day-to-day round, the yearly work, included adjudications of merit and value that, in other places, might long since have been settled.

It turned out, for instance, that a course, English 17, I'd agreed to teach before being hired was one that, like Hester Prynne, had a *past*, but a past of the Harvard kind – which was to say, vouchsafed to the safekeeping of institutional caretakers. Innocuously numbered, English 17 was what remained, I soon learned, of the legendary English 70. The two-semester English 70, its syllabus crammed with New England writers, had been the chief instrument, from Roosevelt through to Reagan, by which departed colleagues had disseminated the New England canon as American literature. Not only, I learned, had thousands of undergraduates passed through it, but it was, as the public eulogy written for its last avatar, Alan Heimert, stated, a "legendary nursery" for scholars of American literature. I, via my own teachers at Columbia, was one of these.

During Alan Heimert's last years, I learned, the existence of this course had been threatened, and Sacvan Bercovitch, at Harvard through the 1990s, had won the battle to keep an American requirement in the curriculum. But the change to the number of my course – from English 70 to the more modest English 17 – reflected a general disapproval for the once excessive claim on undergraduate time that the literature of America, and especially that of New England, had made.

In other words, not everyone liked my course, and I soon realized that its extirpation was on more than a few colleagues' to-do lists. For some, English 17 was merely English 70 lite, and English 70 had represented a redoubt of American exceptionalism and a workshop for the Cold War Manichaeism of its creator, Perry Miller. These regarded English 70 as a stronghold of high-toned jingoism and political complacency, a bastion of canonical homogeneity and religious mystification. No one was ever impolite enough to say these things straight out, of course. But that was the gist of the political critique leveled at English 70, now "reduced" – good Puritan word! – to English 17. Department formalists, meanwhile, had little enough use for my course either. Whether we called it 17 or 70, these colleagues resented the longtime supremacy at Harvard of intellectual history over literary technique. They objected to merely "historical texts" usurping curricular space, and they suspected analysis of rhetorical or "discursive" effects as a cover for the encroachment of ideological programs. What, they argued, *was* this American literature, anyway, once engrossing two full semesters of undergraduate time and still overdrawn on its curricular account? Who were its major authors? For poets: English 17 had Dickinson and Whitman; for novelists, Hawthorne and James. Mightn't we just dispense, then, with the motley mass of sermons and travelogue, with slave narrative and minor poets? They had a point, of course, since a lot of what passed for rhetorical analysis *was* more ideologically interested than not, more agenda-driven. And yet, when they really got going on the "literary," on disinterested aesthetic operations, I found my own hackles rising. I didn't want to see the literature of New England boiled down to a mini-pantheon of "greats." Never mind, I found myself fuming, that the notion of literary greatness, formally guaranteed, was, in most places anyway, long since superannuated! And never mind that the historicist criterion that superseded it was itself a bit long in the tooth.

But I needn't worry, a colleague assured me, about either set of doubters. My English 17, along with its more respectable cousins English 10a and 10b – revered and required surveys of British literature – were the sturdy pillars of a curriculum that predated the department's entire faculty. Inasmuch as, this departmental informant remarked without irony, things at Harvard took "some time" to work themselves through, there'd be time enough for me, a newcomer, to absorb the institutional history, to learn from those of longer tenure the terms of the arguments, pro and con. I was relieved when, casting an ironic look my way, he added that, no, mine was *not* the oldest piece of business still on the docket with the dead.

As it turned out, I taught English 17 only once before deciding it was no good – not so much for the canon represented on the syllabus, but for the pious churchly feel of its lecture format, for its subalternatized section heads (once section "men" of course, and now called "Fellows"), and for the sensation, invariably accompanying my elevation over the upturned faces of my students, of playing myself in some Harvard-themed movie: lecturer ascends Big Podium; students tip chins up thoughtfully, pens raised, from their little chairs. Having come of age at the more entrepreneurial University of Pennsylvania (scrappier school of Benjamin Franklin, New England ex-pat), English 17 stirred something Martin Lutherish and meddlesome in my character: I resolved to spearhead swift reform.

What followed were two spectacularly unsuccessful campaigns, a few years apart, to replace not only my American survey, 17 (née 70), but its even more esteemed cousins, 10a and 10b, with courses more student-friendly and intellectually *au courant*.

Anyone of even slightly longer tenure in Cambridge could have told me, and in truth some did, what they were already telling

Harvard's impatient new President, Larry Summers, who, just weeks after arriving, had taken it upon himself to revamp Harvard's whole College curriculum. He too had imagined such a project would take, perhaps, two or three years. It was good that we were to have each other, as we would learn what long work it would be to change the ways of Harvard. For Larry, the struggle at and with Harvard tended to confirm his Emersonian, his economist's, faith in progress, in development, in the importance of vision opening future-ward. Larry's real Harvard, the institution he tried to lead, was Harvard 2051.

For me, the picture turned out to be mixed. For some mysterious Providence had installed my number-crunching, china-breaking Jewish Harvard President in a house not only old and charming, but storied and literary. This house, Elmwood, one the great art historian Kingsley Porter had deeded to Harvard, had been occupied in the second half of the twentieth century by Harvard presidents Derek Bok and Neil Rudenstine. But before them, and before Porter, it had been the home for a century and a half of a branch of the legendary New England family, the Lowells. Cambridge's warmest, wisest, wittiest literary light, James Russell Lowell – professor, poet, editor, tastemaker – had lived in this house.

The large, square, thick-timbered rooms in which I was courted, the dining room in which I eventually married Larry a few months before we hightailed it with our wedding gifts back to Brookline – these had comprised a sort of nineteenth-century literary White House. Living at Elmwood with James Russell Lowell's own shade, and the shades of his many friends and guests, did to and for me what years in the Harvard English department might never have done. Elmwood, with a little help from its resident president, made me, for a time anyway, a Yankee, a Brahmin, and a Cambridgian of sorts.

It even made me what I'd thought I'd never really be: some manner, some species, anyway, of Harvardian.

To Miss S. B Herrick:

Elmwood, April 19th, 1876

. . . Are you a stout walker? If you are, I will show you my oaks while you are here. If you are not, I will contrive to make you acquainted with them in some more ignominious way. They will forgive you, I dare say, for the same of so old a friend as I. . . . We haven't much to show here. We are a flat country, you know, but not without our charm, and I love Nature, I confess, not to be always on her high horse and with her tragic mask on. Bostonians generally (I am not a Bostonian) seem to have two notions of hospitality – a dinner with people you never saw before nor ever wish to see again, and a drive in Mt Auburn Cemetery, where you will see the worst man can do in the way of disfiguring nature. Your memory of the dinner is supposed to reconcile you to the prospect of the graveyard. (*Letters of James Russell Lowell* 383–384)

By now, I can, more or less blindfolded, lead a guest to James Russell Lowell's own gravesite in Mt Auburn. I can identify and offer anecdotal comment on several of the Lowells among whom he is buried, and on the life of Longfellow, Lowell's dear friend, who, buried on the rise, lies close enough for them to hail one another.

But Lowell's world was, until I moved into it, no part of the New England I had encountered in my reading or teaching. To say I had *never* read Lowell at all would be exaggerating, and yet I'd have been hard pressed to name the poem from which certain one-offs (the jab at Poe, "two fifths genius and three fifths fudge"; the cameo of Emerson, "Greek head on right Yankee shoulders") had actually come.

It was on a shelf in an upstairs bedroom of Elmwood that I found a volume of Lowell's letters, and one of his poetry too; the first edited by Charles Eliot Norton, and the second by the ubiquitous Horace Scudder. The frontispiece of the letters showed Lowell sitting in Elmwood's downstairs library as it had looked in Lowell's time – not so very different than it looked in mine! – while the *Table of Contents* (most considerately annotated for readerly ease) previewed Lowell's correspondence with a cast of literary characters who had already started to seem uncannily near to me. It probably enhanced my sense of personal connection, of immediacy, that the volume of Lowell's *Letters* I found at Elmwood had never been read before. I could tell this was the case because the pages were, as they used to say, "uncut." But once I settled onto a settee in Lowell's own study, an actual knife rescued from a local antique mart in hand, I couldn't imagine why the volume had not been read.

What lover of literature, what student of New England, would not cherish Lowell's salute to William Dean Howells ("My dear boy"), or be charmed by the way Lowell customarily headed his letters? At the left-hand corner Lowell began – always – with the name of the house, *Elmwood*. But sometimes he added, too, a report of climactic conditions around the house on the day of writing. Thus: "Elmwood, Under the Rain, 1869." I felt similar affection for Lowell's bluff, chaffing way of engaging his readers. To James Fields, his publisher, Lowell winningly complains, "I don't see why the New York poets should have all the sonnets to themselves nor why we should not be literary now and then as well as they," and to R.W. Emerson he expresses his affection thus, "emphasizing: how much gratitude for all you have been and are to all us younger men," then signing his letter, "Your liegeman."

My shoulders warmed by the morning sunlight, one winter day I sat and read Lowell's letters straight through. Facing the fireplace, getting the hang of slitting the pages as needed, I encountered, an hour or two into my task, Lowell's description of my own precise situation.

This was in paragraphs to a certain pair of ladies, the Misses Lawrence:

> Elmwood, Cambridge, Mass., Jan. 2, 1890.

> 'Tis a pleasant old house just about twice as old as I am, four miles from Boston, in what was once the country and now is a populous suburb . . . It is a square house with four rooms on a floor, like some houses of the Georgian Era I have seen in English provincial towns. . . . It is very sunny, the sun rising so as to shine (at an acute angle to be sure) through the northern windows, and going round the other three sides in the course of a day. . . . My library occupies two rooms opening into each other by arches at the sides of the

ample chimneys. The trees I look out on are the earliest things I remember. (*Letters of James Russell Lowell* 392)

Turned toward these same arches, what could I do but inhale deeply? I sniffed the wood smoke of last night's fire as it drifted back down the chimney. It was, yes indeed, even in January, just as JRL said, "very sunny" in that room and still, another hundred and more years later, quite square. And what couldn't one view from those Elmwood windows! The trees that formed Lowell's earliest memories were English elms, planted by the house's pre-Revolutionary builders: Tory slave-holding sugar planters, the Olivers. These windows gave views onto the lawn where the crowd, who had already burned down Thomas Hutchinson's house, threatened Peter Oliver with the same. In our time, at Larry's direction, Lowell's study had been returned to its original eighteenth-century function as a receiving room. The decorator had done the room in Federal blue, with some Gilbert Stuarts from the Fogg Museum to set the tone, and she had even found the old wallpaper pattern, called "Elmwood," to hang on the walls. Receiving guests there, Larry enjoyed telling how it was before this very fireplace that, in 1812, Elbridge Gerry, now remembered for the term "gerrymander," had been sworn in as Vice President of the United States under James Madison. Part of the house's charm for Larry was the stately way that, although it had been built by rank Tories, it had joined the nation – a goal he had for Harvard, too. If, after Bunker Hill, king-loving Brattle Street had joined the nation, could not Harvard, so long after Vietnam, do the same?

For my part, though, I liked the house best in its 1840s moods. The staircase landing was painted a colonial yellow, but, in some pamphlets issued by the Cambridge Historical Society, I had learned that under several layers of paint there was a mural, on which every house on Brattle Street was depicted. I longed to peel a corner. Other inscriptions of an earlier age were easier to find. On the other side of the fireplace, on the windows in the smaller parlor, was one of those intriguing scratchings, a signature, etched in the glass by a nineteenth-century bride's diamond ring. At Emerson's house in Concord, The Old Manse, where I sometimes took students on field trips, I made sure to point out the scratches made by Sophia Hawthorne, who had honeymooned there with Nathaniel. What fun it was to have such scratchings of my own to regard of a sunny day! Whether or not the Hawthornes themselves had dined at Elmwood, had trod the very wide boards I walked, was not clear, but I thought it likely. Besides, I had other ways of communicating with Hawthorne's spirit. Simply by passing through the Federal blue sitting room and stepping across the foyer to the dining room, I could stand in front of the fireplace and look at Jared Sparks's picture, painted by Washington Allston. Sparks had courted and married a woman Hawthorne had also loved. Of course, Sparks was best known in Cambridge for his biography of Washington, and best known by New England scholars for having had William Ellery Channing give the sermon that invented Unitarian Christianity at his ordination. I had written paragraphs on this sermon in my first book. But I had never dreamed that Jared Sparks and I might share a dining room.

Would Melville, that radical, I mused, have ever graced the Lowell board? Perhaps he'd paid a call to oblige his wife's father, Lemuel Shaw, since the Shaws were all kin to the Lowells, despite differences over Abolition that sharpened during the 1850s. And what about others? Who else from my syllabus had eaten in our dining room? What about Poe, so impolite to these Boston tastemakers, particularly to Longfellow, whom he called a plagiarist (certainly a case of the pot calling the kettle black). Would poor Poe, I wondered, have been so badly behaved, would ever have acted so burned out, so truly mad, as to insult his Boston hosts by reading his impenetrable rant of a prose-poem, "Eureka," if he had simply been invited to supper? Talking politics at this meal would, I reckoned, have been ill advised. Poe had, of course, been raised a Southerner, while Lowell and his friends were staunch abolitionists. Elmwood had a bunker behind the house, which our children liked to tell their play dates had hidden runaway slaves. Steering by the North Star they'd come to Cambridge and, so my youngest daughter was told, hide out here, near the gas grill.

Perhaps. It was a research project for another day.

One thing I didn't tell this daughter, at least until we'd moved out, was an historical fact I was rather more sure of. This was the mournful tale of Lowell's own bride, the more fiery abolitionist of the two, Maria White Lowell, who had died of tuberculosis in my daughter's very own low-ceilinged room. Maria Lowell may not have shared Poe's politics, but she shared at least two things with him – intimate knowledge of opiates, and the horror of consumption, which gave women so startling a bloom on the cheek before killing them. I reminded this daughter, as I always had her sisters and always reminded my students, of the closeness of the graveyard in the olden days. The century before our own was vastly more perilous than we could imagine. Before antibiotics, before contraception, before anesthesia, one thing or another killed the vulnerable in every family.

In late February of 1650, of 1750, of 1850, the wind off the Charles had been so cold, the glitter of the river so terrible. Not until the twentieth century had there been more than fireplaces and hot bricks in bed at Elmwood to keep a child warm. How miserable, then, to have scraped along the bitter frozen ground to church as Anne Bradstreet had, the wind propelling children before it. But it would have been hard as well to be Du Bois, or Robinson, or Frost, "special students" too poor to pay full tuition, and with little in the way of hearths. On the other hand, hearths themselves were dreadfully risky, and riskiest to those who grew casual about lighting them. Longfellow, happiest and most constant of Elmwood visitors, had watched his wife go up in literal flames, her voluminous skirt catching fire as she preserved her children's curls in wax. An auto-da-fé of sentimentalism one might say, but once I took time to read Longfellow I saw him and his age very differently. Standing at his grave in Mt Auburn with students, I led a discussion of Longfellow's "The Cross of Snow." With its comparison of the poet's heart to a stretch of exposed rock in the West, this poem had to be one of the most mature and affecting elegies I'd ever read.

Elmwood had a lot to do with it, but clearly something was happening to me after only five years at Harvard. Something profound was happening to how I saw and read New England. I began to lose conviction, for one thing, that a poem had to be recondite or difficult to be interesting; I lost conviction that a metaphor's vehicle needed be remote from its tenor, and I began, too, to lose interest in any idea whose main claim to fame was its novelty. Newness, freshness, the cutting edge; progress, innovation, singularity, originality – these began to seem thin to me. I started liking it more and more in class when my students, with awe, discovered time-tested ideas, unearthed toothsome old chestnuts rather than always grasping for new ones. I liked to tempt graduate students with especially fine chapters from superannuated works of criticism.

And most of all, I came to enjoy, and gain refreshment, by allowing myself to extend sympathies and to read (the very phrase seems heretical) uncritically the works of literary cultures quite different from my own. A growing sympathy for Longfellow and Lowell, a deepening interest in the lives of these local poets, recalled to me a complaint, now obviously right, made by a reader of my first book: that I cherished too much affection for poetic extremity, neglecting the middle range of tones. I could see, suddenly, in reading Longfellow what this meant. I could see how I'd let my critical disposition and careerism collude in overestimations of extremity. And thus I had missed a more genial age of New England culture. Here at Lowell's Elmwood so many of the accents were in this middle range – from clever wit to sad resignation, from mature gamesomeness to dutiful cheer. Excluding vulgarity and the drastic, striving to provide consolation and balance, Lowell and company strove to be useful. The metrical stunts of Lowell, his sheer friendliness and bonhomie; Longfellow's pleasing musical effects; Holmes's confidence that literature *was* a matter for the breakfast-table: thus did Cambridge poets of an earlier age serve the greater good. These were poets who'd been humble, more humble than any contemporary poets I knew, and yet they had made poetry a public utility. Mature, bemused, valuing dinner, friendship, talk of faculty matters and tidings from the study, these poets, too, were professors, well taken care of as I was, and so were my academic grand-uncles. Their world was my own. Like me, they were privileged bookworms, installed in America's capital of learning. Together, we made up a long, intellectually consanguineous chain, all beats in the long slow tick-tock, tick-tock of Harvard time. Similar feelings of kinship and Cambridgian cheer infused two winters of turning brittle pages before the fire at Elmwood.

And then – suitably I think – my enthusiasm for the Golden Age of New England authors began to wane.

I first noticed the shift in around the Fall of 2005 or so when, preparing to teach Edward Taylor on the morrow, I realized I'd grown too fond, perhaps, of phrases like "on the morrow." And were not my study bookshelves a little naked, or perhaps not naked enough? Something had gone missing, had been lost, as I learned to talk the talk of Brattle Street circa 1870. What this thing was was the Fall, original sin. Liberal Unitarianism allied to Harvard career-making had little time to spare for damnation. However, when relating the cultural history of New England requires no reference work weightier than the *Harvard Review*; when New England has become too complacently, too optimistically, a place (in Van Wyck Brooks's terms) of "flowerings" – then it was time for a good dose of the sulfur and flame: time for Perry Miller. Time now to recall the flint and forthrightness of Bradford's "starving time"; time to remember not Lowells but Mathers, and to meditate on the more volatile New England personalities, on Roger Williams, Ralph Waldo Emerson, Charles Eliot, Charles Peirce.

They had rattled the cages: and they had paid for it. There was no point in denying those self-regarding, protocol-policing aspects of Harvard. And so now was the time to recall what Felix Frankfurter had noted in 1931 as something "thin and defensive" in Cambridge society, a thinness he ascribed to "ruling traditions that serve to stifle the exercise of passion." To be sure, by this time, I was getting to know the aggressive edge of Harvard's self-regard, the steel underneath its politeness. "Beautiful enough" was Nathaniel Hawthorne's acerbic term for New England's village pride, its inveterate complacency. But if New England bred breeding, I remembered, too, that it bred the radicals and malcontents, the antinomians and angsty innovators who upset its protocols and its mores. It had taken less than five years from Arbella touching shore in 1630 for such complacency to produce Anne Hutchinson – and she merely foreshadowed more such mavericks, more heroes of rebellious spirit. In the 1660s, the 1690s, the 1740s, in the 1780s, and in the 1840s, these disturbers of the peace came forward.

I thus came to think of Perry Miller, who, in a later century, was one of these too. Arriving in the 1930s from Chicago, Miller would not have been alone, and certainly not wrong, in finding both Harvard and New England studies in need of a kick in the pants, a revival of the spirit. A clannish liberalism had blunted Puritan ire, and self-satisfaction had become a habit, one renewed every generation or so (p. 12). One could well imagine, in closing the pages on Van Wyck Brooks, how Perry Miller had *become* himself, and why he had founded a two-semester survey of American literature as a course in the chewing of Calvinist nails, why he had reintroduced rigor – unbeautiful, hardscrabble, theologically drastic rigor – as New England's and the whole nation's defining tone. Hard research in Harvard's unequalled archives was part of why he did it. But it had to have also been sheer exasperation, sheer bloody weariness of the politesse, equability, and belletristic middle range of moderate, middling, meliorate, mediocre Cambridge.

And so I cheered him. What a cultural coup Miller had brought off! What a way to yank the local chain: to de-provincialize, to rediscover forgotten sinew under the softnesses of the Cambridge scene. Miller scratched under the painted swooping cupolas of this charming town and came up with something remarkably, uncomfortably, soberly world-historical. For Miller made the local not only national, but cosmic.

Thus out with the sherried colloquium and in with the General Curriculum! Returning to Miller, after September 11, it was not hard for me to see why, out of the Depression's depths and then out of World War Two, Miller had brought Bradford and Edwards back; had brought back not just the howling Augustinian wilderness but also the un-illusioned, neo-orthodox, character-hardened belief

298

in flaming apocalypse. Nor was Miller alone in bringing Cambridge, and America in turn, face to face with the darker side. Shoulder to shoulder with Miller there was the great F.O. Matthiessen, heralding an American "Renaissance" not gilded and exuberant but guilty and vexed, for whom Hawthorne exemplified "A Haunted Mind" and the "problem of the Artist as New Englander." There was Harry Levin, whose *The Power of Blackness* canonized Melville's assertion that what abounded in Hawthorne was "blackness, ten times black." And Miller himself, professor of the New England mind, weighing in to claim that Hawthorne's fiction expressed not only New England's spirit but the "deepest passions of the continent." Convinced by the Great War, Adolf Hitler, and then the threat of The Bomb that life was as treacherous as a Cambridge sidewalk in winter, these men named evil where they saw it and drank it down neat. One might shake the bitter elixir of whichever Kierkegaardian, Kennanesque, or psychoanalytic flavor one chose, so long as one recognized that the literature of New England was icy truth's native spring. This was the generation that called the romance, and not the realist novel, the quintessential American genre; that identified lonely individualism as the hero's natural habitat; and that declared a shadowy chiaroscuro – métier of Hawthorne, Melville, and Poe – the defining style of American civilization. Magisterial, melancholy, and utterly male, it was the grand old era of American criticism that made Hawthorne our Dante, that found the darkest vein in the sunniest Jamesean mood.

Beyond this, these were literary critics who made themselves culturally indispensable, who raised literary criticism to a worldly prominence it had not had before nor has had since. Out of the lecture hall and into the civic realm and secondary curricula they dispatched an old idea, though one freshly reissued. Rigorous scholarly disciplines and ambitious works of art, when in alliance with the best and the most tough-minded statecraft, could reveal and advance the meaning of America. As Robert Frost, speaking at John Kennedy's Inauguration, put it, the country that had begun flat, "artless," "unstoried," and "unenhanced" was still "realizing" itself.

299

The America that Frost saw as still on pilgrimage, still unfinished, was the one Sacvan Bercovitch would, a few years later, describe in *The American Jeremiad* and *The Puritan Origins of the American Self* – as made, essentially, out of rhetoric. Frost had told America that the best was yet to come; he immortalized the idea that in acts of muscular self-discovery, the nation makes itself. Make's a myth of itself, Bercovitch countered, making glory of struggle and glory of triumph –, and so the revisionist critics of the 1970s and 80s and 90s followed in his stead. I follow in it too, am indebted to it utterly, and yet I now when I walk the streets of Cambridge, I cannot help from hearing in the street names (Appleton, Story, Channing, Sparks; Longfellow, Quincy, Craigie, Bow) some of what I fancy Van Wyck Brooks, or even William James, heard. They sound with a plain sort of poetry. The lilacs along Brattle and the broken spines of books in bookshops with their uneven flooring suggest that "tone" a less critical age than ours valued – while the angled corners of Harvard Square, the slate gray of the sky in March, reminds me of the sharpness Perry Miller, fed up with "tone," reintroduced: the shock of arriving on Cape Cod in December, bushwhacking through brambles and ice, the sharpness of Bradford's terror at his people's audacity and their loneliness. Such sharpness, and perceived in the light of the twentieth century's horrors, would have demanded a criticism dark, authoritative, and cosmological, one that set 1950 and 1650 on Augustine's own timeline. Bradford's phrase "howling wilderness" seems now, in fact, tame when I walk myself through some of those woods on Cape Cod they wandered, full of hollows and wind. Who would not have howled? Why exclude such howling? Our criticism of early New England has not retained sensibility enough, nor sympathy enough for those poetic, most imaginative, most go-for-broke risk-takers – the first New Englanders and their heirs. And we are negligent, too profligate too with the imaginative riches bestowed by critical predecessors, as they, increasingly, were too profligate of theirs. We are not the first to correct the misapprehensions of our predecessors; nor will posterity neglect correcting ours.[1]

It took several more years after I had given up my own crusade, but English 17, that redoubtable institution, is no more. During the

2009–2010 school year, I joined with other colleagues in retiring English 17, along with its august cousins, English 10a and 10b. We have replaced all three now with courses reflecting today's (rather than 1958's) critical ideas, and in so doing, also assisted the Harvard professor off her churchly podium. The course corresponding most closely to English 17 (and its older ancestor, English 70) no longer treats America as New England's annex or afterthought. Instead, it treats the literature of the United States in the broad context of the transatlantic and trans-hemispheric exchanges. This de-parochialization tracks with, in many ways, Harvard's new General Education curriculum, which no longer refers all general knowledge to the norms of the academy and the scholarly disciplines, but rather to the norms of a world beyond Harvard's gates. That both projects of reform took not one year less than the ten full years those wise heads, the Harvard lifers, reckoned is now a source of amusement and inspiration.

It is an immense privilege to study a world, a region, a society so ingrown, perhaps the most ingrown in North America, close up. What triumph I might feel for achieving change in an unchanging place is complicated by how much, in the past ten years, New England's apparent unchangingness has changed, and now, even delights me.

Now, settled in Brookline, Massachusetts, resident in New England for more than a dozen years, I have the pleasure of driving every morning north across the sparkling Charles to Cambridge. Sometimes when I cross the river due North of my house, I cut through Brighton Center, site of New England's largest nineteenth-century cattle fair and slaughter houses, terminus of some of Hawthorne's day-long walks from Brook Farm in West Roxbury. Brighton had, before the nineteenth century, been known as Little Cambridge, for it was there that Cambridgers, or Cantabridgeans, had removed, first building businesses and then a church to save them crossing the icy river on Sundays. Sometimes I cross the river further east – passing through Allston, with its old clapboard houses now all cut up into student apartments and its street scene untidy and interesting. Home to the impecunious young, to musicians and artists – Allston was named for Washington Allston, who painted its fields as they looked to him then, rolling and rural from his window in Cambridgeport. And sometimes, I cross yet further to the east, near Boston University, this route affording me a glimpse down Commonwealth Avenue into Boston. Following that old Avenue as it bears through the Back Bay for just a few minutes takes one to where Boston settlers kept their livestock and held their meetings, the Commons, and where one can admire, as Robert Lowell did, as William James did, Saint-Gaudens's statue of Robert Gould Shaw's men, the black soldiers of the 54th, who died at the assault on Forth Wagner.

The Memorial stands just across from the State House on Beacon Hill. If, from there, you descend the slope of the Common, it is not many minutes on foot to the Harbor, a tramp through some of the oldest settled streets in America, those crooked lanes where Governor John Winthrop, displeased with Salem and then Charleston, had resolved the right place for his Massachusetts Bay settlement. If you take a ferry from that harbor, heading toward the tip of the Cape at Provincetown, you will pass Plymouth where the Mayflower finally docked and let off its passengers, her scouting parties having nosed into various inlets of the wild Cape and found them all too fearsome and inhospitable.

In the evening, as I cross back over the Charles, I like sometimes to follow the river westward with my eyes. The Charles is a quiescent ribbon, one without much current, but to the west there is some higher ground and some falls – some natural, some ingeniously man-made – that clever entrepreneurs of the nineteenth century had harnessed to turn flour and then textile mills – at West Roxbury and Dedham, and at Waltham, where the Lowell family built their first venture. In North Waltham you can pick up the most ancient of east–west routes in Massachusetts, the Concord Turnpike, which will take you past Thoreau's Walden and out into orchards and past the Blue Hills until where it becomes the Mohawk Trail; this is the old Indian route that cuts through the Berkshires and up into the Adirondacks, all the way to Canada. So many of these places one passes in one's car or imagination were once dense with forest, treacherous of cliffs, buried in snow. So many towns now snugly settled three hundred years were once just outposts, vulnerable to depredations of the weather, to disease, to Indian raids. Some remain pristine. Some, spoiled by overly rapid industrialization, economic downturns, are reinventing themselves.

These are all connected in my mind in the loose way the features on my maps of the region connect – as interesting to me in the overall and aggregate as in their particular histories or forms. This New England atlas I keep in my mind is somewhat akin to the larger "field" of New England I have endeavored to open here.

Notes

1 In chronological order: the tradition of New England critics treated in this chapter:

1829: J. Olney, A.M., *A Practical System of Modern Geography; or, a View of the Present State of the World Simplified and Adapted to the Capacity of Youth*

1848: Horace Elisha Scudder (ed.), *The Complete Poetical Works of James Russell Lowell*

1857: D.M. Warren, *The Common School-Geography: An Elementary Treatise on Mathematical, Physical and Political Geography*

1879: Samuel Eliot (ed.), *Selections from American Authors, a Reading Book for School and Home: Franklin, Adams, Cooper, Longfellow*

1893: Nathan Haskell Dole (intro. by), *The Poems of Henry Wadsworth Longfellow*

1893: Charles Eliot Norton (ed.), *Letters of James Russell Lowell*

1901: Horace Elisha Scudder, *James Russell Lowell: A Biography*

1919: William Webster Ellsworth, *A Golden Age of Authors*

1922: Fred Lewis Patee, *Side Lights on American Literature*

1922: Caroline Ticknor, *Glimpses of Authors* (with illustrations),

1927: Vernon Louis Parrington, *Main Currents in American Thought* (in three volumes)

1927: Constance Rourke, *Trumpets of Jubilee*

1929: Kenneth Murdock (ed. and intro by), Michael Wigglesworth's *Day of Doom*

1935: Samuel Eliot Morison, *The Tercentennial History of Harvard College and University, 1636–1936*

1936: Van Wyck Brooks, *The Flowering of New England*

1939: Perry Miller, *The New England Mind: The Seventeenth Century*

1941: Oscar Handlin, *Boston's Immigrants, 1790-1865: A Study in Acculturation* (dissertation)

1941: F.O. Matthiessen, *American Renaissance: Art and Expression in the Age of Emerson and Whitman*

1946: Ferris Greenslet, *The Lowells and Their Seven Worlds*

1951: Oscar Handlin, *The Uprooted*

1958: Harry Levin, *The Power of Blackness: Hawthorne, Poe, Melville*

1963: Reuben Arthur Brower, *The Poetry of Robert Frost: Constellations of Intention*

1965: Samuel Eliot Morison, *The Oxford History of the American People*

1966: Alan Heimert, *Religion and the American Mind: From the Great Awakening to the Revolution*

1966: Richard Poirier, *A World Elsewhere: The Place of Style in American Literature*

1968: Charles R. Anderson, *The Magic Circle of Walden*

1970: John Demos, *A Little Commonwealth: Family Life in Plymouth Colony*

1975: Sacvan Bercovitch, *The Puritan Origins of the American Self*

1977: Ann Douglas, *The Feminization of American Culture*

1978: Sacvan Bercovitch, *The American Jeremiad*

1985: Walter Benn Michales and Donald E. Pease (eds.), *The American Renaissance Reconsidered*

1986: Lawrence Buell, *New England Literary Culture: From Revolution through Renaissance*

1989: Andrew Delbanco, *The Puritan Ordeal*

1989: David Hackett Fischer, *Albion's Seed: Four British Folkways in America*

1990: Donald Weber, "Historicizing the Errand," in *American Literary History*, Vol. 2, No. 1 (review essay of Andrew Delbanco's *The Puritan Ordeal*)

1993: Sacvan Bercovitch, *The Rites of Assent: Transformations in the Symbolic Construction of America*

1995: Lawrence Buell, *The Environmental Imagination: Thoreau, Nature Writing, and the Formation of American Culture*

1998: John Elder, *Reading the Mountains of Home*

2001: Joseph Conforti, *Imagining New England*

2005: Jonathan Arac, *The Emergence of American Literary Narrative, 1820–1860*

References

Anderson, Charles R. *The Magic Circle of Walden.* New York: Holt, Rinehart, and Winston, 1968.

Arac, Jonathan. *The Emergence of American Literary Narrative, 1820–1860.* Cambridge, MA: Harvard University Press, 2005.

Bercovitch, Sacvan, ed. *The American Jeremiad.* Madison: University of Wisconsin Press, 1978.

Bercovitch, Sacvan, ed. *The Puritan Origins of the American Self.* New Haven, CT: Yale University Press, 1975.

Bercovitch, Sacvan, ed. *The Rites of Assent: Transformations in the Symbolic Construction of America.* New York: Routledge, 1993.

Bishop, Elizabeth. *The Complete Poems 1927–1979.* New York: Farrar, 1983.

Brooks, Van Wyck. *The Flowering of New England.* New York: E.P. Dutton & Co., Inc., 1936.

Brower, Reuben Arthur. *The Poetry of Robert Frost: Constellations of Intention.* New York: Oxford University Press, 1963.

Buell, Lawrence. *The Environmental Imagination: Thoreau, Nature Writing, and the Formation of American Culture.* Cambridge, MA: Belknap Press, 1995.

Buell, Lawrence. *New England Literary Culture: From Revolution through Renaissance.* Cambridge: Cambridge University Press, 1986.

Conforti, Joseph. *Imagining New England: Explorations of Regional Identity from the Pilgrims to the Mid-Twentieth Century.* Chapel Hill: University of North Carolina Press, 2001.

Delbanco, Andrew. *The Puritan Ordeal.* Cambridge, MA: Harvard University Press, 1989.

Demos, John. *A Little Commonwealth: Family Life in Plymouth County.* New York: Oxford University Press, 1970.

Douglas, Ann. *The Feminization of American Culture.* New York: Anchor, 1977.

Elder, John. *Reading the Mountains of Home.* Cambridge, MA: Harvard University Press, 1998.

Eliot, Samuel, ed. *Selections from American Authors, a Reading Book for School and Home: Franklin, Adams, Cooper, Longfellow*. New York: Taintor Brothers, Merrill & Co., 1879.

Ellesworth, William Webster. *A Golden Age of Authors: A Publisher's Recollection*. London: Grant Richards, 1919.

Fischer, David Hackett. *Albion's Seed: Four British Folkways in America*. New York: Oxford University Press, 1989.

Frost, Robert. *The Poetry of Robert Frost: The Collected Poems, Complete and Unabridged*. Ed. Edward Connery Lathem. New York: Henry Holt and Company, 1969.

Greenslet, Ferris. *The Lowells and Their Seven Worlds*. Boston: Houghton Mifflin Company, 1946.

Handlin, Oscar. *Boston's Immigrants, 1790–1865: A Study in Acculturation*. Cambridge: Harvard University Press, 1941.

Handlin, Oscar. *The Uprooted*. Boston: Little, Brown and Company, 1951.

Heimert, Alan. *Religion and the American Mind: From the Great Awakening to the Revolution*. Cambridge, MA: Harvard University Press, 1966.

Levin, Harry. *The Power of Blackness: Hawthorne, Poe, Melville*. New York: Knopf, 1958.

Longfellow, Henry Wadsworth. *The Poems of Henry Wadsworth Longfellow*. Intro. by Nathan Haskell Dole. New York: Crowell, 1893.

Lowell, James Russell. *A Fable for Critics*. Boston: Ticknor and Fields, 1856.

Lowell, James Russell. *The Complete Poetical Works of James Russell Lowell*. Ed. Horace Elisha Scudder. Boston: Houghton, Mifflin and Company, 1876.

Lowell, James Russell. *Letters of James Russell Lowell*. Ed. Charles Eliot Norton. New York: Harpers & Brothers, 1893.

Matthiessen, F.O. *American Renaissance: Art and Expression in the Age of Emerson and Whitman*. New York: Oxford University Press, 1941.

Michaels, Walter Benn, and Donald Pease, eds. *The American Renaissance Reconsidered*. Baltimore: The Johns Hopkins University Press, 1998.

Miller, Perry. *The New England Mind: The Seventeenth Century*. Cambridge, MA: Harvard University Press, 1954.

Morison, Samuel Eliot. *The Oxford History of the American People*. New York: Oxford University Press, 1965.

Morison, Samuel Eliot. *The Tercentennial History of Harvard College and University, 1636–1936*. Cambridge, MA: Harvard University Press, 1935.

New, Elisa. *The Line's Eye: Poetic Experience, American Sight*. Cambridge, MA: Harvard University Press, 1998.

New, Elisa. *The Regenerate Lyric: Theology and Innovation in American Poetry.* New York: Cambridge University Press, 1993.

Olney, J. *A Practical System of Modern Geography; or, a View of the Present State of the World Simplified and Adapted to the Capacity of Youth.* 41st ed. New York: Pratt, Woodford, and Co., 1844.

Parrington, Vernon Louis. *Main Currents in American Thought: An Interpretation of American Literature from the Beginnings to 1920.* New York: Harcourt, Brace and Company, 1927.

Patee, Fred Lewis. *Sidelights on American Literature.* New York: The Century Co., 1922.

Poirier, Richard. *A World Elsewhere: The Place of Style in American Literature.* New York: Oxford University Press, 1966.

Rourke, Constance. *Trumpets of Jubilee.* New York: Harcourt, Brace, and Company, 1927.

Scudder, Horace Elisha. *James Russell Lowell: A Biography.* Cambridge, MA: Riverside Press, 1901.

Ticknor, Caroline. *Glimpses of Authors.* Boston: Houghton Mifflin Company, 1922.

Warren, D.M. *The Common School-Geography: An Elementary Treatise on Mathematical, Physical and Political Geography.* Philadelphia: Cowperthwait & Co., 1876.

Weber, Donald. "Historicizing the Errand." *American Literary History* 2:1 (1990): 101–118.

Wigglesworth, Michael. *The Day of Doom: Or a Poetical Description of the Great and Last Judgment.* Ed. and intro. by Kenneth Murdock. New York: The Spiral Press, 1929.

Further Reading

Schweitzer, Ivy. "Anne Bradstreet Wrestles with the Renaissance." *Early American Literature* 23.3 (1988): 291–312.

Winship, Michael P. *The Times and Trials of Anne Hutchinson: Puritans Divided.* Lawrence: University Press of Kansas, 2005.

Index

New England Beyond Criticism: In Defense of America's First Literature, First Edition. Elisa New.
© 2014 Elisa New. Published 2014 by John Wiley & Sons, Ltd.

Index

Bishop, Elizabeth   105
  primordium   135n11
  rhyme   129
  studies of   286–7
  wilderness   108, 120
  works (*see also* "The Moose")
    "At the Fishhouses"   128
    "Brazil, January 1, 1502"   119,
      121–2
    Collected Poems   119
    "The Fish"   125–6
    Geography III   122–3, 126–7,
      267, 287
    North and South   119, 120
    "The Prodigal"   265, 266
    "View of the Capitol from the
      Library of Congress"   120
Black Belt   171, 175, 177–8, 179–80
The Blithedale Romance (Hawthorne)
  154–6
body consciousness   55
Bolts of Melody (Dickinson)   80, 99n2
book as physical object   91–2, 240,
  244, 248, 259–60, 261n1
Book of Martyrs (Foxe)   59
The Bostonians (James, H.)   229–31
Boston's Immigrants (Handlin)   281
boundary-crossing   8, 15, 53–4,
  170–1
A Boy's Will (Frost)   36
Bozeman, Theodore Dwight   41n1,
  43n5, 135n11, 216
Bradford, William   15, 106, 108, 120,
  134–5n10, 300
  Of Plimouth Plantation   105–6, 107,
    109–11, 121, 122
Bradstreet, Anne   295
Brodhead, Richard   144, 195n11
Brooks, Van Wyck   297, 298, 300

Brower, Reuben   286
Brown, Dan   56–7, 70n7
Brown, John   145
Budd, Louis   195n11
Buell, Larry   132n2, 192n3, 194n5
Burke, William   276n1
Bush, Sargent   41n2
Butler, John   71n12

Calvinism
  Bercovitch   282
  Bradford   106
  Dickinson   29, 76, 85, 89–90, 94
  Edwards   216, 250
  Hawthorne   143, 157
  Lowell, R.   201
  Miller, P.   298
  outward behavior   35
  Poe   58, 61, 67
  rationalism   58
  regionalism   168
  Robinson, M.   267, 275, 276n1
  soul   193n3
Cambridge street names   300
Cameron, Sharon   44n11, 91, 92
Canup, John   131n1
Catholicism   70n7, 204–5, 218–19,
  220, 222
Cavell, Stanley   132n4, 133n7,
  133–4n8
census-taking
  Du Bois   174, 175–6
  Frost   187
  soul   164, 174, 191n2
Christ, the Fountain of Life (Cotton)
  38–9
Civil War   162, 195n11, 196n13
Clark, Arthur Corning   212
class factors   4–5, 64, 155

309

310

Index

Index

318

Index

Index